# Lab Manual for
# Network+ Guide to Networks, Sixth Edition

## Todd Verge

COURSE TECHNOLOGY
CENGAGE Learning·

Australia • Brazil • Japan • Korea • Mexico • Singapore • Spain • United Kingdom • United States

**COURSE TECHNOLOGY**
**CENGAGE Learning**

**Lab Manual for Network+ Guide to Networks, Sixth Edition**
**Author: Todd Verge**

Vice President, Career & Computing: Dave Garza

Executive Editor: Stephen Helba

Acquisitions Editor: Nick Lombardi

Managing Editor: Marah Bellegarde

Senior Product Manager: Michelle Ruelos Cannistraci

Developmental Editor: Ann Shaffer

Editorial Assistant: Sarah Pickering

Vice President, Marketing: Jennifer Ann Baker

Marketing Director: Deborah S. Yarnell

Senior Marketing Manager: Mark Linton

Associate Marketing Manager: Erica Glisson

Production Director: Wendy Troeger

Production Manager: Andrew Crouth

Senior Content Project Manager: Andrea Majot

Art Director: GEX

For product information and technology assistance, contact us at
**Cengage Learning Customer & Sales Support, 1-800-354-9706**

For permission to use material from this text or product, submit all requests online at **cengage.com/permissions**
Further permissions questions can be emailed to
**permissionrequest@cengage.com**

Microsoft ® is a registered trademark of the Microsoft Corporation.

Library of Congress Control Number: 2012940981

ISBN-13: 978-1-133-60823-3
ISBN-10: 1-133-60823-X

**Course Technology**
20 Channel Center Street
Boston, MA 02210
USA

Cengage Learning is a leading provider of customized learning solutions with office locations around the globe, including Singapore, the United Kingdom, Australia, Mexico, Brazil, and Japan. Locate your local office at: **international.cengage.com/region**

Cengage Learning products are represented in Canada by Nelson Education, Ltd.

For your lifelong learning solutions, visit **www.cengage.com/coursetechnology.**

Purchase any of our products at your local college store or at our preferred online store **www.cengagebrain.com.**

Visit our corporate website at **cengage.com.**

Printed in the United States of America
1 2 3 4 5 6 7 16 15 14 13 12

# TABLE OF CONTENTS

# PREFACE

Hands-on learning is the best way to master the networking skills necessary for both CompTIA's Network+ exam and a networking career. This book contains dozens of hands-on exercises that apply fundamental networking concepts as they would be applied in the real world. In addition, each chapter offers multiple review questions to reinforce your mastery of networking topics. The organization of this book follows the same organization as Course Technology's *Network+ Guide to Networks, Sixth Edition*. Using the two together will provide an effective learning experience. This book is suitable for a beginning or intermediate networking course. As a prerequisite, students should have at least six months of computer experience and should be familiar with some basic networking components, such as NICs and patch cables. Passing CompTIA's A+ certification exam would suffice in lieu of this experience.

## FEATURES

To ensure a successful experience for instructors and students alike, this book includes the following features:

- **Network+ Certification Objectives**—Each chapter lists the relevant objectives from CompTIA's Network+ N10-005 exam.
- **Lab Objectives**—Every lab has a brief description and list of learning objectives.
- **Materials Required**—Every lab includes information on network access privileges, hardware, software, and other materials you will need to complete the lab.
- **Completion Times**—Every lab has an estimated completion time, so that you can plan your activities more accurately.
- **Step-by-Step Instructions**—Logical and precise step-by-step instructions guide you through the hands-on activities in each lab.
- **Review Questions**—Questions help reinforce concepts presented in the lab.

*Note for instructors: Answers to review questions are available on the Course Technology Web site at http://login.cengage.com*

### New to This Edition

- All labs updated from Windows Vista to Windows 7, with additional steps for Windows XP
- New and expanded labs on topics such as:
  - Virtualization

- Switch and router configuration
- Protocol analyzers
- Telnet and HyperTerminal
- New chapter on virtual networking and remote access
- Updated to the newest versions of equipment and software
- Suggestions for online students
- Updated for CompTIA's new Network+ N10-005 certification
  - Updated mapping of exam objectives
  - Updated practice questions

## HARDWARE REQUIREMENTS

The following is a list of hardware required to complete all the labs in the book. The hardware requirements for many of the individual labs are less extensive, and in the cases where you do not meet the requirements, alternative activities may be possible.

Note that none of the labs require more than three computers at any one time, so all of the labs could be performed with only three physical computers. You might choose to install multiple operating systems on each computer, as this will allow you to boot into a particular operating system when needed.

The minimum requirements for Windows 2008 server computers are as follows:

- Pentium or compatible processor running at 2 GHz or higher
- 1 GB of RAM
- At least 40 GB of available storage
- A CD or DVD-ROM drive
- At least one installed NIC (network interface card)
- Hardware compatible with Windows Server 2008, Standard Edition
  (see *www. microsoft.com/whdc/hcl/default.mspx*)

The minimum requirements for the workstation computers are as follows:

- Pentium or compatible processor running at 1 GHz or higher
- 512 MB of RAM minimum
- At least 2 GB of available storage
- A CD or DVD-ROM drive
- At least one installed NIC (network interface card)

- Hardware compatible with Windows 7 or Windows XP Professional (see *www.microsoft. com/whdc/hcl/default.mspx*)

In addition, at least two computers must be compatible with a current distribution of Linux. The labs assume the student is using a current version of Fedora Linux, which is free for download from *http://fedoraproject.org/*. The minimum requirements for these computers are the same as the workstation requirements.

Other hardware required for various labs include the following:

- Internet access (cable, DSL, or faster preferred)
- One wireless router that can function as a DHCP server and a compatible wireless NIC
- At least five PCI Ethernet network interface cards with RJ-45 connectors
- Category 5 (or better) UTP cabling (or better) for making cables
- At least six straight-through Category 5 (or better) UTP patch cables
- At least three crossover Category 5 (or better) UTP patch cables
- RJ-45 connectors
- A computer professional's toolkit that includes a Phillips screwdriver, a ground strap, and a ground mat
- A networking professional's kit that includes a cable tester, crimper, wire stripper, and a wire cutting tool
- One network printer
- Four 100Base-T (or better) Ethernet switches or hubs
- Two switches with fiber uplink ports and a compatible fiber cable
- Two modems and a dial-up Internet account
- Access to two analog outside phone lines (or two digital lines and two digital-to-analog converters)

## SOFTWARE/SETUP REQUIREMENTS

The following is a list of software required to complete all the labs in the book:

- At least two copies of Windows Server 2008, Standard Edition
- At least two copies of Windows 7 or Windows XP Professional
- At least one current copy of Fedora Linux (note that one copy can be used for each computer)

*Note: Since many students need to work in a virtual environment, the labs assume students are using Windows Server 2008 standard edition, rather than R2, which is only available in a 64-bit edition. In most cases, Server 2008R2 can be substituted for Server 2008 with only minor differences.*

# NOTES ON THE LABS

The following is a list of tips that will assist readers working through the labs:

- Unless otherwise stated, at the beginning of each lab it is assumed that the student has turned on each computer but has not yet logged on.
- On Windows 7/XP computers, Control Panel should be set to Category View, which is the default; the default Start menu should also be used.
- On Windows Server 2008 computers, the default Start menu should be used.
- The Windows firewall may interfere with several of the labs. To disable the firewall, click the **Start button**, click **Control Panel**, click **System and Security**, click **Windows Firewall**, click **Turn Windows Firewall on or off**, select the **Turn off Windows Firewall** radio button, and click **OK**.
- Although these labs were designed using Fedora, most popular distributions are quite similar at the command line and could easily be substituted.

# DISTANCE LEARNING STUDENTS

Some students may not have access to all of the suggested equipment. In most cases, some simple equipment substitutions can be made, although the reader may need to consult the Internet to find the correct steps. In any event, students will still find it useful to read through all of the labs. The following is a list of tips for students who are attempting a lab without all of the required resources:

- For labs requiring Server 2008, Server 2008R2 can be substituted with only minor differences. In some cases, it's possible to substitute Server 2008 with Windows 7.
- Readers with only one computer can attempt many of the labs by installing multiple operating systems in a virtual environment such as VMware, Virtual Box, or Virtual PC. Details of these programs can easily be found on the Internet.
- In labs where the Ping or Tracert utility is used to test a network connection, an ISP's home router can be substituted for a second computer on the network.

# ABOUT THE AUTHOR

Todd Verge has worked as a technologist and teacher for over 20 years and is the author of several Course Technology titles on information technology and mathematics. He graduated with a Bachelor of Science in Physics from Dalhousie University, a Masters Degree in Philosophy from Carleton University, and a Diploma in Adult Education from the Nova Scotia Community College.

# ACKNOWLEDGMENTS

Thank you to the many helpful people on the Course Technology/Cengage Learning staff who made the sixth edition a reality. My sincere appreciation goes out to: Nick Lombardi, Acquisitions Editor; Michelle Ruelos Cannistraci, Senior Product Manager; Andrea Majot, Senior Content Product Manager. Thanks also to Ann Shaffer, Developmental Editor at Shaffer Technical Editing, LLC, for her guidance and encouragement throughout the editorial process. For their amazing attention to detail, I am grateful to our three Technical Editors for Manuscript Quality Assurance: Serge Palladino, Susan Pedicini, and Danielle Shaw. Many warm thanks to Suwathiga Velayutham of Integra Communications, who oversaw the production process, and to our very helpful copy editor, Christine Clark. A huge thank you goes to the following instructors, who faithfully reviewed every chapter and made numerous helpful suggestions and corrections: Tom Gibson, Wichita Technical Institute; Nancy Jones, Coastline College; Jane Perschbach, Central Texas College; Stephan Shelton, Wichita Technical Institute; and Richard Smolenski, Westwood College.

Screenshots of software programs and operating systems included in the text are courtesy of the following companies: Microsoft, Fedora Linux, Wireshark, PuTTY, and OfficeSIP.

Finally, I'd like to thank my friends and colleagues at the Nova Scotia Community College for inspiring me with their love of learning.

# AN INTRODUCTION TO NETWORKING

## Labs included in this chapter

- Lab 1.1 Understanding Elements of a Network
- Lab 1.2 Building a Simple Peer-to-Peer Network
- Lab 1.3 Building a Simple Client/Server Network
- Lab 1.4 Sharing a Network Printer

## Network+ Exam Objectives

| Objective | Lab |
| --- | --- |
| 2.6 Given a set of requirements, plan and implement a basic SOHO (Small Home and Office) network. | 1.2, 1.3, 1.4 |
| 3.1 Categorize standard media types and associated properties. | 1.1 |
| 3.2 Categorize standard connector types based on network media. | 1.1 |
| 3.5 Describe different network topologies. | 1.1 |
| 3.7 Compare and contrast different LAN technologies. | 1.1 |
| 4.5 Describe the purpose of configuration management documentation. | 1.1 |
| 5.3 Explain methods of user authentication. | 1.3 |

# Lab 1.1 Understanding Elements of a Network

## Objectives

When first learning about network components, it is often helpful to observe a live network and talk with experienced networking professionals. The concepts of segments, connectivity devices, or structured wiring techniques, for example, can be more easily demonstrated on a real network than in a textbook. The goal of this lab is to explore some real-life examples of basic networking concepts. To complete this lab, you are required to tour your school's computer laboratory or network and identify various networking components at that site. Alternately, your instructor might arrange to allow your class to tour another network, guided by a willing network professional.

After completing this lab, you will be able to:

- Identify and sketch an organization's network topology
- Identify the nodes on a real-life network
- Identify a network's client and network operating systems
- Identify protocols used by a network

## Materials Required

This lab requires the following:

- A network professional or instructor willing to give you a tour of your school's computer laboratory or data center, or a network professional willing to give you a tour of a network at a business or other site
- Pencil and paper
- Access to software such as Microsoft Visio that can be used for creating network diagrams (optional)

Estimated completion time:   **1–3 hours**

## Activity

1. If you cannot tour your school's computer laboratory or data center, contact a business, school, or other organization and ask to interview the person in charge of their network. Explain that your purpose is purely educational and that you want to learn more about networking. Also explain that you need to take notes. Because revealing information about a network might pose a security risk, some network professionals might not be willing to share this information. If this is the case, you might need to ask your instructor to create a fictitious network and play the role of the network administrator.

2. Make the visit and, with the guidance of the network administrator, observe the organization's network. Remember to ask for details about the network's transmission media, physical topology, hardware, operating systems, services, and protocols.

3. On a separate piece of paper, draw the site's network topology, using boxes to represent the network components such as computers and printers. Draw lines to connect the components. You might also use network-diagramming software such as Microsoft Visio to diagram the network.

4. On your diagram, label servers with the letter "S," workstations with the letter "W," and printers with the letter "P." Label devices used to connect other devices together (such as switches) with a "C." If you are unsure about a network component, label the box with the letter "O" for other.

5. Ask the networking professional or instructor for specifics about the network operating system (NOS) running on the server(s) as well as the operating system running on the workstations. Record this information.

6. Ask for information on the media that physically connect the network components. Record the details of any wires, connectors, and network interface cards (NICs). Are the workstation NICs integrated or are they removable? Note how many different types of network connections this network uses. If the number of different types is high (for example, over six), ask the network administrator if this variability affects network maintenance and troubleshooting.

7. Ask the networking professional or instructor if any wireless LANs are used on this network. Record information about any wireless devices used.

8. Record the protocols used in the network.

9. Ask the networking professional or instructor what sorts of measures they take to make the network secure. Ask them about the possible effects of an intrusion or the loss of data. Record this information.

10. If you toured an outside organization's network, thank the person you interviewed. Follow up later with a letter of thanks.

## Certification Objectives

Objectives for the Network+ Exam:

- 3.1 Categorize standard media types and associated properties.
- 3.2 Categorize standard connector types based on network media.
- 3.5 Describe different network topologies.
- 3.7 Compare and contrast different LAN technologies.
- 4.5 Describe the purpose of configuration management documentation.

## Review Questions

1. Which of the following best describes a network's physical topology?

   a. the method by which multiple nodes transmit signals over a shared communications channel

   b. the physical layout of a network

   c. the distance spanned by a network's cable and wireless infrastructure

   d. the software used to ensure reliable connections between nodes on a network

2. Which of the following is the most popular type of modern network architecture for businesses?

   a. client/server

   b. terminal/mainframe

   c. peer-to-peer

   d. mainframe/dial-up

3. Which of the following elements is *not* required for a client to connect to a server on a client/server LAN?

   a. protocols

   b. media

   c. e-mail account

   d. client software

4. Which of the following are capable of acting as a network server? (Choose all that apply.)

   a. Windows XP Professional

   b. Windows Server 2008

   c. Windows 7

   d. Linux/UNIX

5. Network protocols are used to do which of the following? (Choose all that apply.)

   a. ensure reliable delivery of data

   b. determine the nearest printer for a print job

   c. interpret keyboard commands

   d. indicate the source and destination addresses for data packets

6. On a client/server network, clients may have only one protocol installed at any time. True or False?

7. A significant difference between the peer-to-peer and client/server network types is that a peer-to-peer network:

   a. is more difficult to set up

   b. does not allow for resource sharing between workstations

   c. does not usually provide centralized management for shared resources

   d. is more secure

8. Why is it necessary for each client on a client/server network to have a unique address?

# Lab 1.2 Building a Simple Peer-to-Peer Network

## Objectives

Peer-to-peer networks are commonly found in offices where only a handful of users have access to networked computers because these networks do not scale well and do not provide good security. However, peer-to-peer networks are an excellent choice in a few situations because they are simple and inexpensive to configure. A home office with three to five computers and only a couple of users, for example, would make a good candidate for peer-to-peer networking. Even in client/server networks, users might find it convenient to allow other users to access files on their computers. This is often a security risk, however, because a user might share files without sufficient security or even without any security.

The goal of this lab is for you to become familiar with the methods for establishing a simple peer-to-peer network. During this lab, you are introduced to the hardware and software required to connect two workstations so they can share resources, such as files and DVD drives.

After completing this lab, you will be able to:

- Build a simple peer-to-peer network

## Materials Required

This lab requires the following:

- Two computers running Windows 7 or Windows XP Professional, with RJ-45 network connections; neither computer should be configured as a member of a domain
- A DVD/CD-ROM drive for one of the computers
- Access to both computers with an administrative account (with different passwords)
- Client for Microsoft Networks and File and Printer Sharing for Microsoft Networks installed on both computers
- Either a crossover Category 5 (or better) UTP cable with RJ-45 connectors at either end, or two straight-through Category 5 (or better) UTP cables with RJ-45 connectors and a hub compatible with the Ethernet port, or NICs on both computers
- A DVD/CD with data files on it

 This lab can also be completed with two virtual workstations using virtualization software such as VMware or VirtualBox, although separate Windows licenses are still required.

Estimated completion time: **45 minutes**

## Activity

1. If you are using a crossover cable, plug one end of the crossover cable into the NIC in one machine and the other end into the NIC in the other machine. If you are using straight-through cables and a hub, plug one end of the first cable into the NIC in the first

computer and the other end into the hub. Repeat with the second cable and the second computer. A link light on both NICs illuminates, indicating that each NIC has successfully connected.

2. On each machine, if necessary, press **Ctrl+Alt+Del**. The Log On to Windows dialog box opens.

3. Log on to both machines as an **administrator**. The Windows desktop appears.

4. Insert the DVD or CD in the DVD drive. If both machines have a DVD-ROM drive, select one at random. In this activity, the machine with the DVD or CD in its DVD drive is referred to as *WORKSTATION1*, and the other is referred to as *WORKSTATION2*.

If you are using Windows 7, follow these steps:

1. On *WORKSTATION1*, click the **Start** button, and then click **Control Panel**.

2. Click **System and Security**, and then click **System**.

3. Click **Change settings**. The System Properties dialog box opens.

4. Click the **Change** button. Type **WORKSTATION1** in the Computer name text box.

5. In the Member of section, select **Workgroup** and type **NETPLUS** in the Workgroup name text box.

6. Click **OK** in the next dialog box, close any open windows, and restart the computer when prompted.

7. Log on with an administrative account. Click the **Start** button, and then click **Computer**. The Computer window opens.

8. Right-click the icon for the DVD-ROM drive, move your mouse pointer over **Share with**, and select **Advanced sharing**. The Properties dialog box opens, with the Sharing tab displayed.

9. Click the **Advanced Sharing** button. The Advanced Sharing dialog box opens, as shown in Figure 1-1.

10. Check the **Share this folder** check box and click **Add**. Enter **DVD-ROM** in the **Share name** text box and click **OK**.

11. Click **OK**. The Advanced Sharing dialog box closes. Click **Close** to close the Properties dialog box.

12. Repeat Steps 1 through 6 on *WORKSTATION2*, using **WORKSTATION2** as the name of the computer in Step 4.

13. On *WORKSTATION2*, click the **Start** button, click **Computer**, and then click **Network**. The Network window opens.

14. Double-click the icon for **WORKSTATION1** to open it. If the Connect to WORKSTATION1 dialog box opens, type **Administrator** in the User name text box, type the password for *WORKSTATION1* in the Password text box, and then click **OK**.

15. Right-click the icon for the CD-ROM drive on *WORKSTATION1*, and click **Open**. The files on the CD on *WORKSTATION1* are listed.

16. Log off both computers.

**Figure 1-1**   Advanced Sharing dialog box in Windows 7

*(Source: Microsoft Windows 7)*

If you are using Windows XP, follow these steps:

1. On *WORKSTATION1*, click the **Start** button, and then click **Control Panel**.

2. Click **Network and Internet Connections**. The Network and Internet Connections window opens.

3. Click **Set up or change your home or small office network**. The Network Setup Wizard opens.

4. Click **Next**. The next wizard window asks you to connect to the network.

5. Click **Next**. The next wizard window asks you to select a connection method.

6. Click the **Other** option button. Click **Next**.

7. Select the **This computer belongs to a network that does not have an Internet connection** option button, and then click **Next**. The next wizard window asks you to name your computer.

8. Type **Network+ Lab** in the Computer description text box. Type **WORKSTATION1** in the Computer name text box. Click **Next**. The next wizard window asks you to name your network.

9. Type **NETPLUS** in the Workgroup name text box. Click **Next**. The next wizard window asks you whether or not to turn on file and printer sharing. Verify that the **Turn on file**

**and printer sharing** option button is selected, and then click **Next**. A dialog box opens, summarizing the settings you have chosen.

10. Click **Next**. A dialog box opens, asking you to wait. The next wizard window indicates that you are almost finished.

11. Click the **Just finish the wizard; I don't need to run the wizard on other computers** option button, and then click **Next**. The Completing the Network Setup Wizard dialog box opens.

12. Click **Finish**. The Network Setup Wizard closes, and the System Settings Change dialog box opens.

13. Click **Yes** to restart the computer.

14. If necessary, press **Ctrl+Alt+Del**. The Log On to Windows dialog box opens. Log on to *WORKSTATION1* again as an administrator. The Windows XP desktop appears.

15. Click the **Start** button, and then click **My Computer**. The My Computer window opens.

16. Right-click the icon for the DVD drive, and select **Sharing and Security** from the shortcut menu. The Properties dialog box opens, with the Sharing tab displayed.

17. Click **If you understand the risk but still want to share the root of the drive, click here.** (Because the DVD/CD is read-only, this action does not present a security risk.)

18. If necessary, click the **Share this folder on the network** check box. A check mark appears in the box. Replace the existing entry in the Share name text box with **DVD-ROM**.

19. If necessary, click the **Allow network users to change my files** check box to remove the check mark.

20. Click **OK**. The Properties dialog box closes.

21. Repeat Steps 1 through 13 on *WORKSTATION2*, using **WORKSTATION2** as the name of the computer in Step 8.

22. On *WORKSTATION2*, click the **Start** button, if necessary, click **My Computer**, and then click **My Network Places**. The My Network Places window opens.

23. Right-click the icon for the DVD-ROM drive on *WORKSTATION1* and click **Explore** in the shortcut menu. If the Connect to WORKSTATION1 dialog box opens, go to the next step. Otherwise, go to Step 25.

24. Type **Administrator** in the User name text box, and type the password for *WORKSTATION1* in the Password text box. Click **OK**.

25. A folder containing the files on the CD on *WORKSTATION1* opens.

26. Log off both computers.

## Certification Objective

Objective for the Network+ Exam:

- 2.6 Given a set of requirements, plan and implement a basic SOHO network.

## Review Questions

1. What physical topology would you use to create your peer-to-peer network where all the workstations are connected to a single hub or switch?

   a. bus

   b. tree

   c. star

   d. cube

2. Which of the following operating systems allow you to create a peer-to-peer network from a group of workstations? (Choose all that apply.)

   a. MS-DOS

   b. Windows XP Professional

   c. Linux

   d. Windows 7

3. Which of the following components are *not* necessary to create a peer-to-peer network from a group of workstations? (Choose all that apply.)

   a. client operating system

   b. NIC or motherboard with onboard NIC

   c. network media

   d. Web browser

   e. network operating system

4. What is the primary difference between peer-to-peer and client/server architectures?

5. On a peer-to-peer network consisting of four Windows XP workstations, each user can individually control which of her local data files she wants to share with other users. True or False?

# Lab 1.3 Building a Simple Client/Server Network

## Objectives

Client/server networks are found in all but the smallest organizations. Although client/server networks are more difficult to configure than a peer-to-peer network, they are more scalable and can grow larger than peer-to-peer networks. With more than a handful of computers, a peer-to-peer network quickly becomes unwieldy. In a client/server network, however, you can manage user accounts and network resources such as printers from a single machine. For instance, to change the printer used by all users on a peer-to-peer network, you would need to go to each machine and configure the new printer. Imagine having to do this on 500 machines! In a client/server network, however, you can typically change this setting on the server for all users.

The goal of this lab is to become familiar with the methods for establishing a simple client/server network. During this lab, you are introduced to the hardware and software required to connect one or more workstations to a server. As part of the setup for this lab, both the server and the workstation need to be configured with an IP address. Computers and other network devices use the IP address to find other computers. You learn about addressing beginning in Chapter 2.

After completing this lab, you will be able to:

- Build a simple client/server network
- Add a Windows 7 or XP client computer to a Windows Server 2008 domain

## Materials Required

This lab requires the following:

- One computer named *SERVER1* running Windows Server 2008, Standard Edition (or better) with an Ethernet port or NIC, configured with an IP address of 192.168.54.1
- *SERVER1* configured as the domain controller for the netpluslab.net domain
- Access to the Windows Server 2008 computer and the netpluslab.net domain as the administrator
- On *SERVER1*, a DVD/CD-ROM drive with a DVD or CD in it
- A user account named *netplus* in the Users group in the netpluslab.net domain on *SERVER1*
- One computer named *WORKSTATION1* running Windows 7 or Windows XP Professional with an Ethernet port or NIC, configured with an IP address of 192.168.54.2; this computer should not be configured as a member of a domain
- Access to *WORKSTATION1* as a regular user
- *WORKSTATION1* configured to use 192.168.54.1 as its DNS server
- An Ethernet hub or switch compatible with both NICs
- Two straight-through Category 5 (or better) UTP cables with RJ-45 connectors at either end

Estimated completion time: **60 minutes**

## Activity

1. Plug one end of one of the cables into the hub. Plug the other end of the cable into one of the computers. The link light on both the hub and on the NIC in the back of the computer should illuminate.
2. Repeat Step 1 to connect the other computer to the hub.
3. On *SERVER1* (the Windows Server 2008 computer), press **Ctrl+Alt+Del**. The Log On to Windows dialog box opens.
4. Type **Administrator** in the User name text box, and type the password for this account in the Password text box. Click the **Log on to** list button, and then click **NETPLUSLAB**. Click **OK**. The Windows Server 2008 desktop appears.

5. Click the **Start** button, and then click **Computer**.

6. Right-click the icon for the DVD/CD-ROM drive, and then click **Share** in the shortcut menu.

7. Click the **Advanced Sharing** button, and then check the **Share this folder** option button. Record the name that appears in the Share name text box. This is the name by which the shared DVD/CD-ROM drive is identified on the other computer. Click **OK**, and then click **Close**.

If you are using Windows 7, follow these steps:

1. Log on as an administrator. The Windows desktop appears.

2. Click the **Start** button, and then click **Control Panel**. The Control Panel opens.

3. Click **System and Security**, and then click **System**. The System window opens.

4. In the lower-right corner, click **Change settings**. You see the System Properties dialog box shown in Figure 1-2.

5. Click **Network ID**.

**Figure 1-2**  System Properties dialog box in Windows 7

6. Select the **This computer is part of a business network; I use it to connect to other computers at work** option button. Click **Next**.

7. Click the **My company uses a network with a domain** option button. Click **Next**.

8. Click **Next**.

9. Type **netplus** in the User name text box. Type the password for the netplus account in the Password text box. Type **NETPLUSLAB.NET** in the Domain Name text box. Click **Next**.

10. Now you enter information about the Windows 7 computer itself. In the Computer name text box, type **WORKSTATION1** if necessary. In the Computer domain text box, type **NETPLUSLAB.NET**. Click **Next**. The Domain User Name and Password dialog box opens.

11. In the User name text box, type **Administrator**. Type the password for this account in the Password text box. Type **NETPLUSLAB.NET** in the Domain text box. Click **OK**.

12. The wizard asks you to add a user account to this computer. The wizard should have already selected the **Add the following domain user account** option button, displayed **netplus** in the User name text box, and displayed **NETPLUSLAB.NET** in the User domain text box. If not, complete these settings now. Click **Next**.

13. The wizard asks you what sort of access the netplus user should have to this computer. Make sure the **Standard account** option button is selected, and then click **Next**.

14. Click **Finish**. A window opens, informing you that you must restart the computer for the changes to take effect.

15. Click **OK** in the System Properties dialog box and then click **Restart Now** to reboot the computer.

16. When the computer has rebooted, enter **netplus** in the User name text box. In the Password text box, enter the password for this account. Select **NETPLUSLAB** from the Log on to drop-down menu. Click **OK**.

17. Click the **Start** button, click **Computer**, and then click **Network**. If an information bar appears at the top of the window indicating that network discovery and file sharing are turned off, click **Turn on network discovery and file sharing**.

18. Double-click the **SERVER1** icon. If necessary, enter the administrator user name and password. A list of all the folders shared on **SERVER1** appears.

19. Right-click the folder name you recorded for the CD on the server. Click **Explore** in the shortcut menu. You see a list of the contents of the CD.

20. Log off both computers.

On a Windows XP computer:

1. If necessary, press **Ctrl+Alt+Del** to display the Log On to Windows dialog box. Log on as an administrator. The Windows desktop appears.

2. Click the **Start** button, and then click **Control Panel**. The Control Panel opens. Click **Performance and Maintenance**.

3. Click **System**. The System Properties dialog box opens.

4. Click the **Computer Name** tab.

5. Click **Network ID**. The Network Identification Wizard opens. Click **Next**.

6. Click the **This computer is part of a business network, and I use it to connect to other computers at work** option button. Click **Next**.

7. Click the **My company uses a network with a domain** option button. Click **Next**.

8. Click **Next**.

9. Type **netplus** in the User name text box. Type the password for the netplus account in the Password text box. Type **NETPLUSLAB.NET** in the Domain text box. Click **Next**.

10. Now you enter information about the Windows XP computer itself. In the Computer name text box, if necessary type **WORKSTATION1**. In the Computer domain text box, type **NETPLUSLAB.NET**. Click **Next**. The Domain User Name and Password dialog box opens.

11. In the User name text box, type **Administrator**. Type the password for this account in the Password text box. Type **NETPLUSLAB.NET** in the Domain text box. Click **OK**.

12. The wizard asks you to add a user account to this computer. The wizard should have already selected the **Add the following user** option button, displayed **netplus** in the User name text box, and displayed **NETPLUSLAB.NET** in the User domain text box. If not, complete these settings now. Click **Next**.

13. The wizard asks you what sort of access the netplus user should have to this computer. Make sure the **Standard user** option button is selected, and then click **Next**.

14. Click **Finish**. The Computer Name Changes dialog box opens, informing you that you must restart the computer for the changes to take effect.

15. Click **OK**. The Computer Name Changes dialog box closes.

16. Click **OK** again. The System Properties dialog box closes.

17. The System Settings Change dialog box opens, asking if you want to restart your computer now. Click **Yes** to reboot the computer.

18. When the computer has rebooted, press **Ctrl+Alt+Del**, if necessary, to display the Log On to Windows dialog box. If the Log on to drop-down menu is not visible, click **Options**. In the User name text box, if necessary enter **netplus**. In the Password text box, enter the password for this account. Select **NETPLUSLAB** from the Log on to drop-down menu. Click **OK**.

19. Click the **Start** button, and then click **My Computer**. The My Computer window opens.

20. Click **My Network Places** in the left pane.

21. Click **Entire Network** in the left pane.

22. Double-click the **Microsoft Windows Network** icon.

23. Double-click the **Netpluslab** icon.

24. Double-click the **SERVER1** icon. A list of all the folders shared on *SERVER1* appears.

25. Right-click the folder name you recorded earlier in this lab. Click **Explore** in the shortcut menu. The files and folders on the disc are displayed.

26. Log off both computers.

## Certification Objectives

Objectives for the Network+ Exam:

- 2.6 Given a set of requirements, plan and implement a basic SOHO network.
- 5.3 Explain methods of user authentication.

## Review Questions

1. Which of the following are or could be shared as resources across a network? (Choose all that apply.)

   a. Microsoft Word and other Office software

   b. printers

   c. documents

   d. network interface cards

2. Even in a client/server network, it is possible to share documents between individual users' computers as you can in a peer-to-peer network. True or False?

3. You are the network administrator for a small company. When users take vacations, they would like to allow other users to update the files stored on their computers. In addition, several users have complained that they accidentally deleted important files on their local computer and would like some way to recover them. How would you recommend that they store their files?

   a. Make multiple copies on their local hard drive.

   b. Store the files on the server, which is backed up nightly.

   c. Make copies of the file on a USB thumb drive.

   d. Burn the files onto a CD.

4. A very large organization might have thousands of servers. Do the benefits of client/server networks still apply to such an organization?

   a. No, because managing so many servers is difficult.

   b. No, because the organization can rely on a large peer-to-peer network to share files instead.

   c. Yes, because it is easier to manage thousands of servers than it is to manage the hundreds of thousands of workstations such an organization might have.

   d. Yes, because managing thousands of servers is no more difficult than managing a few servers.

5. In this lab, what kind of network service did you configure on your client/server network?

   a. management service

   b. mail service

   c. Internet service

   d. file service

6. Which two of the following issues make peer-to-peer networks less scalable than client/server networks?

   a. Each time a new user is added, the peer-to-peer network cabling must be reinstalled between nodes.

   b. Adding nodes to a peer-to-peer network results in diminished overall network performance.

   c. Adding nodes to a peer-to-peer network increases the risk that an intruder can compromise a shared data folder.

   d. Adding new resource-sharing locations and ensuring that all authorized users have access to new resources becomes less manageable as the peer-to-peer network grows.

# Lab 1.4 Sharing a Network Printer

## Objectives

The ability to share network resources among all the users in an organization is an important reason networks are so widely used. To print a document without a network, a user would need a printer directly attached to her computer, or she would need to copy the document to a form of portable media such as a CD-R or USB drive and find a computer with an attached printer. In an organization with even a few employees, this can be both expensive and time consuming. In an organization with thousands of employees, this can waste an enormous amount of time and cost a great deal of money.

In this lab, you share a network printer so that users can access it. In the process, you become familiar with the methods used to share network resources. Depending on the make and model of the printer, the steps required to install printer drivers might vary from the steps provided here.

After completing this lab, you will be able to:

- Share a networked printer on a Windows Server 2008 client/server network

## Materials Required

This lab requires the following:

- The network and computers required for Lab 1.3
- A printer that is compatible with Windows Server 2008, Standard Edition
- Drivers for the printer that are compatible with Windows Server 2008; these drivers should be available either among the default drivers installed with Windows Server 2008 or in a known location on a disk or DVD/CD
- Drivers for the printer that are compatible with Windows 7 or Windows XP Professional; these drivers should be available either among the default drivers installed with Windows or in a known location on a CD
- A printer cable that you can use to attach the printer to the Windows Server 2008 computer

- A printer port, such as USB or TCP/IP, available on the Windows Server 2008 computer
- Paper in the appropriate printer tray

Estimated completion time:  **30 minutes**

## Activity

1. Attach one end of the printer cable to the printer. Attach the other end of the printer cable to the Windows Server 2008 computer.
2. If necessary, power on the printer.
3. Press **Ctrl+Alt+Del** and log on to the Windows Server 2008 computer as the administrator. The Windows Server 2008 desktop appears.
4. Windows Server 2008 might detect and install the printer automatically. If it does, read through the steps, and then skip to Step 11. Otherwise, continue with the following steps.
5. Click the **Start** button, click **Control Panel**, and then click **View devices and printers** under Hardware. The Devices and Printers window opens.
6. Click the **Add Printer** icon. The Add Printer window opens.
7. Select **Add a local printer**.
8. Select the appropriate printer port from the drop-down menu and click **Next**.
9. Now you must select a printer driver. If the printer drivers are known to be among the default drivers installed with Windows Server 2008, select the manufacturer for the printer in the Manufacturer list, select the printer model in the Printers list, click **Next**, and then skip ahead to Step 11. If the drivers for the printer are on a CD, insert the CD into the appropriate drive, and click **Have Disk**. The Install From Disk dialog box opens.
10. Click **Browse**, select the location of the printer drivers, highlight the name of the printer driver, and click **Open**. Click **OK**, and then click **Next**.
11. Type **NetplusPrinter** in the Printer name text box. Click **Next**.
12. In the Printer Sharing window, accept the default share name of **NetplusPrinter**, enter **Network+ Laboratory** in the Location text box, and click **Next**.
13. Click **Print a test page**. The NetplusPrinter dialog box opens, indicating that the test page is being printed. The test page prints. Click **Close**, and then click **Finish** to close the Add Printer window.
14. Right-click the printer's icon, click **Printer Properties** to open the Properties dialog box, and then click the **Sharing** tab. Click the **List in the directory** check box to select it, and then click **OK**.

In Windows 7:

1. On *WORKSTATION1*, click the **Start** button, and then click **Devices and Printers**. The Devices and Printers window opens.
2. Click **Add a printer**. The Add Printer dialog box opens, as shown in Figure 1-3.

Source: Microsoft Windows 7

**Figure 1-3**    Add Printer dialog box in Windows 7

3. Click **Add a network, wireless or Bluetooth printer**. The printer you just added to the Windows Server 2008 computer appears in the list of available printers.

4. Select **NetplusPrinter on SERVER1** and click **Next**.

5. Make sure the **Set as the default printer checkbox** is checked and click **Next**.

6. Click **Print a test page**. The NetplusPrinter on SERVER1 dialog box opens, indicating that you have printed a test page. The test page prints.

7. Click **Close**, and then click **Finish** in the Add Printer dialog box.

8. Close any open windows. You have successfully accessed a printer shared on a Windows Server 2008 computer from a client workstation.

9. Log off both computers.

In Windows XP:

1. On *WORKSTATION1*, press **Ctrl+Alt+Del**, if necessary, to display the Windows XP logon screen. Enter **netplus** in the User name text box and the password for this account in the Password text box. Make sure that **NETPLUSLAB** is selected from the drop-down menu next to Log on to. Click **OK**. The Windows XP desktop appears.

2. Click the **Start** button, and then click **Printers and Faxes**. The Printers and Faxes window opens.

3. Below the Printer Tasks heading, click **Add a printer**. The Add Printer Wizard opens.

4. Click **Next**.

5. Make sure that the **A network printer, or a printer attached to another computer** option button is selected. Click **Next**.

6. Now you must select a printer. Make sure that the **Find a printer in the directory** (or, depending on your computer setup, the **Browse for a printer** option button) is selected, and click **Next**. The Find Printers dialog box opens.

7. Enter **NetplusPrinter** in the Name text box. Verify that **Entire Directory** is selected in the **In** drop-down menu. Click **Find Now**.

8. Click **NetplusPrinter** to highlight it and click **OK**. Click the **No** option button when asked if you want to make this the default printer, and then click **Next**.

9. Click **Finish**. The Add Printer Wizard closes, and the "NetplusPrinter on SERVER1" icon appears in the Printers and Faxes window.

10. Right-click the **NetplusPrinter on SERVER1** icon and select **Properties** from the shortcut menu.

11. Click **Print Test Page**. The NetplusPrinter on SERVER1 dialog box opens, indicating that you have printed a test page. The test page prints.

12. Click **OK**.

13. Click **OK** again. You have successfully accessed a printer shared on a Windows Server 2008 computer from a client workstation.

14. Log off both computers.

## Certification Objective

Objective for the Network+ Exam:

- 2.6 Given a set of requirements, plan and implement a basic SOHO network.

## Review Questions

1. Many printers come with network cards so that they do not need to be attached to a computer. How would the process of sharing such a printer differ from sharing a printer attached to a computer? (Choose all that apply.)

   a. You would need to configure the printer with an address so that other computers can find it.

   b. The process would not differ.

   c. You would have to add the printer to the Windows Server 2008 domain, just as you did the Windows computer in Lab 1.3.

   d. You would not need to connect the printer to another computer via a cable.

2. Users may share printers in a peer-to-peer network. What are the potential disadvantages of this? (Choose all that apply.)

   a. A user could easily misconfigure or turn off his workstation, preventing all other users from accessing the attached printer.

   b. No one will be able to use the printer if the network is down.

   c. The printer will not be backed up.

   d. The printer will not be under centralized control.

3. In this lab, what kind of network service did you configure on your client/server network?

   a. management service

   d. mail service

   c. print service

   d. file service

4. Suppose that you configured software on a Windows Server 2008 computer that checked printers on the network to make sure that they were operating correctly. What sort of network service would this software provide?

   a. file service

   b. print service

   c. management service

   d. mail service

5. How can you tell whether a printer is shared or not?

   a. The word *shared* is written on the printer icon.

   b. There is no way to tell.

   c. There is a small icon at the bottom of the printer icon.

   d. Each shared printer appears in the Shared Printers folder.

# NETWORKING STANDARDS AND THE OSI MODEL

## Labs included in this chapter

- Lab 2.1 IP Address Assignments
- Lab 2.2 Configuring TCP/IP for a Windows Computer
- Lab 2.3 Finding the MAC Address of Another Computer
- Lab 2.4 Looking at Network Connections on a Windows Computer
- Lab 2.5 Viewing Ethernet Frames

## Network+ Exam Objectives

| Objective | Lab |
|---|---|
| 1.1 Compare the layers of the OSI and TCP/IP models. | 2.5 |
| 1.3 Explain the purpose and properties of IP addressing. | 2.1, 2.2, 2.3, 2.4 |
| 1.6 Explain the function of common networking protocols. | 2.3 |
| 4.3 Given a scenario, use appropriate software tools to troubleshoot connectivity issues. | 2.1, 2.2, 2.3, 2.4, 2.5 |
| 5.2 Explain the methods of network access security. | 2.4 |

# Lab 2.1 IP Address Assignments

## Objectives

A Regional Internet Registry (RIR) is an organization that assigns IP addresses to public and private organizations. There are five RIRs: the American Registry for Internet Numbers (ARIN), the Asia-Pacific Network Information Centre (APNIC), the Latin American and Caribbean Internet Addresses Registry (LACNIC), Réseaux IP Européens (RIPE), and the African Network Information Centre (AfriNIC). Each RIR assigns IP addresses in a different area.

As a network administrator, you might sometimes find that you need to track down the owner of a particular IP address. For instance, you might discover that a host at an IP address outside your network is generating excessive amounts of traffic to your Web server, sending your mail server unsolicited commercial e-mail, or otherwise abusing your network. To ask the owner of this host to stop, you must be able to contact that owner. You can use the Web site of an RIR to find this information. All of the RIRs maintain a Web site and a WHOIS database, which tracks IP assignments. You can find the Web sites for each organization at *www.arin.net, www.apnic.net, www.lacnic.net, www.ripe.net,* and *www.afrinic.net.* Often, IP address assignments are divided further. An Internet service provider (ISP), for instance, usually delegates some of its IP addresses to its customers.

In this lab, you use the `nslookup` command to find the IP address of a site. Then you look up that IP address on the ARIN site.

Note that the steps in this lab were correct at the time this book was published. If ARIN changes its Web site significantly, the steps might not work exactly as written. However, you should still be able to go to *www.arin.net* and follow the links for WHOIS.

After completing this lab, you will be able to:

- Describe the function of an RIR
- Track down the organization owning an IP address

## Materials Required

This lab requires the following:

- A computer running Windows 7 or Windows XP Professional with a connection to the Internet (and instructions on how to access it, if necessary)
- Internet Explorer configured as needed to access Web sites on the Internet
- A Web site address (such as *www.cisco.com)* whose IP address was assigned by ARIN; your instructor should tell you which Web site to use

Estimated completion time: **20–25 minutes**

## Activity

1. Log on to the Windows computer. The desktop appears. If necessary, perform whatever steps are needed to access the Internet.

**Figure 2-1**  Typical output from the `nslookup` command

2. In Windows 7, click the **Start** button, type **cmd** in the Search programs and files text box, and then press **Enter**. (In Windows XP, click the **Start** button, point to **All Programs,** point to **Accessories,** and then click **Command Prompt.**) A command prompt window opens.

3. In the command prompt window, type **nslookup** followed by a space and then the name of the Web site assigned to you by your instructor. (For instance, if you were assigned *www.google.com,* you would type **nslookup   www.google.com.**) Press **Enter.** The output of this command should look similar to Figure 2-1.

4. In the **Non-authoritative answer** section you should see the IP address of the Web site directly under the name of the Web site. In some cases the Web site's name may vary slightly from its alias. In Figure 2-1, for instance, the IP address of *www.l.google.com* is 173.194.73.106. Below, record the IP address you found. Some Web sites might have multiple IP addresses. If this is the case, record the last IP address found.

5. Open Internet Explorer.

6. In the Address bar, type **http://www.arin.net/whois/** and then press **Enter.** The ARIN WHOIS Database Search page opens.

7. In the Search ARIN WHOISRWS text box, type the IP address you recorded in Step 4 and press **Enter.** The query results appear.

8. Record the name of the organization to which the IP address belongs. In some cases, more than one organization might be listed. For instance, an organization and its ISP might be listed.

9. Close any open windows and log off the computer.

## Certification Objectives

Objectives for the Network+ Exam:

- 1.3 Explain the purpose and properties of IP addressing.

- 4.3 Given a scenario, use appropriate software tools to troubleshoot connectivity issues.

## Review Questions

1. A host has been overwhelming your Web server. You look up the IP address on *www.arin.net* to determine its owner, but ARIN's Web site tells you that LACNIC owns the IP address. What should you do?

   a. Complain to the owner of the *www.lacnic.net* Web site.

   b. Look up LACNIC in the Regional Internet Registry.

   c. Look up the owner of the IP address on the LACNIC Web site.

   d. Look up the owner of the IP address on the APNIC Web site.

2. What might happen if no organization were responsible for IP addressing on the Internet? (Choose all that apply.)

   a. Organizations might try to use the same ranges of IP addresses.

   b. Addressing on the Internet would be physically impossible.

   c. Nothing

   d. The Internet would use another protocol besides IP.

3. You look up an IP address on *www.arin.net* and two organizations are listed. What does this mean?

   a. The two organizations share the IP address assignment.

   b. One organization sold the IP address to the second.

   c. The RIR made a mistake.

   d. One organization delegated the IP address to the second.

4. What is a Regional Internet Registry responsible for?

   a. Maintaining Internet connectivity

   b. Registering Internets

   c. Assigning IP addresses

   d. Signing up users with ISP accounts

5. Which of the following are situations when contacting the owner of an IP address would be useful? (Choose all that apply.)

   a. A host outside your network has been attempting to log on to your servers without your permission.

   b. A host inside your network has been attempting to log on to your servers without your permission.

   c. A host outside your network has been attempting to send large amounts of unsolicited commercial e-mail, or spam.

   d. A host outside your network has been accessing your Web site once an hour.

# Lab 2.2 Configuring TCP/IP for a Windows Computer

## Objectives

Whereas addressing at the Data Link layer usually does not require configuration, addressing at the Network layer usually does. Without properly configured network addresses, two hosts can't communicate with each other over the network using Network layer protocols. The network address is a logical address and does not correspond to any physical attribute of the computer.

On a TCP/IP network, the Network layer address is the IP address. It consists of four numbers with values between 0 and 255 separated by dots. For instance, 10.172.255.93 is a valid IP address. When written in binary, each number in an IP address is eight bits long, and these numbers are often called octets. The subnet mask is also important. The subnet mask also consists of four octets separated by dots. However, only certain values are allowed. A host with an improperly configured subnet mask might not be able to communicate with some or any hosts. In this lab, you use the Ipconfig utility to display a computer's IP configuration.

In this lab, you also configure an IP address and subnet mask on a host so that it can communicate with other hosts on a network. You then use the Ping (Packet Internet Groper) utility to verify that two hosts can communicate with each other at the Network layer in a TCP/IP network. The ping command sends one or more packets using the Internet Control Message Protocol (ICMP) to a remote computer. If the remote computer receives these packets, it sends a reply. If the sender receives the replies, the ping command was successful. After completing this lab, you will be able to:

- Configure an IP address on a Windows computer

## Materials Required

This lab requires the following:

- A hub or switch
- A computer running Windows Server 2008 Standard Edition, Windows 7, or Windows XP Professional configured with an IP address of 192.168.54.1 and with a NIC connected to the hub or switch with a straight-through Category 5 (or better) cable
- A computer named *WORKSTATION1* running Windows 7 or Windows XP Professional with a NIC connected to the hub or switch with a straight-through Category 5 (or better) UTP cable but with no IP address configured
- Access to the Windows 7 or Windows XP computer as an administrator

> Estimated completion time: **20 minutes**

## Activity

1. On the workstation computer, log on as an administrator. The Windows desktop appears.

2. In Windows 7, click the **Start** button, click **Control Panel**, click **Network and Internet**, click **Network and Sharing Center**, and click **Change adapter settings**. (In Windows XP,

Click **Start,** point to **All Programs,** point to **Accessories,** point to **Communications,** and then click **Network Connections.**) The Network Connections window opens.

3. Right-click the **Local Area Connection** icon, and then click **Properties** in the shortcut menu.

4. In Windows 7, double-click **Internet Protocol Version 4 (TCP/IPv4).** (In Windows XP, double-click **Internet Protocol (TCP/IP).**) The Internet Protocol Version 4 (TCP/IPv4) Properties dialog box opens. (In Windows XP, the Internet Protocol (TCP/IP) Properties dialog box opens.)

5. Click the **Use the following IP address** option button.

6. Enter **192.168.54.2** in the IP address text box.

7. Enter **255.255.255.0** in the Subnet mask text box.

8. Enter **192.168.54.1** in the Default gateway text box.

9. Click the **Use the following DNS server addresses** option button.

10. In the Preferred DNS server text box, enter **192.168.54.1.** At this point, your Internet Protocol Version 4 (TCP/IPv4) Properties dialog box should match the one shown in Figure 2-2.

11. Click **OK** to close the Internet Protocol Version 4 (TCP/IPv4) Properties dialog box.

12. Click **OK** to close the Local Area Connection Properties window.

13. Now you verify that you have successfully configured an IP address for the Windows computer. In Windows 7, click the **Start** button, type **cmd** in the Search programs and files box, and then press **Enter.** (In Windows XP, click the **Start** button, point to **All Programs,** point to **Accessories,** and then click **Command Prompt.**) A command prompt window opens.

**Figure 2-2**   Internet Protocol Version 4 (TCP/IPv4) Properties dialog box

14. Type **ping 192.168.54.1** and press **Enter**. The Windows computer sends four ICMP packets to 192.168.54.1 and indicates that it has received four replies from the remote computer.

15. Type **ipconfig** and press **Enter**. The computer displays its IP address, subnet mask, and default gateway. Does this match the information you entered in the Internet Protocol Version 4 (TCP/IPv4) Properties dialog box in Steps 6, 7, and 8?

16. Log off.

## Certification Objectives

Objectives for the Network+ Exam:

- 1.3 Explain the purpose and properties of IP addressing.
- 4.3 Given a scenario, use appropriate software tools to troubleshoot connectivity issues.

## Review Questions

1. Which of the following information is included in the results of the ping command? (Choose all that apply.)

   a. The operating system used by the remote computer

   b. The IP address or name of the remote computer

   c. The number of packets that were lost

   d. The time it took for the reply to be received

2. Which of the following commands can you use to print information about a computer's Network layer configuration?

   a. **netstat**

   b. **ipconfig**

   c. **arp**

   d. **ping**

3. How can you verify that two hosts are connected and communicating properly?

   a. From one host, run the **ping** command to the other host.

   b. From a third host, run the **ping** command to both hosts.

   c. Run the **arp** command on both hosts.

   d. Run the **ipconfig** command on both hosts.

4. What type of protocol does the **ping** command use?

   a. TCP/IP

   b. UDP

   c. ICMP

   d. ARP

5. A Dynamic Host Configuration Protocol (DHCP) server can be used to assign IP addresses automatically. Why might this be useful to a network administrator?

6. On many networks, DHCP is used to assign workstations their IP addresses. However, DHCP is rarely used to assign addresses for servers. Why?

   a. DHCP is too expensive.

   b. DHCP is not scalable enough.

   c. Servers are frequently moved around, whereas workstations are not.

   d. Workstations are frequently moved around, whereas servers are not.

# Lab 2.3 Finding the MAC Address of Another Computer

## Objectives

The MAC address operates at the Media Access Control sublayer of the Data Link layer. It is a unique address the manufacturer assigned when the NIC was built. In TCP/IP networks, the Address Resolution Protocol (ARP) allows a computer to associate another computer's MAC address at the Data Link layer with its IP address at the Network layer. A computer keeps track of these associations in its ARP cache. If a computer does not see packets from one of the computers whose MAC address is in its ARP cache for a certain period of time, the computer removes that MAC address from its ARP cache. This is called the ARP cache timeout.

A MAC address consists of two parts. The first part, known as the block ID, consists of six characters assigned to the vendor by the IEEE. The second part, known as the device ID, consists of six characters assigned by the vendor. Each MAC address should be unique. Each character in a MAC address is a hexadecimal number, consisting of numbers from 0 through 9 and letters from *a* through *f*. A MAC address is often represented with colons or dashes between every pair of characters, such as 00:60:97:7F:41:A1 or 00-60-97-7F-41-A1.

You can use the **arp** command to look at the entries in a computer's ARP cache and to find the MAC addresses of other computers with which it has communicated on its local network segment. Incorrect ARP entries can prevent two computers from communicating. For instance, on very rare occasions, two computers are found on the same network with identical MAC addresses (generally due to manufacturer error). These computers will have difficulty communicating with other computers on that network. More commonly, replacing a computer's NIC might prevent that computer from communicating with other computers on the network until their ARP cache entries time out.

In this lab, you use the **arp** command to find the MAC address of another computer. After completing this lab, you will be able to:

- Use the **arp** command to find and set the MAC address of another computer

## Materials Required

This lab requires the following:

- The network required in Lab 1.4, consisting of a computer named *SERVER1* running Windows Server 2008, Standard Edition with an IP address of 192.168.54.1, a computer named *WORKSTATION1* running Windows 7 or Windows XP Professional with an IP address of 192.168.54.2, a hub or switch, and two straight-through Category 5 (or better) UTP cables connecting the NICs on the computers to the hubs

- Access to the Windows Server 2008 computer as an administrator
- Access to the Windows 7 or Windows XP Professional computer as an ordinary user

Estimated completion time:  **20–30 minutes**

## Activity

1. Log on to *WORKSTATION1* as an ordinary user. The Windows desktop appears.

2. In Windows 7, click the **Start** button, type **cmd** in the Search programs and files text box, and then press **Enter**. (In Windows XP, click the **Start** button, point to **All Programs**, point to **Accessories**, and then click **Command Prompt**.) A command prompt window opens.

3. You now test network connectivity between *WORKSTATION1* and *SERVER1*. Type **ping  192.168.54.1** in the command prompt window and press **Enter**. The computer indicates that it has received four replies from 192.168.54.1. See Figure 2-3 for an example of the output produced. This indicates that the two computers can communicate with each other over the network. If they could not, the **ping** command would display an error message such as "Request timed out."

4. Repeat Steps 1 through 3 on *SERVER1,* logging on as an administrator. Use the IP address **192.168.54.2** in Step 3.

5. On *SERVER1,* type **arp  -a** in the Command Prompt window and press **Enter**. The computer prints a list of IP addresses and the physical addresses, or MAC addresses, associated with each. Record the MAC address for 192.168.54.2, the Windows 7 or Windows XP computer.

6. Now you replace the actual MAC address of the Windows 7 or Window XP computer with a bogus MAC address and see how it affects the ability of the two machines to

**Figure 2-3**   Typical output from the **ping** command

communicate with each other. In the command prompt window, type **netsh inter-face ipv4 add neighbors "Local Area Connection" 192.268.54.2 00-11-22-33-44-55** and press **Enter**. The Windows Server 2008 computer changes the MAC address it knows for *WORKSTATION1*.

7. Type **arp -a** and press **Enter**. What is the MAC address for *WORKSTATION1* now?

8. On the Windows 7 or Windows XP computer, repeat Step 3. Are you able to ping *SERVER1* successfully?

9. In the command prompt window, type **ipconfig /all**. The computer prints detailed information about its network configuration, including its MAC address. Does this MAC address match the one for *WORKSTATION1* that you found in Step 5?

10. Now you delete the ARP entry you created for *WORKSTATION1*. On *SERVER1*, type **arp -d** and press **Enter**. All ARP entries are deleted. For your reference, Table 2-1 lists some options for the **arp** command in Windows.

**Table 2-1    Options for the `arp` command in Windows**

| Command | Action |
|---------|--------|
| arp -a | Displays all the addresses in the ARP cache |
| arp -s | Adds a static, or permanent, entry to the ARP cache |
| arp -d | Deletes entries from the ARP cache |

© Cengage Learning 2013

11. On *WORKSTATION1*, repeat Step 3. Are you able to communicate with the Windows Server 2008 computer successfully now?

12. Log off both computers.

## Certification Objectives

Objectives for the Network+ Exam:

- 1.3 Explain the purpose and properties of IP addressing.
- 1.6 Explain the function of common networking protocols.
- 4.3 Given a scenario, use appropriate software tools to troubleshoot connectivity issues.

## Review Questions

1. What do the first six characters of a MAC address indicate?

   a. The device ID assigned by the vendor

   b. The block ID assigned by IEEE

   c. The logical address assigned by DHCP

   d. The logical address assigned by DNS

2. Which of the following is a valid MAC address?

   a. 01-ba-cd-dh-83-21

   b. 01-ba-cd-de-83-21-42

c. 01-ba-cd-de-83-21-42-a0

    d. 01-ba-cd-de-83-21

3. Which of the following commands can you use to find a Windows XP computer's MAC address from a command prompt window on that computer?

    a. `ipconfig`

    b. `ipconfig /all`

    c. `arp -a`

    d. `netstat`

4. Which of the following commands can you use to find the MAC address of another computer on the same network?

    a. `ipconfig`

    b. `ipconfig /all`

    c. `arp -a`

    d. `netstat`

5. Under what circumstances is it possible for a computer to have more than one MAC address?

    a. Never

    b. If a computer has more than one NIC

    c. If a computer has more than one NIC, but only if it is acting as a router

    d. If a computer is a router

6. You have just replaced the NIC on a server, making no other changes. It can communicate with all the computers on its network but one. What is the most likely explanation for this?

    a. The new NIC is not working properly.

    b. Both computers have the same MAC address.

    c. The remote computer has the old MAC address entry in its ARP cache.

    d. The remote computer has a bad NIC.

7. Which of the following is a function of the Data Link layer?

    a. Arranging data in proper sequence at the destination

    b. Encrypting data prior to transmission

    c. Dividing data into distinct frames

    d. Issuing electrical signals onto a wire

8. What part of a data frame checks to make sure that the data arrived exactly as it was sent?

    a. CRC

    b. Start delimiter

    c. Payload

    d. Padding

# Lab 2.4 Looking at Network Connections on a Windows Computer

## Objectives

The Transport layer ensures that data travels from the source host to the destination host. Transport layer protocols might check for errors. They also might ensure that data arrives in the proper order. In the TCP/IP stack, TCP is the protocol operating at the Transport layer. Because TCP is a connection-oriented protocol, the computers on both ends of a TCP connection must keep track of the status of the connection.

You can use the **netstat** command on Windows, UNIX, and other operating systems to look at active connections. This command can show detailed information about active network connections, including their status, the number of bytes sent over the network, and other information. UDP, on the other hand, is a connectionless protocol and does not keep track of the connection. As a result, the **netstat** command provides much less information about UDP connections.

After completing this lab, you will be able to:

- Use the **netstat** command to view information about the Transport layer

## Materials Required

This lab requires the following:

- The network required in Lab 1.4, consisting of a computer named *SERVER1* running Windows Server 2008, Standard Edition with an IP address of 192.168.54.1, a computer named *WORKSTATION1* running Windows 7 or Windows XP Professional with an IP address of 192.168.54.2, a hub or switch, and two straight-through Category 5 (or better) UTP cables connecting the NICs on the computers to the hubs

- Terminal Services running on *SERVER1* and the computer configured to allow users to log on remotely

- Access to both computers as an administrator

Estimated completion time: **20 minutes**

## Activity

1. On the Windows 7 or Windows XP computer, press **Ctrl+Alt+Del**, if necessary.

2. Log on to *WORKSTATION1* as an administrator. The Windows desktop appears.

3. In Windows 7, click the **Start** button, type **cmd** in the Search programs and files text box, and then press **Enter**. (In Windows XP, click the **Start** button, point to **All Programs**, point to **Accessories**, and then click **Command Prompt**.)

4. Type **netstat** and press **Enter**. The computer displays information about all open connections on the computer or returns to the prompt if there are none.

5. Now you open a new TCP connection by using the Remote Desktop Connection. This program is used to log on to Windows machines remotely. In this lab, you use it only to create a

TCP connection. In Windows 7, click the **Start** button, click **All Programs**, click **Accessories**, and then click **Remote Desktop Connection**. (In Windows XP, click **Start**, point to **All Programs**, point to **Accessories**, point to **Communications**, and then click **Remote Desktop Connection**. You might not have to point to Communications if Remote Desktop Connection appears on the Accessories menu.) The Remote Desktop Connection window opens.

6. Type **192.168.54.1** in the Computer text box. Click **Connect**. The Windows Security dialog box for the Windows Server 2008 computer opens.

7. Log on as an administrator. If necessary, click **Yes** in the trust certificate. The Windows Server 2008 desktop appears.

8. Click the **Minimize** button on the horizontal bar at the top of the window to minimize the Remote Desktop session.

9. In the command prompt window, type **netstat** and press **Enter**. The computer displays information about the connection, indicating the protocol used, the state of the connection, the local address, the destination address, and the ports or service name used by each side of the connection. The state of the connection should be ESTABLISHED. What protocol does the Remote Desktop Connection use? Figure 2-4 shows the output of the **netstat** command.

10. On *SERVER1*, press **Ctrl+Alt+Del**, if necessary, and log on as an administrator. The Windows Server 2008 desktop appears.

11. Open the command prompt.

12. In the command prompt window, type **netstat** and press **Enter**. How are the results of the **netstat** command different when run on the server?

13. Type **netstat -e** and press **Enter**. The computer displays information about the number of bytes sent and received and about the number of packets sent and received. Table 2-2 shows options for the **netstat** command.

14. Type **ping 192.168.54.2** and press **Enter**. The computer indicates that it has received four replies from 192.168.54.2.

15. Type **netstat -e** again and press **Enter**. Has the number of packets sent and received increased?

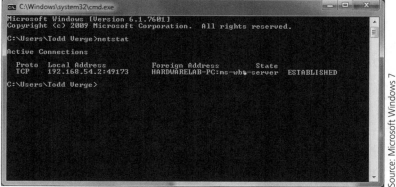

**Figure 2-4**   Typical output from the **netstat** command

**Table 2-2** Options for the `netstat` command

| Command | Action |
|---|---|
| netstat -a | Displays all connections and listening ports |
| netstat -e | Displays Ethernet statistics |
| netstat -s | Displays statistics per protocol |
| netstat -r | Displays the routing table |
| netstat -n | Displays numbers instead of names (usually used with the **-a** or **-r** options) |

© Cengage Learning 2013

16. Type **netstat -s** and press **Enter**. The computer displays information about individual protocols used.

17. Close the Remote Desktop Connection dialog box and log off both computers.

## Certification Objectives

Objectives for the Network+ Exam:

- 1.3 Explain the purpose and properties of IP addressing.
- 4.3 Given a scenario, use appropriate software tools to troubleshoot connectivity issues.
- 5.2 Explain the methods of network access security.

## Review Questions

1. What protocol does Remote Desktop Connection use?

   a. ICMP

   b. TCP

   c. UDP

   d. IP

2. About which protocols does the **netstat -s** command print information? (Choose all that apply.)

   a. ARP

   b. ICMP

   c. TCP

   d. UDP

3. At what layer of the OSI model does TCP work?

   a. Physical layer

   b. Data Link layer

   c. Network layer

   d. Transport layer

4. At what layer of the OSI model does IP work?

   a. Physical layer

   b. Data Link layer

   c. Network layer

   d. Transport layer

5. A user is having difficulty connecting to a remote Web site. After the user attempts to connect, the `netstat` command tells you that the connection state is established. Where in the OSI model is the problem probably located?

   a. The Data Link layer

   b. The Network layer

   c. The Transport layer

   d. Somewhere above the Transport layer

6. Why doesn't the `netstat` command display any information about ICMP connections?

   a. ICMP does not function at the Transport layer.

   b. ICMP is not a true protocol.

   c. ICMP is a connectionless protocol.

   d. ICMP is considered unimportant.

# Lab 2.5 Viewing Ethernet Frames

## Objectives

A network protocol analyzer is software or a hardware device that reads packets or frames directly from a computer's NIC and allows you to view them or to save them for later viewing. This process is called capturing the frames. A network protocol analyzer also decodes the frames captured so that you can look at the individual parts of the frame. Even though a network protocol analyzer captures frames, the packets are typically of the most interest to a network administrator.

Microsoft Network Monitor is a network protocol analyzer available on Windows Server 2008, as well as on other versions of Windows. You can use a network protocol analyzer to examine the traffic on a network one frame at a time, or one part of a frame at a time. As you gain experience looking at network traffic, you can also use Network Monitor to look for potential problems. For instance, you can look at Transport layer information in a series of packets to determine if the computer on the other end is sending data too quickly. With a little experience, Network Monitor or other network protocol analyzers can be invaluable troubleshooting tools.

It is important to keep in mind that a network protocol analyzer such as Network Monitor can be used to violate a user's privacy. As such, it should not be used carelessly or lightly.

After completing this lab, you will be able to:

• Use Network Monitor to look at captured frames

## Materials Required

This lab requires the following:

- The network required in Lab 1.4, consisting of a computer named *SERVER1* running Windows Server 2008, Standard Edition, with an IP address of 192.168.54.1, a computer named *WORKSTATION1* running Windows 7 or Windows XP Professional with an IP address of 192.168.54.2, a hub or switch, and two straight-through Category 5 (or better) UTP cables connecting the NICs on the computers to the hubs

- The latest version of Network Monitor downloaded from the Microsoft download center and installed on *SERVER1*

- Access to *SERVER1* as an administrator

- Access to *WORKSTATION1* as any ordinary user

---

| Estimated completion time: | **60 minutes** |
| --- | --- |

---

## Activity

1. Log on to *WORKSTATION1* as an ordinary user. The Windows desktop appears.

2. Open the command prompt.

3. Type `ping -t 192.168.54.1` and press **Enter**. This sends ICMP packets continuously to *SERVER1* and ensures that packets are available when you open Network Monitor.

4. Log on to SERVER1 as an administrator. The Windows Server 2008 desktop appears.

5. Click the **Start** button, point to **All Programs**, click **Microsoft Network Monitor 3.4**, and then click **Microsoft Network Monitor 3.3** on the submenu. (Your version number might be different.) The Microsoft Network Monitor window opens, as shown in Figure 2-5.

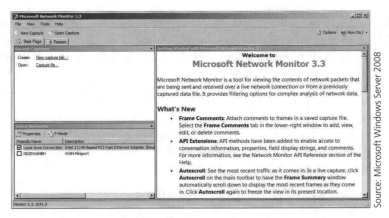

**Figure 2-5**    Microsoft Network Monitor

**Figure 2-6** A network capture

6. In the Select Networks pane, ensure that **Local Area Connection** is checked.

7. Click **New Capture** on the toolbar, and then click the **Start** button. Network Monitor begins to capture packets, as shown in Figure 2-6. The Frame Summary pane shows information about the packets Network Monitor captured.

8. When the number of frames captured is above 100, click **Stop** on the toolbar.

9. Locate a frame with "ICMP" in the Protocol field and click that row. The list of frames remains in the Frame Summary pane, while a detailed description of each part of the selected frame appears in the Frame Details pane, and a representation of the frame in hexadecimal appears in the Hex Details pane. See Figure 2-7 for an example of a captured frame.

10. By clicking the plus signs (+) in the Frame Details pane, you can display detailed information about each part of the packet. In the Frame Detail section, Network Monitor shows detailed information about the frame itself. What is the total frame length for the frame you chose?

**Figure 2-7** An individual frame in a network capture

11. Click the **plus sign (+)** next to Ethernet. Network Monitor shows detailed information about the Ethernet portion of the frame. What is the source address of the packet? What is the destination address of the packet? What is the Ethernet type?

12. Click the **plus sign (+)** next to Ipv4. Network Monitor shows detailed information about the IP portion of the packet. What is the source address of the packet? What is the destination address of the packet? Is there a checksum in the IP portion of the packet?

13. Click the **plus sign (+)** next to Icmp. Network Monitor shows detailed information about the ICMP portion of the packet. Is there another checksum for this portion of the packet?

14. Close Network Monitor. Click **No** when asked if you want to save the capture. Click **No** if asked to save unsaved entries in the database. On *WORKSTATION1*, press **Ctrl+C** to stop the **ping** command.

15. Log off both computers.

## Certification Objectives

Objectives for the Network+ Exam:

- 1.1 Compare the layers of the OSI and TCP/IP models.
- 4.3 Given a scenario, use appropriate software tools to troubleshoot connectivity issues.

## Review Questions

1. At what layer in the OSI model were the source and destination addresses for the packet in Step 11 located?

2. In the frame you examined in Steps 9 through 13, which portions of the packet calculated a CRC checksum? What layers of the OSI model do they correspond to?

3. A user is unable to reach your company's Web site. From the user's workstation, you can ping the remote Web server. How might you use Network Monitor or another network protocol analyzer to troubleshoot the problem? (Choose all that apply.)

   a. By checking to see if the workstation is sending packets to the Web server

   b. By checking to see if the server is sending packets to the workstation

   c. By checking the workstation's IP configuration

   d. By checking the workstation's ARP configuration

4. Which protocols can be seen using Network Monitor? (Choose all that apply.)

   a. ICMP

   b. ARP

   c. TCP

   d. UDP

5. About which OSI layer does Network Monitor *not* provide information?

   a. Physical layer

   b. Data Link layer

   c. Network layer

   d. Transport layer

# TRANSMISSION BASICS AND NETWORKING MEDIA

## Labs included in this chapter

- Lab 3.1 Learning Media Characteristics
- Lab 3.2 Creating a UTP Crossover Cable to Connect Two Computers
- Lab 3.3 Comparing Throughput
- Lab 3.4 Understanding How a Category 5 Cable Fails
- Lab 3.5 Connecting Two Switches with Fiber-Optic Cable

## Network+ Exam Objectives

| Objective | Lab |
| --- | --- |
| 3.1 Categorize standard media types and associated properties. | 3.1, 3.2, 3.4, 3.5 |
| 3.2 Categorize standard connector types based on network media. | 3.1, 3.2, 3.4, 3.5 |
| 3.6 Given a scenario, troubleshoot common physical connectivity problems. | 3.2 |
| 3.7 Compare and contrast different LAN technologies. | 3.3 |
| 4.2 Given a scenario, use appropriate hardware tools to troubleshoot connectivity issues. | 3.2 |

# Lab 3.1 Learning Media Characteristics

## Objectives

In this lab, you learn about the costs and characteristics of network media and networking and computer equipment. This gives you experience in comparing costs of network components and network media. It also gives you an idea of the equipment needed to set up a network and of the total costs involved.

Bear in mind that the cost of a particular medium includes not only the cost of the cable, but also the installation cost, the maintenance costs, and the cost of replacing the medium if it becomes obsolete in the future. In addition, the cost of networking and computer equipment and software varies widely, depending on the vendor, the equipment chosen, and the licensing terms.

After completing this lab, you will be able to:

- Identify the costs and characteristics of Category 5 UTP cable

## Materials Required

This lab requires the following:

- Access to a retail or online store that sells computer networking equipment
- Pencil and paper

Estimated completion time: **30–90 minutes**

## Activity

1. Visit a retail computer store (such as Best Buy or CompUSA) that sells Ethernet Category 5 cable, computers, software, and networking supplies. Alternately, visit a Web site (such as *www.cdw.com*) that specializes in computers, software, and networking supplies. In Figure 3-1, record the Web address or the name of the store.

2. In Figure 3-1, record the cost of Category 5 cable sold by the foot. If the store does not sell cable by the foot, divide the price of the longest Category 5 cable you can find by its length in feet.

3. In Figure 3-1, record the cost of the highest-quality cable available (Category 5e, Category 6, Category 6a, or Category 7), as you did in the previous step.

4. In Figure 3-1, record the cost and model information for a low-end, four-port Ethernet hub or switch with RJ-45 connections.

5. In Figure 3-1, record the cost and model information for a 16-port hub or switch with RJ-45 connections.

6. In Figure 3-1, record the cost and model information for an 802.11n wireless access point or a home router that includes a wireless access point.

7. In Figure 3-1, record the cost and model information for a typical desktop computer. If you have difficulty deciding on a model, choose one that is intermediate in price.

8. In Figure 3-1, record the cost and model information for a typical laptop computer. If you have difficulty deciding on a model, choose one that is intermediate in price.

9. In Figure 3-1, record the cost of an Ethernet NIC with an RJ-45 connection for a desktop. If your desktop computer already has an onboard NIC, record the cost as "Included."

10. In Figure 3-1, record the cost and model information for a PCMCIA or USB NIC with an RJ-45 connection for a laptop. If your laptop computer already has an onboard NIC, record the cost as "Included."

11. In Figure 3-1, record the cost and model information for a wireless network card that is compatible with the desktop computer you listed in Step 7. If your desktop computer already has an integrated wireless card, record the cost as "Included."

12. In Figure 3-1, record the cost and model information for a wireless network card that is compatible with the laptop you listed in Step 8. If your laptop already has an integrated wireless card, record the cost as "Included."

13. In Figure 3-1, record the cost of the full version of Windows 7 Professional.

14. Assume that you need to connect 50 workstations and 20 laptops to a network and that all of them must run Windows 7 Professional. Calculate the cost of these computers and their operating systems, assuming you use the computers you identified in Steps 7 and 8. Record this information in Figure 3-1.

15. Assume that each workstation and each laptop require 50 feet of cable. Calculate the cost of the total amount of Category 5 cable needed and record this information in Figure 3-1.

16. For comparison, calculate the cost of the total amount of the Category 5e, Category 6, Category 6a, or Category 7 cable you found in Step 3. Record this information in Figure 3-1.

17. Assume that each workstation uses a wired connection and that each laptop uses both a wired and a wireless connection. Calculate the total cost of all of the wired and wireless NICs. Record this information in Figure 3-1.

18. Assume that one wireless access point is required. (Additional wireless access points might be required depending on the physical layout of the building and other factors.) How many hubs or switches are required to connect all the workstations and all the laptops to the network at the same time? Calculate the total cost for hubs or switches and the wireless access point. Record this information in Figure 3-1.

19. Calculate the total cost of the network using Category 5 cable by adding up the totals you calculated in Steps 14 through 17. Record this information in Figure 3-1. Do not include in the total the cost of the other cabling you calculated in Step 14.

20. For comparison, calculate the total cost of the network using the highest-quality cable you could find (Category 6 or 7). Record this information in Figure 3-1. Do this by summing the totals you calculated in Steps 13 through 17. Do not include in the total the cost of the Category 5 cabling.

| Store or Web site name: | | |
|---|---|---|
| **Item** | **Cost** | **Notes** |
| Category 5 cable | | Per foot |
| Highest-quality cable available | | Per foot |
| Low-end, four-port Ethernet hub or switch with RJ-45 connections | | Model: |
| 16-port hub or switch with RJ-45 connections | | Model: |
| 802.11n wireless access point or a home router that includes a wireless access point | | Model: |
| Desktop computer | | Model: |
| Laptop computer | | Model: |
| Ethernet NIC for a desktop | | Model: |
| PCMCIA or USB NIC for a laptop | | Model: |
| Wireless network card for a desktop | | Model: |
| Wireless network card for a laptop | | Model: |
| Windows 7 Professional | | |

© Cengage Learning 2013

**Figure 3-1**   Cost information for Lab 3.1                    (*Continues*)

| Store or Web site name: | | |
| --- | --- | --- |
| Item | Cost | Notes |
| 50 workstations and 20 laptops with operating systems | | |
| Category 5 cable to connect all 50 workstations and 20 laptops | | |
| Category 5e, 6, 6a, or 7 cable to connect all 50 workstations and 20 laptops | | |
| Wired and wireless NICs for desktops and laptops | | |
| One wireless access point and a sufficient number of hubs or switches to connect all the workstations and laptops to the network | | |
| Total cost of the network with Category 5 cable | | |
| Total cost of the network with highest-quality cable available | | Type of cable: |

© Cengage Learning 2013

**Figure 3-1**    Cost information for Lab 3.1 (*Continued*)

## Certification Objectives

Objectives for the Network+ Exam:

- 3.1 Categorize standard media types and associated properties.
- 3.2 Categorize standard connector types based on network media.

## Review Questions

1. What type of connector does a 100Base-T network require?

   a. RJ-11

   b. BNC

   c. AUI

   d. RJ-45

2. Which of the following is commonly used to protect UTP cable from EMI?

  a. Conduit

  b. STP

  c. Crossover cable

  d. Lead shielding

3. What is the maximum throughput of a 100Base-TX network?

  a. 5 Mbps

  b. 10 Mbps

  c. 50 Mbps

  d. 100 Mbps

4. On a 10Base-T network, attenuation is addressed through the use of which of the following?

  a. Amplifiers

  b. Multiplexers

  c. Repeaters

  d. RF generators

5. What is the maximum allowable segment length on a 1000Base-T network?

  a. 85 feet

  b. 85 meters

  c. 185 feet

  d. 100 meters

6. Which of the following contributes to latency?

  a. The twist ratio of the cable

  b. Cable length

  c. EMI

  d. Attenuation

# Lab 3.2 Creating a UTP Crossover Cable to Connect Two Computers

## Objectives

You might find it necessary to make cables from time to time. The phrase "making cables" actually refers to the process of properly attaching connectors to the ends of a length of cable. Many companies make their own cables to save money. In addition, knowing how to make cables makes it easier to troubleshoot cabling problems.

Normal patch cables, also known as straight-through cables, have identical wire terminations on either end. Another kind of cable is a crossover cable. In this type of cable, the transmit and receive pins in one of the cable's plugs must be reversed. A crossover cable allows two workstations to connect directly to each other (without a connectivity device between them).

After completing this lab, you will be able to:

- Make a crossover Category 5 cable
- Directly connect two computers with an RJ-45 crossover cable by plugging one end of the cable into the NIC of one computer and the other end of the cable into the NIC of the second computer
- Use a cable tester to ensure cable integrity

## Materials Required

This lab requires the following:

- At least 10 feet of Category 5 (or better) UTP cable without connectors
- Two RJ-45 connectors (or more, if necessary)
- Two computers named *WORKSTATION1* and *WORKSTATION2* running Windows 7 or Windows XP Professional, configured to be in a workgroup named NETPLUS, with an Ethernet NIC
- Administrative access to both computers
- A network crimper
- A wire stripper
- A cable tester
- A wire-cutting tool

Estimated completion time: **60 minutes**

## Activity

1. Use the wire cutter to make a clean cut at both ends of the UTP cable.

2. Use the wire stripper to remove one inch (or less) of the sheath from one end of the UTP cable. Do not strip the insulation from the individual wires inside the UTP cable, and take care not to damage the insulation on the twisted pairs inside the cable.

3. Slightly separate the four wire pairs, but keep the pairs twisted around each other.

4. Hold the RJ-45 connector so that the opening faces you and the plastic flap is on the bottom. Push the wires into the RJ-45 connector so that each wire is in its own slot in the connector, in the order shown in Table 3-1. Use a crimping tool to punch down the cable. You have now completed one end of the cable.

**Table 3-1    Pin numbers and color codes for creating a TIA/EIA 568A straight-through cable end**

| Pin number | Pair number | Use | Color |
|---|---|---|---|
| 1 | 2 | Transmit | White with green stripe |
| 2 | 2 | Receive | Green |
| 3 | 3 | Transmit | White with orange stripe |
| 4 | 1 | Receive | Blue |
| 5 | 1 | Transmit | White with blue stripe |
| 6 | 3 | Receive | Orange |
| 7 | 4 | Transmit | White with brown stripe |
| 8 | 4 | Receive | Brown |

© Cengage Learning 2013

5. Repeat Steps 2 and 3 for the other end of the twisted-pair cable.

6. Hold the RJ-45 connector so that the opening faces you and the plastic flap is on the bottom, just as you did in Step 4. If you flip the RJ-45 connector over, the cable will not work. Push the wires into the RJ-45 connector so that each wire is in its own slot in the order shown in Table 3-2. Use a crimping tool to punch down the cable. This crosses the transmit and receive wires (both positive and negative), which allows the computers to communicate when connected. After completing this step, your crossover cable is ready to use. Figure 3-2 shows an example of a crossover cable.

**Table 3-2    Pin numbers and color codes for creating a TIA/EIA 568B crossover cable end**

| Pin number | Pair number | Use | Color |
|---|---|---|---|
| 1 | 3 | Transmit | White with orange stripe |
| 2 | 3 | Receive | Orange |
| 3 | 2 | Transmit | White with green stripe |
| 4 | 1 | Receive | Blue |
| 5 | 1 | Transmit | White with blue stripe |
| 6 | 2 | Receive | Green |
| 7 | 4 | Transmit | White with brown stripe |
| 8 | 4 | Receive | Brown |

© Cengage Learning 2013

7. Plug each end of the cable into the cable tester. If the cable tester determines there are any problems with your cable, remove the ends of the cable with a wire cutter and repeat the first six steps of this lab. Otherwise, skip to the next step. Making a cable properly on the first try is difficult.

8. Remove the cable ends from the cable tester.

**Figure 3-2**   Crossover cable

9. Connect one end of the cable to the NIC of *WORKSTATION1*.

10. Connect the other end of the same cable to the NIC of *WORKSTATION2*. The lights on each NIC turn on.

11. Log on to *WORKSTATION1* using an administrative account. The Windows desktop appears.

12. Click the **Start** button, click **Control Panel**, click **Network and Internet**, click **Network and Sharing Center**, and click **Change adapter settings**. (In Windows XP, click the **Start** button, point to **All Programs**, point to **Accessories**, point to **Communications**, and then click **Network Connections**.)

13. Right-click the **Local Area Connection** icon. Select **Properties** from the shortcut menu that appears. The Local Area Connection Properties window opens.

14. Double-click **Internet Protocol Version 4(TCP/IPv4)**. (In Windows XP, double-click **Internet Protocol (TCP/IP)**.) The Internet Protocol Version 4 (TCP/IPv4) Properties dialog box opens. (In Windows XP, the Internet Protocol (TCP/IP) Properties dialog box opens.)

15. Click the **Use the following IP address** option button. In the IP address text box, enter **192.168.54.2**. In the Subnet mask text box, enter **255.255.255.0**. Click **OK** and then click **OK** again.

16. Repeat Steps 11 through 15 on *WORKSTATION2*, using an IP address of **192.168.54.3**.

17. On *WORKSTATION2*, click the **Start** button, type **cmd** in the Search programs and files text box, and then press **Enter**. (In Windows XP, click the **Start** button, point to **All Programs**, point to **Accessories**, and then click **Command Prompt**.) A command prompt window opens.

18. Type **ping 192.168.54.2** and press **Enter**. The computer indicates that it has received four replies, demonstrating that the two computers can communicate with each other over the new cable.

19. On *WORKSTATION1*, open a command prompt window.

20. Type **ping 192.168.54.3** and press **Enter**. The computer indicates that it has received four replies from the remote computer.

21. Log off both computers.

## Certification Objectives

Objectives for the Network+ Exam:

- 3.1 Categorize standard media types and associated properties.
- 3.2 Categorize standard connector types based on network media.
- 3.6 Given a scenario, troubleshoot common physical connectivity problems.
- 4.2 Given a scenario, use appropriate hardware tools to troubleshoot connectivity issues.

## Review Questions

1. What is one use for a crossover cable?

   a. To connect a hub and a workstation

   b. To connect a workstation to a wall jack

   c. To connect two workstations directly

   d. To connect a workstation to a modem

2. Which of the following tools would be useful in creating a patch cable for a 100Base-T network?

   a. Screwdriver

   b. Crimper

   c. Soldering iron

   d. Pliers

3. In twisted-pair wire, how does the twist ratio affect transmission? (Choose all that apply.)

   a. The more twists per inch, the less cross talk transmission suffers.

   b. The more twists per inch, the slower the transmission.

   c. The more twists per inch, the more attenuation transmission suffers.

   d. The more twists per inch, the faster the transmission.

4. What is the maximum speed at which Category 3 UTP can transmit data?

   a. 1 Mbps

   b. 10 Mbps

   c. 100 Mbps

   d. 1 Gbps

5. What type of cable would connect a workstation to the wall jack in the work area of a 100Base-T network?

   a. Straight-through cable

   b. Crossover cable

   c. Coaxial cable

   d. Punch-down cable

6. What type of cable is required for 100Base-FX?

   a. Coaxial cable

   b. UTP

   c. STP

   d. Fiber-optic cable

7. Which of the following would be the best medium for an environment that is subject to heavy EMI?

   a. Fiber-optic cable

   b. RF

   c. Infrared

   d. UTP

# Lab 3.3 Comparing Throughput

## Objectives

As a network administrator, you often have to choose among different types of media, even within the same network. Throughput is often an important consideration in choosing among different network media. For instance, servers typically require faster media than most workstations, and some workstations require faster media than others. In addition, the types of applications in use on the network play a role in the types of media used. Some applications, such as streaming video, require more bandwidth than others.

When comparing media types, it is often helpful to look at the actual transmission rates under realistic conditions. The *actual* transmission rates often differ from the theoretical transmission rates. Many factors prevent a computer from transmitting or receiving data at the theoretical rate. These include the quality of the cabling, noise, and the ability of the computer on either end to send or receive data. In addition, the bandwidth used by other computers on the network can limit the available bandwidth. Also, you often need to verify that many applications work as expected with the intended media. With applications such as streaming video or IP telephony (VoIP), factors such as latency and transmission rate make a big difference in whether users can successfully use the application. Testing new applications under realistic conditions can help you make the best decision possible about the type of network media you use in your network.

After completing this lab, you will be able to:

- Measure the throughput on an Ethernet network
- Compare throughput on networks using different media
- Recognize that actual throughput might not reach the maximum throughput specified for a network

## Materials Required

This lab requires the following:

- A computer named *SERVER1* running Windows Server 2008, Standard Edition and configured as a domain controller for the netpluslab.net domain with an IP address of 192.168.54.1 and a subnet mask of 255.255.255.0
- A computer named *WORKSTATION1* running Windows 7 or Windows XP Professional in the netpluslab.net domain and configured with an IP address of 192.168.54.2 and a subnet mask of 255.255.255.0
- Access as the administrator to *SERVER1*
- Two hubs capable of at least 100 Mbps or two switches with RJ-45 ports configured so that each port is in the same VLAN
- Ethernet NICs with RJ-45 connectors in each computer so that each computer can transmit data at the rate of the hubs or switches
- Two straight-through Category 5 (or better) UTP cables that can be used to connect the computers to a hub
- One crossover Category 5 (or better) UTP cable that can be used to connect the two hubs directly
- On *SERVER1,* a shared folder named NETPLUS that can be accessed by the netplus user in the netpluslab.net domain; this folder should contain a large file (>50MB) such as a video file or a compressed folder

> Estimated completion time:  **25–30 minutes**

## Activity

1. Connect the computers to the first hub or switch.
2. On *SERVER1,* log on as the administrator. The Windows Server 2008 desktop appears.
3. Click the **Start** button, point to **All Programs,** click **Administrative Tools,** and then click **Performance Monitor.**
4. Select the **Performance Monitor** icon in the left pane.
5. Right-click the graph in the right pane. Select **Add Counters** from the shortcut menu. The Add Counters dialog box opens, as shown in Figure 3-3.
6. Click **Network Interface** in the list of available counters, and then click the computer's NIC in the Instances of selected object list box.

**Figure 3-3**   Add Counters dialog box

7. Expand the **Network Interface** category, and click **Bytes Total/sec** in the list below Network Interface. Click **Add**. The Bytes Total/sec counter is added to the list of counters being monitored.

8. Click **OK**. The Add Counters dialog box closes.

9. If the Performance window shows any counters besides Bytes Total/sec at the bottom of the right pane of the Performance window, click these counters to highlight them. Press the **Delete key** to delete them. You now see the NIC's current bandwidth.

10. Log on to *WORKSTATION1* with an administrative account. The Windows desktop appears.

11. Click the **Start** button, and then click **Computer** (or **My Computer** in Windows XP). The Computer window opens.

12. Click **Map network drive** on the toolbar. (In Windows XP, click **Tools** on the menu bar, and then click **Map Network Drive**.) The Map Network Drive window opens.

13. If necessary, choose drive letter **Z:** from the drop-down menu next to the Drive list box. Type **\\192.168.54.1\netplus** in the Folder text box, and then click **Finish**.

14. A message box opens, indicating that you are attempting to connect to \\192.168.54.1\ netplus. The Connect to 192.168.54.1 window opens. (The window might not appear if the password is the same on both computers. If so, go to Step 16.)

15. In the User name text box, enter **netplus@netpluslab.net**. In the Password text box, enter the password for the netplus account. Click **OK**. A window showing the contents of the shared netplus folder on the server is displayed.

16. Click the **Start** button, type **cmd** in the Search programs and files text box, and then press **Enter**. (In Windows XP, click the **Start** button, point to **All Programs**, point to **Accessories**, and then click **Command Prompt**.) A command prompt window opens.

17. Type **mkdir C:temp** and press **Enter**. The computer creates a new directory.

18. Type **notepad test.bat** and press **Enter**. A dialog box opens asking if you want to create the file.

19. Click **Yes**. The Notepad window opens.

20. In Notepad, enter the following three lines, substituting the correct filename for *filename*:

```
:Copy
copy Z:\filename C:\temp
goto COPY
```

21. Exit Notepad. A dialog box opens, asking if you want to save your changes. Click **Save**. (In Windows XP, click **Yes**.)

22. At the command prompt, type **test** and press **Enter**. The batch file continuously copies the file to *WORKSTATION1* from the shared folder on the Windows Server 2008 computer.

23. Look at the graph on *SERVER1*. If the line is flat and at the very bottom or the very top of the graph, right-click the graph and select **Properties** from the shortcut menu. Otherwise, go to Step 26.

24. On *SERVER1*, click the **Graph** tab. In the Maximum text box, enter **500** and click **OK**. The computer redraws the graph with the new scale. If the line on the graph is still flat, repeat the previous step and this step using 5000 and then 50,000 until the line is in the middle of the graph.

25. After a minute, look at the Average box at the bottom of the graph and record the number of bytes received per second. Multiply this number by 8 to find the number of bits received per second. Record the number of bits received per second and compare it with the bandwidth of the hub.

26. At the command prompt on *WORKSTATION1*, press **Ctrl+C** to stop the batch file. Type **Y** and press **Enter** when asked to terminate the batch job.

27. Leave *WORKSTATION1* connected to the first hub, but connect *SERVER1* to the second hub. Connect the two hubs directly with a crossover cable. The lights on each NIC turn on.

28. At the command prompt on *WORKSTATION1*, type **test** and press **Enter**.

29. Watch the graph on *SERVER1*. After a minute, record the number of bytes received per second. Multiply this number by 8 to find the number of bits received per second and compare it with the bandwidth of the hubs.

30. At the command prompt on *WORKSTATION1*, press **Ctrl+C** to stop the batch file. Type **Y** and press **Enter** when asked to terminate the batch job. On *SERVER1*, close the Performance Monitor window.

31. Compare the number of bits received per second through the single hub you recorded in Step 25 with the number of bits received per second through two hubs you recorded in Step 29.

32. Log off both computers.

## Certification Objective

Objective for the Network+ Exam:

- 3.7 Compare and contrast different LAN technologies.

## Review Questions

1. What might cause a 100Base-TX network to experience an average throughput of less than 100 Mbps? (Choose all that apply.)

   a. Heavy traffic on the network

   b. Excessive noise

   c. Too many protocols bound on the server

   d. A mix of different network operating systems on the servers

2. What is the maximum number of repeaters a data packet may traverse on a 100Base-T network?

   a. 2

   b. 3

   c. 4

   d. 5

3. What does the "T" in 10Base-T and 100Base-T stand for?

   a. Transmission

   b. Transport layer

   c. Twisted-pair

   d. Transparent

4. Which of the following is not capable of full duplexing?

   a. 10Base-T

   b. 100Base-TX

   c. 100Base-T4

   d. 100Base-FX

5. What type of media do wireless networks use? (Choose all that apply.)

   a. UTP

   b. Alpha wave

   c. Infrared

   d. Radio frequency

6. What type of cable is required for a 100Base-T network?

   a. CAT 3 or higher

   b. CAT 5 or higher

   c. CAT 6 or higher

   d. CAT 7 or higher

7. Where would you find a plenum cable?

   a. Above the ceiling tiles in an office

   b. In an outdoor cable trench that leads to a building

   c. Between a hub and a punch-down panel

   d. Between a workstation and a wall jack

# Lab 3.4 Understanding How a Category 5 Cable Fails

## Objectives

Verifying the integrity of network cabling is often an important first step in solving network problems. In the OSI model, the network media is at the Physical layer. If the network media is not functioning properly, the layers above the Physical layer will not function properly either. It is important to keep in mind that damage to cabling might not be immediately obvious and might result in odd or intermittent problems. For instance, a damaged cable might cause excess noise. Although data might be transmitted through the cable, protocols at higher levels of the OSI model will need to retransmit data. The problem might also become worse over time, eventually preventing data from being transmitted through the cable at all.

Network cabling should be protected as much as possible. It can be damaged slowly over time by factors such as excessive heat or pressure, or it can be damaged quickly by a user's foot or a backhoe. The better protected network cabling is, the longer it lasts.

In this lab, you simulate a failed cable by building an incorrectly made cable. Although cables can be damaged in many different ways, it is also important to verify that network cabling is properly installed in the first place. If you do not verify proper installation of network cabling, you might find it difficult to distinguish between a problem with the original installation and cabling damaged after the installation. This can prevent you from finding the ultimate source of the problem and fixing it properly.

After completing this lab, you will be able to:

- Identify the problem associated with an incorrectly wired Category 5 (or better) UTP cable

- Use a basic RJ-45 network cable tester (optional)

## Materials Required

This lab requires the following:

- At least 10 feet of Category 5 (or better) UTP cable

- Four RJ-45 connectors

- A computer named *WORKSTATION1* running Windows 7 or Windows XP Professional in the NETPLUS workgroup with an Ethernet NIC with RJ-45 connectors, configured with an IP address of 192.168.54.2 and a subnet mask of 255.255.255.0

- A computer named *WORKSTATION2* running Windows 7 or Windows XP Professional in the NETPLUS workgroup with an Ethernet NIC with RJ-45 connectors, configured with an IP address of 192.168.54.3 and a subnet mask of 255.255.255.0

- File and Printer Sharing for Microsoft Networks installed on both computers

- Administrative access to both computers

- A network crimper

- A wire stripper

- A wire-cutting tool

- A basic RJ-45 network cable tester (optional)
- A miswired Category 5 UTP cable created by your instructor (optional)
- Completion of Lab 3.2

Estimated completion time: **60 minutes**

## Activity

1. If you already have a miswired cable, skip to Step 5. Otherwise, you can create one with the following steps.

2. Perform Steps 1 through 4 of Lab 3.2 for one end of the twisted-pair cable.

3. Repeat Steps 1 through 3 of Lab 3.2 for the other end of the twisted-pair cable.

4. On the second end of the twisted-pair cable, push the wires into the RJ-45 connector so that each wire is in its own slot and so that the colors match the pin numbers listed in Table 3-3. Using a crimping tool, punch down the end of the cable. This results in an incorrectly made cable.

**Table 3-3   Pin numbers and color codes for creating an incorrect cable end**

| Pin number | Pair number | Color |
|---|---|---|
| 1 | 4 | Brown |
| 2 | 4 | White with brown stripes |
| 3 | 1 | White with blue stripes |
| 4 | 3 | White with orange stripes |
| 5 | 3 | Orange |
| 6 | 1 | Blue |
| 7 | 2 | White with green stripes |
| 8 | 2 | Green |

© Cengage Learning 2013

5. Connect one end of the cable to each computer. If the network adapter lights on each computer do not illuminate, proceed with the next step. If they do, you accidentally made a correctly wired cable, and you need to begin this lab again.

6. Log on to *WORKSTATION1* with an administrative account. The Windows desktop appears.

7. Click the **Start** button, type **cmd** in the Search programs and files text box, and then press **Enter**. (In Windows XP, click the **Start** Button, point to **All Programs**, point to **Accessories**, and then click **Command Prompt**.) A command prompt window opens.

8. Type **ping 192.168.54.3** and press **Enter**. The computer indicates that the request timed out four times.

9. Repeat Steps 6 through 8 on *WORKSTATION2*, attempting to ping the IP address 192.168.54.2 instead.

10. If you have a basic cable tester, use it to test the cable for problems. What information does the cable tester give you?

11. Using the wire-cutting tool, cut the incorrectly wired end of the cable about one inch from the RJ-45 connector. The RJ-45 connector should drop off.

12. Rewire and recrimp the connector to make a crossover cable, as described in Lab 3.2. This connector should be wired according to Table 3-1. Test the cable again if you have a cable tester, and then connect one end of the cable to the NIC in each of the computers.

13. In the command prompt window on *WORKSTATION1*, type **ping 192.168.54.3** and press **Enter**. The computer indicates that it has received four replies from *WORKSTATION2*.

14. In the command prompt window on *WORKSTATION2*, type **ping 192.168.54.2** and press **Enter**. The computer indicates that it has received four replies from *WORKSTATION1*.

15. Log off both computers.

## Certification Objectives

Objectives for the Network+ Exam:

- 3.1 Categorize standard media types and associated properties.
- 3.2 Categorize standard connector types based on network media.

## Review Questions

1. What pin number is used for transmitting a positive signal on an RJ-45 straight-through-patch cable?

   a. 1

   b. 2

   c. 5

   d. 6

2. Which of the following could be a symptom of a damaged patch cable between a workstation and the wall jack on a UTP network? (Choose all that apply.)

   a. The workstation cannot send or receive data to or from the network.

   b. The workstation and other workstations in the same office cannot send or receive data to or from the network.

   c. The workstation can send data to the network but cannot receive data from the network.

   d. All workstations on the same segment can send data to the network but cannot receive data from the network.

3. How does bend radius affect transmission?

   a. Transmission is not successful until the bend radius has been reached.

   b. Transmission cannot occur at the bend radius.

   c. Transmission is unreliable after the bend radius is exceeded.

   d. Transmission is less secure after the bend radius is exceeded.

4. How many wire pairs are in a typical Category 5 cable?

   a. 2

   b. 3

   c. 4

   d. 6

5. What problem could be caused by laying cable in the ceiling tiles six inches above a bank of fluorescent lights?

   a. Increased latency

   b. EMI

   c. Fire hazard

   d. Decreased bend radius

6. What organization is responsible for establishing structured wiring standards?

   a. TIA/EIA

   b. ANSI

   c. ITU

   d. FCC

# Lab 3.5 Connecting Two Switches with Fiber-Optic Cable

## Objectives

In this lab, you connect two switches with fiber-optic cable. Although UTP cable is less fragile, less expensive, and easier to handle than fiber, fiber can allow the transfer of more information over greater distances than UTP cable. In addition, electrical interference does not affect fiber.

A port used to connect two switches is often called an uplink port. An uplink port often uses faster media than the other ports on the switch, but not always. Traffic between the two switches is transmitted through the uplink ports. If the other ports on the switch transmit a lot of traffic between the two switches, the uplink port might become saturated. This reduces throughput for any traffic that must go through the two switches. If the uplink ports use a faster media than the other ports on the switch, it becomes more difficult (or impossible) to saturate the link between the two ports.

After completing this lab, you will be able to:

• Connect two switches using multimode fiber

## Materials Required

This lab requires the following:

- A computer named *WORKSTATION1* running Windows 7 or XP Professional with a NIC and with an IP address of 192.168.54.2 and a subnet mask of 255.255.255.0

- A computer named *WORKSTATION2* running Windows 7 or Windows XP Professional with a NIC and with an IP address of 192.168.54.3 and a subnet mask of 255.255.255.0

- Administrative access to both computers

- A shared folder on *WORKSTATION2* named NETPLUS

- Two switches, named *SWITCH1* and *SWITCH2*, with fiber uplink ports (with any necessary configuration to act as uplink ports), the appropriate connectors, and all ports configured in the same VLAN

- Installation of any adapters, such as Gigabit Interface Converters (GBICs), necessary for operation of the uplink ports

- A length of fiber-optic cable with the appropriate connectors to attach to the two switches

- Two Category 5 (or better) UTP cables with RJ-45 connectors

Other fiber connectors may be used as appropriate.

Estimated completion time: **20 minutes**

## Activity

1. Plug the RJ-45 connector at one end of a UTP cable into the NIC of *WORKSTATION1*. Plug the RJ-45 connector at the other end of the cable into one of the RJ-45 ports on *SWITCH1*. Link lights on the switch and on the NIC light up.

2. Repeat the previous step, connecting *WORKSTATION2* to *SWITCH2*.

3. If necessary, remove the plugs from one of the fiber uplink ports on *SWITCH1*. Fiber ports often come with a plug to protect the port from dust and other damage.

Fiber ports may emit invisible laser radiation when they do not contain a cable, so do not stare into an open port. If possible, avoid looking into one while the switch is powered on.

4. Grasp the connector at one end of the fiber-optic cable. Making sure that the SC connector is properly oriented, push it into the uplink port on *SWITCH1* until the connector snaps into place. Link lights on both switches light up.

5. Log on to *WORKSTATION1* using an administrative account. The Windows desktop appears.

6. Click the **Start** button, type **cmd** in the Search programs and files text box, and then press **Enter**. (In Windows XP, click the **Start** button, point to **All Programs**, point to **Accessories**, and then click **Command Prompt**.) A command prompt window opens.

7. Type **ping 192.168.54.3** and press **Enter**. The computer indicates that it has received four replies.

8. Repeat Steps 5 through 7 on *WORKSTATION2*, and then ping the IP address **192.168.54.2**.

9. Log off both computers.


## Certification Objectives

Objectives for the Network+ Exam:

- 3.1 Categorize standard media types and associated properties.
- 3.2 Categorize standard connector types based on network media.


## Review Questions

1. Which of the following is *not* an advantage of fiber cables over UTP cables?

   a. Fiber is not susceptible to electric interference, whereas UTP cable is.

   b. Fiber is less fragile than UTP cable.

   c. Fiber is less expensive than UTP cable.

   d. Fiber can transmit data over longer distances than UTP cable.

2. In which of the following situations would it be possible to use a UTP cable standard such as 1000Base-CX over a fiber-optic cable standard such as 1000Base-LX or 1000Base-T?

   a. When connecting two data centers over distances of 2 km or less

   b. When connecting short distances of 25 meters or less between network devices and servers inside a single data center

   c. When connecting short distances of 200 meters or less between network devices and workstations inside a building

   d. When connecting buildings inside a campus over distances of 500 meters or less

3. Which of the following problems could cause optic loss in fiber-optic cable?

   a. Cross talk between strands of fiber in multimode fiber cables

   b. Cross talk between cables in single-mode fiber cables

   c. Electromagnetic interference caused by power lines near the cables

   d. Oil accidentally placed in a connection during splicing

4. 100Base-FX requires multimode fiber cable with two or more strands. How are these strands used to transmit and receive data? (Choose all that apply.)

   a. One strand is used for both transmission and reception in both full and half duplex.

   b. Both strands are used for transmission and reception in full duplex.

   c. One strand is used for transmission, and the other is used for reception in half duplex.

   d. Both strands are used for transmission and reception in full duplex, whereas there is no half duplex for 100Base-FX.

5. You work for a small ISP. Which fiber technology would be best for connecting to your telecommunications carrier over a distance of 2.8 miles?

   a. 1000Base-LX

   b. 1000Base-SX

   c. 10GBase-SR

   d. 1000Base-T

# INTRODUCTION TO TCP/IP PROTOCOLS

## Labs included in this chapter

- Lab 4.1 Configuring IP Addresses and Subnet Masks
- Lab 4.2 Automatically Assigning IP Addresses with DHCP
- Lab 4.3 Configuring Domain Name System (DNS) Properties
- Lab 4.4 Using FTP
- Lab 4.5 Understanding Port Numbers
- Lab 4.6 Disabling Unnecessary Protocols

## Network+ Exam Objectives

| Objective | Lab |
| --- | --- |
| 1.3 Explain the purpose and properties of IP addressing. | 4.1 |
| 1.5 Identify common TCP and UDP default ports. | 4.5 |
| 1.6 Explain the function of common networking protocols. | 4.2, 4.3, 4.4, 4.6 |
| 2.3 Explain the purpose and properties of DHCP. | 4.2 |
| 4.3 Given a scenario, use appropriate software tools to troubleshoot connectivity issues. | 4.1, 4.2, 4.3 |

# Lab 4.1 Configuring IP Addresses and Subnet Masks

## Objectives

To address a TCP/IP host properly, you need both an IP address and a subnet mask. The subnet mask is used to further divide a network. This allows a network administrator to control access or traffic between two subnetworks (or subnets). A router or layer-3 switch is required to route network traffic between the two subnets. For instance, you might want to prevent users from directly accessing a Web server. If you put the users and the Web server on different subnets, you can then use a router to control user access to the Web server.

An IP address consists of four numbers separated by dots. Each number in the address is called an octet. For instance, in the IP address 10.172.11.145, the first octet is 10, the second octet is 172, and so on. IP addresses have traditionally been divided into classes based on the first octet. The first octet of Class A addresses is between 1 and 127, the first octet of Class B addresses is between 128 and 191, and the first octet of Class C addresses is between 192 and 223. Class D addresses, whose first octet ranges from 224 to 239, are reserved for multicast. Class E addresses, whose first octet ranges from 240 to 254, are reserved for experimental purposes. Finally, addresses whose first octet is 255 are reserved for broadcasts.

Subnet masks can be used to conserve IP addresses. The size of a subnet mask determines the number of hosts that can be placed on a network. Using subnet masks, you can allocate IP address blocks that fit the number of hosts you have. The default subnet mask of a Class B network is 255.255.0.0, and it can have up to 65,534 hosts. A Class A network has a default subnet mask of 255.0.0.0, and it can have up to 16,777,214 hosts. Without subnetting, you would not be able to divide these very large networks into smaller networks. With subnetting, you can carve a larger network into many different subnets. For instance, suppose you were assigned a Class B network. If you subdivided this network into smaller networks with subnet masks of 255.255.255.0 (the default subnet mask for Class C networks), you would be able to divide the Class B network into 256 smaller networks.

After completing this lab, you will be able to:

- Configure IP addresses and subnet masks in Windows 7 or Windows XP Professional
- Discuss the purpose of subnet masks

## Materials Required

This lab requires the following:

- Two computers running Microsoft Windows 7 or Windows XP Professional, both configured as members of the NETPLUS workgroup
- Access to each computer as an administrator
- Both computers connected to a hub or switch with Category 5 (or better) UTP cables

> Estimated completion time: **20 minutes**

## Activity

1. Log on to both computers as an administrator.
2. On one computer, click the **Start** button, click **Control Panel**, click **Network and Internet**, click **Network and Sharing Center**, and click **Change adapter settings**. (In Windows XP, click

**Figure 4-1**  Entering the IP address manually

the **Start** button, point to **All Programs**, point to **Accessories**, point to **Communications**, and then click **Network Connections**.) The Network Connections window opens.

3. In the Network Connections window, right-click **Local Area Connection** and select **Properties** from the shortcut menu. The Local Area Connection Properties window opens.

4. Double-click **Internet Protocol Version 4 (TCP/IPv4)**. The Internet Protocol (TCP/IPv4) Properties dialog box opens. (In Windows XP, double-click **Internet Protocol (TCP/IP)**. The Internet Protocol (TCP/IP) Properties dialog box opens.)

5. Click the **Use the following IP address** option button.

6. Enter **172.20.1.1** in the IP address text box.

7. Enter **255.255.255.0** in the Subnet mask text box. See Figure 4-1. If necessary, clear the Default gateway and DNS server fields.

8. Click **OK** and then click **OK** again. The Local Area Connection Properties window closes.

9. Now you configure the second computer in a different network. Repeat Steps 2 through 8 on the second computer, using **172.20.2.1** as the IP address and **255.255.255.0** as the subnet mask. Table 4-1 shows the IP addresses and subnet masks on each computer.

10. You now have configured the two computers on two different subnets. To demonstrate this, on the second computer click the **Start** button, type **cmd** in the Search programs

**Table 4-1  IP address and subnet mask assignments in different networks**

| Computer | IP address | Subnet mask |
| --- | --- | --- |
| First computer | 172.20.1.1 | 255.255.255.0 |
| Second computer | 172.20.2.1 | 255.255.255.0 |

© Cengage Learning 2013

and files box, and then press **Enter**. (In Windows XP, click the **Start** button, point to **All Programs**, point to **Accessories**, and then click **Command Prompt**.) A command prompt window opens.

11. In the command prompt window, type **ping 172.20.1.1** and press **Enter**. You see a message indicating that the remote computer is unreachable. The message appears on the screen four times.

12. Repeat Steps 10 and 11 on the first computer, attempting to ping **172.20.2.1**.

13. Now you change the subnet mask so that both computers are on the same network. Repeat Steps 2 through 8 on the first computer, keeping the IP address the same but changing the subnet mask to **255.255.0.0**.

14. Repeat Steps 2 through 8 on the second computer, keeping the IP address the same but changing the subnet mask to **255.255.0.0**. Table 4-2 summarizes the new IP address assignments for the network.

**Table 4-2  New IP address assignments in the same network**

| Computer | IP address | Subnet mask |
|---|---|---|
| First computer | 172.20.1.1 | 255.255.0.0 |
| Second computer | 172.20.2.1 | 255.255.0.0 |

© Cengage Learning 2013

15. Repeat Step 11 on the second computer, attempting to ping **172.20.1.1**. The computer receives four replies, indicating that there is network connectivity between the two computers.

16. Repeat Step 11 on the first computer, attempting to ping **172.20.2.1**.

17. Log off both computers.

## Certification Objectives

Objectives for the Network+ Exam:

- 1.3 Explain the purpose and properties of IP addressing.
- 4.3 Given a scenario, use appropriate software tools to troubleshoot connectivity issues.

## Review Questions

1. What class of network did you configure in this activity?

   a. Class A

   b. Class B

   c. Class C

   d. Class D

2. What is the purpose of a subnet mask?

   a. To indicate which protocols a particular network uses

   b. To further subdivide a network

c. To mask, or prevent access to, portions of a network

    d. To limit the protocols used in a particular network

3. A network has a subnet mask of 255.255.255.0. How many usable IP addresses are available for network hosts?

    a. 65,535

    b. 65,534

    c. 256

    d. 254

4. Assuming that it has the default subnet mask, why can't you assign the IP address 192.168.54.255 to a host?

    a. This address is reserved for multicast.

    b. This address is reserved for experimental uses.

    c. This address describes the network.

    d. This address is the broadcast address.

5. Which of the following commands can you use in Windows to display information about the subnet mask configured for a particular NIC?

    a. `ipconfig`

    b. `ping`

    c. `cmd`

    d. `netstat`

# Lab 4.2 Automatically Assigning IP Addresses with DHCP

## Objectives

In this lab, you assign IP addresses to client workstations automatically with a Dynamic Host Configuration Protocol (DHCP) server. DHCP allows you to assign IP addresses from a central location without having to configure each workstation individually. In all but the smallest networks, this saves you time. You can also configure additional information, such as the default gateway and any DNS or WINS servers to be used.

DHCP works by assigning a pool of IP addresses to a network. When a workstation requests an IP address, the DHCP server assigns one of the available addresses from the pool. Most network administrators do not use DHCP to address their servers, routers, or other network devices like printers. You might find it useful to set aside a range of IP addresses on each network for devices with static IP addresses. Servers and most network devices typically have static IP addresses, and are not often moved. However, you can use DHCP to assign static addresses based on a device's MAC address.

If a Windows computer configured to use DHCP is unable to obtain IP address information from a DHCP server, it uses Automatic Private IP Addressing (APIPA) to assign itself an IP address. However, the DHCP client periodically attempts to reach the DHCP server until it can obtain an IP address. APIPA addresses are in the range from 169.254.0.0 to 169.254.255.255 and have a subnet mask of 255.255.0.0. The APIPA address pool is a Class B address set aside by the Internet Assigned Numbers Authority (IANA), so network administrators cannot use it for any other purpose. Although APIPA can simplify address assignment on simple networks, it does not work well in networks with more than one subnet or that need to connect to the Internet.

To configure the Windows DHCP server, you create a DHCP scope. Each scope consists of a range of IP addresses to be assigned, addresses to be excluded from the scope, and other information to be assigned to clients. Multiple DHCP scopes are typically used when a DHCP server needs to assign addresses for multiple subnets.

After completing this lab, you will be able to:

- Configure the DHCP server on Windows Server 2008
- Understand DHCP and dynamic addressing

## Materials Required

This lab requires the following:

- A computer named *SERVER1* running Windows Server 2008, Standard Edition, configured as a DNS server and a domain controller for the netpluslab.net domain, with an IP address of 192.168.54.1 and a subnet mask of 255.255.255.0
- Access to the computer as the administrator
- DHCP installed on *SERVER1* but not configured
- A computer running Windows 7 or Windows XP Professional in the netpluslab.net domain, without a specified IP address
- Administrative access to the Windows 7 or Windows XP Professional computer
- Both computers connected to a hub with straight-through Category 5 (or better) UTP cables

Estimated completion time: **30 minutes**

## Activity

1. Log on to *SERVER1* as the administrator. The Windows Server 2008 desktop appears.
2. Click the **Start** button, point to **Administrative Tools,** and then click **DHCP.** The DHCP window opens.
3. Click **server1.netpluslab.net** in the left pane of the window. Right-click **IPv4,** and click **New Scope.** The New Scope Wizard opens.
4. Click **Next.**
5. Enter **Net Plus Lab** in the Name text box. Enter **Test** in the Description text box. Click **Next.**
6. Now you configure the DHCP server to assign clients IP addresses from 192.168.54.10 to 192.168.54.200. This range allows for servers and network devices with static IP addresses from 192.168.54.1 to 192.168.54.9 and 192.168.54.201 to 192.168.54.254. In the Start IP address text box, enter **192.168.54.10.** In the End IP address text box,

**Figure 4-2** New Scope Wizard

enter **192.168.54.200**. In the Subnet mask text box, enter **255.255.255.0,** if necessary. Figure 4-2 shows the New Scope Wizard. Click **Next.**

7. Now you exclude the IP address 192.168.54.100 from the DHCP scope. In the Start IP address text box, enter **192.168.54.100.** This allows you to reserve this static IP address for the existing server in the middle of the range of IP addresses to be used for the DHCP scope. Click **Add.** The computer excludes the address from the DHCP scope. Click **Next.**

8. Now you can assign the amount of time that a client can use an IP address assigned to it from the DHCP server before it needs to renew the address. Enter **10** in the Days text box. Click **Next.**

9. Now you have the opportunity to configure further options. Click the **Yes, I want to configure these options now** option button, if necessary. Click **Next.**

10. Now you can specify the default gateway used by clients. Click **Next** because this network has no default gateway.

11. Now you can specify information about domain name resolution for clients. In the Parent domain text box, enter **netpluslab.net** if necessary. In the IP address text box, enter **192.168.54.1,** and click **Add.** Clients can now use this server as their DNS server. Click **Next.**

12. In this window, you can specify WINS servers. Click **Next.**

13. Now you must activate the DHCP scope. Make sure that the **Yes, I want to activate this scope now** option button is selected, click **Next,** and then click **Finish.**

14. If the server1.netpluslab.net icon is a white circle with a red arrow in the center, right-click **IPv4** in the left pane, and select **Authorize** from the shortcut menu. Wait a few seconds, and press **F5.** If the server1.netpluslab.net icon in the left pane is not a green circle with a white check mark in the center, press **F5** every few seconds until it is. A green circle with a white check mark indicates that the scope is active, whereas

a red arrow indicates that it is not. The DHCP server is now authorized to assign IP addresses in the netpluslab.net domain.

15. Log on to the Windows 7 or XP computer as an administrator. The Windows desktop appears.

16. Click the **Start** button, click **Control Panel**, click **Network and Internet**, click **Network Sharing**, right-click **Network**, and click **Properties**. Click **Change adapter settings in the left hand panel**. (In Windows XP, click the **Start** button, point to **All Programs**, point to **Accessories**, point to **Communications**, and then click **Network Connections**.) The Network Connections window opens.

17. Right-click the **Local Area Connection** icon, and select **Properties** from the shortcut menu. The Local Area Connection window opens.

18. Double-click **Internet Protocol Version 4 (TCP/IPv4)**. The Internet Protocol (TCP/IPv4) Properties dialog box opens. (In Windows XP, double-click **Internet Protocol (TCP/IP)**. The Internet Protocol (TCP/IP) Properties dialog box opens.)

19. Click the **Obtain an IP address automatically** and **Obtain DNS server address automatically** option buttons. Click **OK**, and then click **OK** again to close the Local Area Connection Properties window.

20. Click the **Start** button, type **cmd** in the Search programs and files box, and then press **Enter**. (In Windows XP, click the **Start** button, point to **All Programs**, point to **Accessories**, and then click **Command Prompt**.) A command prompt window opens.

21. Type **ipconfig** and press **Enter**. What is the current IP address of this computer?

22. Type **ipconfig/release** and press **Enter**. The computer releases any current address assigned by DHCP.

23. Type **ipconfig/renew** and press **Enter**. The computer obtains an IP address from the DHCP server and prints it. What is the new IP address?

24. Type **ipconfig/all** and press **Enter**. Record the name or address of the DNS server, the DHCP server, and the time the DHCP lease expires.

25. Now you examine what happens when a computer running Windows fails to get an IP address through DHCP. Disconnect the cable connecting *SERVER1* to the hub or switch. (Do not disconnect *WORKSTATION1* from the hub or switch.)

26. In the command prompt window, type **ipconfig/release** and press **Enter**. The computer prints information for the NIC indicating that the IP address and subnet mask are both 0.0.0.0.

27. Type **ipconfig/renew** and press **Enter**. After a couple of minutes, the computer indicates that it was unable to contact the DHCP server.

28. Type **ipconfig/all** and press **Enter**. The computer prints the new IP address and subnet mask for the computer. What are the IP address and subnet mask now? What DNS servers and domain name are now configured for the server?

29. Connect *SERVER1* to the hub again. Wait a couple of minutes and type **ipconfig** in the command prompt window. Repeat this step until the computer is able to obtain an IP address from the DHCP server.

30. Log off both computers.

## Certification Objectives

Objectives for the Network+ Exam:

- 1.6 Explain the function of common networking protocols.
- 2.3 Explain the purpose and properties of DHCP.
- 4.3 Given a scenario, use appropriate software tools to troubleshoot connectivity issues.

## Review Questions

1. What was the IP address the Windows computer obtained in Step 23?

2. When does the DHCP lease you obtained in this lab expire?

3. Which of the following are valid methods of assigning IP addresses to workstations, servers, and network devices? (Choose all that apply.)

   a. Manual configuration

   b. DHCP

   c. BOOTP

   d. POST

4. You would like to assign a WINS server to each workstation. Can you accomplish this via DHCP?

5. Your colleague placed a second DHCP server on the network by mistake. What might happen as a result? (Choose all that apply.)

   a. The second DHCP server might lease duplicate addresses to some hosts.

   b. The second DHCP server might give its clients incorrect settings.

   c. DHCP might stop working on the first DHCP server.

   d. You might need to configure IP addresses on some hosts manually.

6. Which of the following information could not be given out by a DHCP server?

   a. WINS server address

   b. DNS server address

   c. Default gateway

   d. Additional network protocols to be used

7. All of the following configuration information can be supplied by a DHCP server. Which of the following cannot be supplied by APIPA? (Choose all that apply.)

   a. IP address

   b. Subnet mask

   c. DNS servers

   d. Default gateway

# Lab 4.3 Configuring Domain Name System (DNS) Properties

## Objectives

The Domain Name System (DNS) is a method of associating an IP address with a host name. It is an alternative to the hosts file, and is much easier to manage and maintain over many servers. For that reason, DNS is used throughout the Internet. When you open a Web browser and attempt to connect to *www.comptia.com,* for example, the Web browser first queries a DNS server to find the IP address of the Web site. If the DNS server your computer is configured to use does not know the IP address associated with *www.comptia.com,* it queries the authoritative name server for the comptia.com domain (or zone). The authoritative name server is the DNS server with the definitive DNS information for that domain. When the authoritative DNS server responds with the IP address to your DNS server, your DNS server sends that information to your computer. The Web browser on your computer then uses that IP address to connect to the Web site.

In addition to finding the IP address belonging to a particular host name (a process known as a forward DNS lookup), DNS is also used to find the host name belonging to a particular IP address. This process is known as a reverse DNS lookup. A computer can use a reverse DNS lookup to determine the name of a computer attempting to access its network resources. However, reverse DNS lookups are not a reliable way of determining this information.

One tool you can use to find DNS information directly is the **nslookup** command. This command allows you to find the IP address associated with a particular host name and other information.

Keep in mind that beginning with Windows 2000 Server, DNS has become tightly integrated with Active Directory. Before Windows 2000 Server, making a mistake when configuring DNS might prevent you from accessing a server by name. Now, making a mistake configuring DNS can prevent Active Directory from working properly. It is important to keep DNS working properly in networks that use Windows Server 2008.

After completing this lab, you will be able to:

- Add a DNS server to DNS
- Add a DNS zone
- Add a DNS host
- Configure a computer to refer to the DNS server
- Access a computer using its DNS name

## Materials Required

This lab requires the following:

- A computer running Windows Server 2008, Standard Edition named *SERVER1* configured with an IP address of 192.168.54.1 and a subnet mask of 255.255.255.0
- The Windows Server 2008 computer configured as a domain controller for the netpluslab.net domain with the DNS server role installed
- A reverse lookup zone configured for the 192.168.54.x subnet

- A computer running Windows 7 or Windows XP Professional named *WORKSTATION1* configured with an IP address of 192.168.54.3 and a subnet mask of 255.255.255.0 but without a DNS server configured

- A second computer running Windows 7 or Windows XP Professional named *WORKSTATION2* configured with an IP address of 192.168.54.5 and a subnet mask of 255.255.255.0 but without a DNS server configured

- Administrative access to both computers

- Each computer connected to a hub or switch with straight-through CAT 5 (or better) UTP cables

Estimated completion time: **30 minutes**

## Activity

1. Log on to *SERVER1* as the administrator. The Windows Server 2008 desktop appears.

2. Click the **Start** button, point to **Administrative Tools**, and then click **DNS**. The DNS Manager window opens.

3. If necessary, click the **plus sign (+)** next to the server name to expand the tree underneath it. Right-click the name of the server. Click **New Zone**. The New Zone Wizard opens.

4. Click **Next**. The next window in the wizard asks you to select the type of zone you want to configure.

5. Make sure that the **Primary zone** option button is selected, and click **Next**. The next window in the wizard asks you to choose whether you want to create a forward or reverse lookup zone.

6. Make sure that the **Forward lookup zone** option is selected, and click **Next**. The wizard now asks you to choose a name for the zone.

7. In the Zone name text box, type **otherorg.net**, and then click **Next**. The next window asks if you want to create a new zone file or use an existing one.

8. Make sure the **Create a new file with this file name** option button is selected, and then click **Next**. The next window in the wizard asks you to select the type of DNS updates to be used.

9. Click **Next** to select the default option. The next window in the wizard summarizes the options you have chosen and indicates that you have finished.

10. Click **Finish**. The New Zone Wizard closes.

11. In the left pane of the DNS Manager window, click the **plus sign (+)** next to the Forward Lookup Zones folder. The tree expands, showing a list of domains for which this DNS server is authoritative, including the new otherorg.net domain.

12. In the left pane, click the **otherorg.net** folder to select it. Right-click the **otherorg.net** folder, and click **New Host (A or AAAA)** from the shortcut menu. The New Host dialog box opens.

13. In the Name text box, type **workstation1**. In the IP address text box, type **192.168.54.3**. Place a check in the **Create associated pointer (PTR) record** check box. Figure 4-3 shows the DNS Manager window and the New Host dialog box.

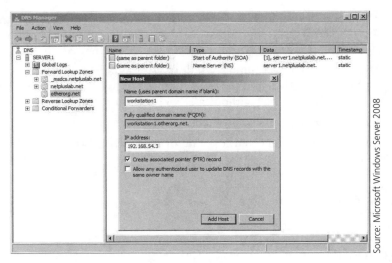

Source: Microsoft Windows Server 2008

**Figure 4-3**   The DNS Manager window and New Host dialog box

14. Click the **Add Host** button. The DNS dialog box opens, indicating that the host record workstation1.otherorg.net was successfully created.

15. Click **OK**. The DNS dialog box closes.

16. Click **Done**. The New Host dialog box closes.

17. Click the **netpluslab.net** folder to select it, right-click the **netpluslab.net** folder, and then click **New Host (A or AAAA)** from the shortcut menu. The New Host dialog box opens.

18. In the New Host dialog box, repeat Steps 13 through 15, creating the domain name **workstation2.netpluslab.net** with an IP address of **192.168.54.5**.

19. Click **Done**.

20. Log on to *WORKSTATION1* as an administrator. The Windows desktop appears.

21. Click the **Start** button, click **Control Panel**, click **Network and Internet**, and then click **Network Sharing Center**. Click **Change adapter settings**. (In Windows XP, click the **Start** button, point to **All Programs**, point to **Accessories**, point to **Communications**, and then click **Network Connections**.) The Network Connections window opens.

22. Right-click **Local Area Connection** and click **Properties** from the shortcut menu. The Local Area Connection Properties window opens.

23. Double-click **Internet Protocol Version 4 (TCP/IPv4)**. The Internet Protocol (TCP/IPv4) Properties dialog box opens. (In Windows XP, double-click **Internet Protocol (TCP/IP)**. The Internet Protocol (TCP/IP) Properties dialog box opens.)

24. Click the **Use the following DNS server addresses** option button, if necessary. In the Preferred DNS server text box, type **192.168.54.1**.

25. Click **OK** and then click **Close** to exit the Local Area Connection Properties window.

26. Click the **Start** button, type **cmd** in the Search programs and files box, and then press **Enter**. (In Windows XP, click the **Start** button, point to **All Programs**, point to **Accessories**, and click **Command Prompt**.) A command prompt window opens.

27. In the command prompt window, type **nslookup workstation2.netpluslab.net** and press **Enter**. The computer displays the name *workstation2.netpluslab.net* and its IP address as well as the IP address of the DNS server answering the request.

28. Type **ping workstation2.netpluslab.net** and press **Enter**. The computer indicates that it has received four replies from the remote computer and displays its IP address.

29. Repeat Steps 27 and 28, pinging **workstation1.otherorg.net**.

30. Log off all three computers.

## Certification Objectives

Objectives for the Network+ Exam:

- 1.6 Explain the function of common networking protocols.
- 4.3 Given a scenario, use appropriate software tools to troubleshoot connectivity issues.

## Review Questions

1. What is the purpose of a name server?

   a. To maintain the DNS database for an entire zone

   b. To supply clients with IP address resolution for requested hosts

   c. To track and record all TCP/IP host name information for a network

   d. To track and record all NetBIOS naming information for a network

2. What is the term for the group of devices that a name server manages?

   a. Hierarchy

   b. Tree

   c. Zone

   d. Directory

3. Which of the following are examples of top-level domains? (Choose all that apply.)

   a. .net

   b. .com

   c. .uk

   d. .aut

4. When a DNS server retrieves the host name associated with an IP address, what type of lookup is it accomplishing?

   a. Forward

   b. Adjacent

   c. Backward

   d. Reverse

5. What is one advantage of using DNS instead of hosts files?

  a. DNS does not require manual updating of files on multiple networked nodes.

  b. DNS is more compatible with Linux systems.

  c. DNS maps both NetBIOS and TCP/IP host names to IP addresses, whereas hosts files map only TCP/IP host names to IP addresses.

  d. Using DNS is more secure than using hosts files.

# Lab 4.4 Using FTP

## Objectives

In this lab, you connect to a File Transfer Protocol (FTP) server on a remote host. FTP is used throughout the Internet to make files available for downloading. A network administrator who wants to make files available to the general public can create an anonymous FTP server. Users can log on to an anonymous FTP server by using a special account named "anonymous" without knowing the password.

FTP servers are available on nearly all platforms. If you run an anonymous FTP server, you should be careful when allowing anonymous users to upload files (that is, transfer files to the server) because malicious users could fill up your server's disk drive with their files. Another potential problem with FTP is that it sends passwords in unencrypted text, so they could be captured by a malicious user.

A variety of FTP clients are available for almost all modern operating systems. Command-line FTP clients are built into most modern operating systems, including Linux and Windows, but various GUI clients are also available. A GUI client automates the FTP process for you and might include additional features such as the ability to resume interrupted downloads.

After completing this lab, you will be able to:

- Log on to an FTP site
- Download files from an FTP site
- Copy files to an FTP site
- Define security policies for an FTP site

## Materials Required

This lab requires the following:

- A computer running Windows Server 2008, Standard Edition named *SERVER1,* configured as a domain controller for the netpluslab.net domain with an IP address of 192.168.54.1 and a subnet mask of 255.255.255.0

- Internet Information Services (IIS) version 7 installed and running on *SERVER1* with the File Transfer Protocol (FTP) service installed, with a root of C:\Inetpub\ftproot for the FTP service and with the default configuration and sample files in place

- The folder C:\Inetpub\ftproot configured so that users in the Domain Users group have Read, Write, and Execute permissions

- Access to *SERVER1* as the Administrator

- A user account named netplus in the Domain Users group in the netpluslab.net domain

- A computer running Windows 7 or Windows XP Professional named *WORKSTATION1*, configured with an IP address of 192.168.54.3 and a subnet mask of 255.255.255.0

- Both computers connected to a hub with CAT 5 (or better) UTP cables

Estimated completion time: **35 minutes**

## Activity

1. Log on to *SERVER1* as the administrator. The Windows Server 2008 desktop appears.

2. Click the **Start** button, point to **All Programs**, click **Accessories**, and then click **Command Prompt**. A command prompt window opens.

3. In the command prompt window, type `echo your name > C:\Inetpub\ftproot\ netplus.txt` and press **Enter** (substituting your name for *your name*). This creates a file named netplus.txt containing your name in the C:\Inetpub\ftproot directory.

4. At the command prompt, type `copy C:\Inetpub\wwwroot\welcome.png C:\Inetpub\ftproot` and press **Enter**. The computer copies the file from one directory to the other. This image file is now available on the FTP site configured on this computer.

5. Log on to *WORKSTATION1* as the netplus user. The Windows desktop appears.

6. Click the **Start** button, type `cmd` in the Search programs and files box, and then press **Enter**. (In Windows XP, click the **Start** button, point to **All Programs**, point to **Accessories**, and then click **Command Prompt**.) A command prompt window opens.

7. In the command prompt window, type `ftp 192.168.54.1` and press **Enter**. The computer indicates that you have connected to 192.168.54.1 and that the remote computer is running the Microsoft FTP service. The prompt changes to `User (192.168.54.1:(none)):`.

8. At the `User (192.168.54.1:(none)):` prompt, type `anonymous` and press **Enter**. The computer indicates that anonymous access is allowed and asks you to type an e-mail address or other form of identity as a password. The password prompt also appears. At the Password prompt, type an e-mail address or a brief phrase, and then press **Enter**. Note that the letters you type do not echo to the screen. The computer indicates that you have logged on successfully, and the prompt changes to `ftp>`. Figure 4-4 shows a user logging on to an FTP server.

9. Type `dir` and press **Enter**. A list of the files found on the remote computer, including welcome.png and netplus.txt, is displayed.

10. Type `ls` and press **Enter**. A list of the files found on the remote computer is displayed.

11. At the prompt, type `get netplus.txt` and press **Enter**. The computer indicates that it is opening an ASCII mode data connection. ASCII mode allows FTP to transfer plain text files more quickly and ensures that a plain text file is readable by the computer that downloads it. An ASCII mode transfer corrupts files that are not in plain text, such as image or program files. It also corrupts many word processor files, such as Microsoft Word documents, because these are not stored as plain text files by the word processor.

**Figure 4-4**    Logging on to an FTP server

12. To transfer the image file, type **binary** at the prompt, and then press **Enter**. The computer now transfers files using binary mode. In a binary mode transfer, an exact copy of the file is transferred from the server.

13. Type **get welcome.png** at the prompt, and then press **Enter**. The computer indicates that the file is being transferred in binary mode. The **ftp>** prompt returns when the transfer is complete.

14. Type **!copy netplus.txt upload.txt** and press **Enter**. The computer displays the message "1 file(s) copied." The exclamation mark (!) tells the FTP program that you want to run a command on *WORKSTATION1* that copies the file netplus.txt to upload.txt in the directory in which you are working on *WORKSTATION1*.

15. To try to upload a file to the remote server, type **put upload.txt** and press **Enter**. The computer indicates that access is denied.

16. Type **quit** and press **Enter** to exit the FTP site.

17. Now you remove anonymous FTP access to the server and allow users to upload files. On *SERVER1*, click the **Start** button, point to **Administrative Tools**, and then click **Internet Information Services (IIS) Manager** (*not* IIS 6.0 Manager). The Internet Information Services (IIS) Manager window opens.

18. Click the **SERVER1 (netpluslab\Administrator)** icon in the left pane. Icons for services run by IIS appear in the right pane, including an icon for FTP Sites.

19. Double-click the **FTP Sites** icon in the right pane. An icon for Default FTP Site appears.

20. Right-click **Default FTP Site** and click **Properties**. The Default FTP Site Properties window opens.

21. Click the **Security Accounts** tab. Uncheck the **Allow anonymous connections** check box. The IIS Manager dialog box opens, indicating that the authentication option you have selected will result in unencrypted passwords being transmitted over the network.

22. Click **Yes** to close the IIS Manager dialog box.

23. Click the **Home Directory** tab. Select the **Write** check box. At this point, you are ready to upload files. Click **OK**.

24. Right-click **SERVER1 (netpluslab\Administrator)** in the left pane, point to **All Tasks**, and click **Restart IIS**. The Stop/Start/Restart dialog box opens.

25. Make sure that **Restart Internet Services on SERVER1** is selected in the "What do you want IIS to do?" drop-down menu, and click **OK**. The Shutting Down dialog box opens briefly, indicating that the computer is shutting down IIS. An hourglass appears while Internet services are restarted, and then the Internet Information Services dialog box reopens.

26. In the command prompt window on *WORKSTATION1,* type `ftp 192.168.54.1` and then press **Enter**. The logon prompt appears. Type `anonymous` and then press **Enter**. Type a password and then press **Enter**. The `ftp>` prompt indicates that user anonymous cannot log on and that the logon failed.

27. Type `quit` and press **Enter**.

28. Type `ftp 192.168.54.1` and then press **Enter**. The logon prompt appears. Type `netplus` and press **Enter**. At the Password prompt, type the password for the netplus account and press **Enter**. You are now logged on to the remote server.

29. Type `put upload.txt` and press **Enter**. The computer indicates that the file is being uploaded to the remote computer in ASCII mode data connection.

30. Type `quit` and then press **Enter**.

31. On *SERVER1,* click the **Start** button and then click **Computer**. The Computer window opens.

32. Double-click the **Local Disk (C:)** icon. Double-click the **Inetpub** folder. Double-click the **ftproot** folder. The C:\Inetpub\ftproot folder opens, showing the upload.txt text file and the other files on the FTP server.

33. Log off both computers.

## Certification Objective

Objective for the Network+ Exam:

- 1.6 Explain the function of common networking protocols.

## Review Questions

1. Which of the following commands would you type at the `ftp>` prompt to copy a file named "textfile.doc" from your C:\ directory to an FTP server?

   a. `copy "textfile.doc"`

   b. `put C:\textfile.doc`

   c. `get C:\textfile.doc`

   d. `move C:\textfile.doc`

2. On what Transport layer protocol does FTP rely?

   a. TCP

   b. UDP

   c. ICMP

   d. NTP

3. What is the term for an FTP site that allows any user to access its directories?

   a. Anonymous

   b. Restricted

   c. Private

   d. Unlimited

4. What command allows you to list the contents of a directory on an FTP server?

   a. `list`

   b. `lf`

   c. `ls`

   d. `la`

5. What would you type at the `ftp>` prompt to view a list of available FTP commands? (Choose all that apply.)

   a. `list`

   b. `?`

   c. `help`

   d. `commands`

6. What two file types can you specify when transferring files via FTP?

   a. ASCII and binary

   b. Alphabetical and numeric

   c. Program and data

   d. Dynamic and static

# Lab 4.5 Understanding Port Numbers

## Objectives

In TCP/IP, servers use port numbers to identify processes associated with different services. For instance, a server might run several different services over TCP, including HTTP and FTP. Based only on the IP address, there is no way to distinguish between the two services. However, requests from client computers can connect to different port numbers. The default port number for the HTTP service, for example, is 80, whereas the default port number for the FTP control service is 21.

Most client software is designed to look for the default port number when connecting to a service. For example, by default, Web browsers attempt to find Web servers at port 80. However, you can usually configure a service to run on another port and configure the client software to look for that service on the new port.

You can tell a Web browser to look for a Web server at a nondefault port by adding a colon and the port number after the Web site name or IP address in the URL. For instance, to go to the Microsoft Web site using the default port (80), you would use the URL *www. microsoft. com*. To look for a Web server at the same site on port 7777, you would use the URL *www. microsoft.com:7777* instead. Port numbers in UDP work the same way as port numbers in TCP.

After completing this lab, you will be able to:

- Identify default port numbers for several services
- Modify a service's default port numbers
- Connect to a service using a nondefault port number

## Materials Required

This lab requires the following:

- A computer running Windows Server 2008, Standard Edition named *SERVER1*, con-figured as a domain controller for the netpluslab.net domain with an IP address of 192.168.54.1 and a subnet mask of 255.255.255.0

- Internet Information Services (IIS) 6.0 installed and running on *SERVER1* with the default configuration; to ensure that the default configuration is enabled, you can remove and reinstall the software

- A text file in *SERVER1*'s Web root (C:\Inetpub\wwwroot) named default.htm and containing the text "This is a test page"

- Access as the administrator to *SERVER1*

- A computer running Windows 7 or Windows XP Professional named *WORKSTATION1*, configured with an IP address of 192.168.54.3 and a subnet mask of 255.255.255.0

- Access with an ordinary user account to the client computer

- Both computers connected to a hub or switch with straight-through CAT 5 (or better) UTP cables

Estimated completion time: **20 minutes**

## Activity

1. Log on to *WORKSTATION1* with an ordinary user account. The Windows desktop appears.

2. Open Internet Explorer.

3. In the Address bar, type **http://192.168.54.1** and press **Enter**. A Web page opens containing the text "This is a test page."

4. If you are not already logged on to *SERVER1* as the administrator, do so now.

5. On *SERVER1*, click the **Start** button, point to **Administrative Tools**, and then click **Internet Information Services (IIS) 6.0 Manager**. The Internet Information Services (IIS) Manager 6.0 window opens.

6. In the left pane of the window, click **SERVER1 (NETPLUSLAB/Administrator)**. Icons for services controlled by the IIS Manager appear in the right pane.

7. In the right pane, double-click the **Web Sites** icon. The Default Web Site icon appears in the right pane.

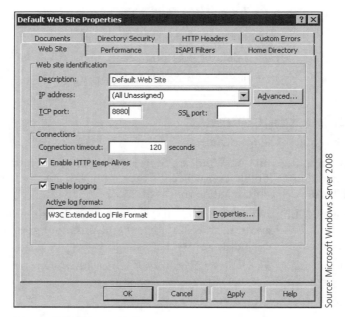

**Figure 4-5**    The Default Web Site Properties dialog box

8. Right-click the **Default Web Site** icon in the right pane of the window, and then click **Properties**. The Default Web Site Properties dialog box opens.

9. In the TCP port text box, change the number from 80 to **8880**. This tells IIS to run the Web server on port 8880 instead of on port 80. Figure 4-5 shows the Default Web Site Properties dialog box. Click **OK**.

10. In the left pane of the Internet Information Services (IIS) Manager window, right-click **SERVER1**. In the shortcut menu, point to **All Tasks**, and then click **Restart IIS**. The Stop/Start/Restart dialog box opens.

11. Make sure that **Restart Internet Services on SERVER1** is selected in the "What do you want IIS to do?" drop-down menu. Click **OK**. The Shutting Down dialog box opens, indicating that the computer is attempting to shut down IIS, and then closes. An hourglass appears briefly, and then the computer restarts IIS.

12. On the menu bar, click **File** and then click **Exit** to close the IIS Manager.

13. On *WORKSTATION1*, close Internet Explorer. This ensures that Internet Explorer does not use its disk cache of the Web page when you try to load the Web page again.

14. Click the **Start** button, point to **All Programs**, and then click **Internet Explorer**. Internet Explorer opens.

15. In the Address bar, type `http://192.168.54.1` and then press **Enter**. An error message appears indicating that the page cannot be displayed.

16. In the Address bar, type `http://192.168.54.1:8880` and then press **Enter**. A Web page displays the text "This is a test page."

17. Log off both computers.

## Certification Objective

Objective for the Network+ Exam:

- 1.5 Identify common TCP and UDP default ports.

## Review Questions

1. What symbol is used to separate the computer name from the port number in a URL (assuming that IP version 4 is in use)?

   a. ;

   b. :

   c. #

   d. .

2. What is the default port number for the FTP service?

   a. 20

   b. 21

   c. 22

   d. 23

3. What is the default port number for the HTTP service?

   a. 40

   b. 44

   c. 60

   d. 80

4. What range of port numbers comprises the well-known port numbers?

   a. 0 to 64

   b. 0 to 128

   c. 0 to 1023

   d. 0 to 8880

5. What is a socket?

   a. A virtual connector that associates a URL with its IP address

   b. A method of identifying the IP addresses belonging to clients as they connect to servers

   c. A logical address assigned to a specific process running on a computer

   d. A discrete unit of data

6. Which of the following addresses could represent the SMTP service using its default port on a mail server?

   a. 188.65.79.80:25

   b. 188.65.79.80...24

   c. 188.65.79.80$24

   d. 188.65.79.80;25

# Lab 4.6 Disabling Unnecessary Protocols

## Objectives

The goal of this lab is to help you learn how to disable protocols that are not being used. You often can configure multiple network clients to use only one or two network protocols. Disabling or removing a protocol reduces network traffic and the load on your servers. On a computer with multiple NICs, you might find it useful to disable a protocol on one network interface card and leave it enabled on another. The clients on the network attached to one NIC might need that protocol, whereas the clients on the network attached to the other NIC do not. After completing this lab, you will be able to:

- Disable unnecessary protocols

## Materials Required

This lab requires the following:

- One computer named *WORKSTATION1* running Windows 7 or Windows XP Professional with an Ethernet NIC, configured with an IP address of 192.168.54.2; this computer should not be configured as a member of a domain
- *WORKSTATION1* should have the Reliable Multicast Protocol already installed
- Access to the Windows computer as an administrator
- One computer named *SERVER1* running Windows Server 2008, Standard Edition with an Ethernet NIC, configured with an IP address of 192.168.54.1
- *SERVER1* should have the Reliable Multicast Protocol already installed
- An Ethernet hub or switch compatible with both NICs
- Two straight-through Category 5 (or better) UTP cables with RJ-45 connectors at either end

Estimated completion time: **15–20 minutes**

## Activity

1. Log on to *WORKSTATION1* as an administrator. The Windows desktop appears.
2. Click the **Start** button, click **Control Panel**, click **Network and Internet**, and then click **Network Sharing Center**. Click **Change adapter settings**. (In Windows XP, click the **Start** button, point to **All Programs**, point to **Accessories**, point to **Communications**, and click **Network Connections**.) The Network Connections window opens.
3. Right-click the **Local Area Connection** icon and select **Properties** from the shortcut menu. The Local Area Connection Properties window opens.
4. Click **Reliable Multicast Protocol** to highlight it.
5. Click **Uninstall**. A dialog box opens, indicating that uninstalling a network component removes it from all network connections. Figure 4-6 shows the process of uninstalling a network protocol

**Figure 4-6**   Uninstalling a protocol

6. Click **Yes** to remove the protocol. The computer removes Reliable Multicast Protocol. The Local Network dialog box may open, indicating that you must shut down the computer before the changes take effect.

7. Click **Yes**. The computer reboots.

8. Log on to *SERVER1* as the administrator. The Windows Server 2008 desktop appears.

9. Click the **Start** button, click **Control Panel**, click **Network and Internet**, click **Network Sharing Center**, click **Change adapter settings**, and then double-click **Local Area Connection**. The Local Area Connection Status window opens.

10. Click the **Properties** button. The Local Area Connection Properties window opens.

11. Repeat Steps 4 through 7. You have successfully removed the Reliable Multicast Protocol from the Windows Server 2008 computer.

12. Log off both computers.

## Certification Objective

Objective for the Network+ Exam:

- 1.6 Explain the function of common networking protocols.

## Review Questions

1. It is prudent to install and bind all four major protocol suites on your server, regardless of whether they are going to be used. True or False?

2. Why would a network administrator choose to disable one of two network interface cards on a server?

   a. It is infrequently used.

   b. It is faulty.

   c. It is not as fast as the other one.

   d. It is incapable of handling certain protocols.

3. A computer uses both the IPX/SPX and TCP/IP protocols. Which of the following would be true if IPX/SPX were disabled?

   a. Clients would not be able to access the server's resources via IPX/SPX.

   b. Clients would not be able to access the server at all.

   c. Only those clients running TCP/IP would be able to access the server's resources.

   d. Clients would be able to access the server's resources via both TCP/IP and IPX/SPX, but TCP/IP-based services would be slower.

4. Why would a network administrator choose to unbind a protocol on a server?

   a. It is only occasionally used, and as long as it remains bound, it uses server resources.

   b. It is no longer used, and as long as it remains bound, it uses server resources.

   c. It is interfering with traffic using other protocols.

   d. It has proven to be unstable with certain applications.

5. Besides TCP/IP, what must be bound to a client's NIC before the client can log on to a Windows Server 2008 server?

   a. Client for Microsoft Networks

   b. Gateway Services for NetWare

   c. IPX/SPX

   d. NWLink

6. Why is NetBEUI not routable?

   a. It does not contain a subprotocol at the Application layer of the OSI model.

   b. It does not contain Network layer addressing information.

   c. It is incompatible with modern routing techniques.

   d. Its data frames are too large and slow to be practically routed.

# TOPOLOGIES AND ETHERNET STANDARDS

## Labs included in this chapter

- Lab 5.1 The Parallel Backbone
- Lab 5.2 Building a Daisy Chain
- Lab 5.3 Examining Ethernet Frames
- Lab 5.4 Capturing Network Data

## Network+ Exam Objectives

| Objective | Lab |
| --- | --- |
| 1.2 Classify how applications, devices, and protocols relate to the OSI model layers. | 5.3, 5.4 |
| 1.6 Explain the function of common networking protocols. | 5.3, 5.4 |
| 3.5 Describe different network topologies. | 5.1, 5.2 |
| 4.6 Explain different methods and rationales for network performance optimization. | 5.1 |

# Lab 5.1 The Parallel Backbone

## Objectives

In this lab, you build a network that includes a variation of the parallel backbone. In a parallel backbone, each network segment has two or more connections to the central router or switch. If one connection fails, each segment can still connect to the rest of the network through the other connection.

The disadvantage to using a parallel backbone is cost. Depending on the type of devices used in the network and on the logical topology, it might require additional cabling, additional network devices, or additional configuration of network devices. As a network administrator, you must often choose between price and reliability. In most networks, only the most important devices have redundant network connections. For instance, a failure of the server that handles a company's billing might cost the company a substantial amount of money. The cost of a parallel backbone can be offset by the money that could be lost during such an outage. For a workstation, however, a parallel backbone might not be cost effective.

After completing this lab, you will be able to:

- Create a parallel backbone network

## Materials Required

This lab requires the following:

- Two computers running Windows Server 2008, Standard Edition, one named *SERVER1* and the other named *SERVER2,* each with two NICs with RJ-45 connectors but without IP addresses configured

- Routing and Remote Access Services (RRAS) installed but not enabled on both computers

- Access as the administrator to both computers

- Two Ethernet switches

- Four straight-through Cat 5 (or better) UTP cables

> Estimated completion time: **60 minutes**

## Activity

1. Power on the two computers and the two switches.

2. Plug one of the cables into a NIC in *SERVER1*. Plug the other end of the cable into one of the switches. The link lights on the switches and on the NIC illuminate.

3. Plug another cable into the second NIC in *SERVER1*. Plug the other end of this cable into the other switch (that is, the switch you did not use in Step 2). Both NICs on *SERVER1* are now connected to different switches. The link lights on the switch and on the NIC illuminate.

4. Plug a third cable into a NIC on *SERVER2*. Plug the other end of this cable into one of the switches.

© Cengage Learning 2013

**Figure 5-1**   Parallel backbone

5. Plug the fourth cable into the second NIC on *SERVER2*. Plug the other end of this cable into the other switch. Both NICs on *SERVER2* are now plugged into different switches, and each server is now connected to each switch. Figure 5-1 shows the network cabling for this lab.

6. Log on to *SERVER1* as the administrator. The Windows Server 2008 desktop appears.

7. Click the **Start** button, click **Control Panel**, double-click **Network and Sharing Center**, click **Manage network connections,** and then double-click **Local Area Connection**. The Local Area Connection Status window opens.

8. Click **Properties**. The Local Area Connection Properties window opens.

9. Double-click **Internet Protocol Version 4 (TCP/IPv4)**. The Internet Protocol Version 4 (TCP/IPv4) Properties window opens.

10. Select the **Use the following IP address** option button. Enter **192.168.54.1** in the IP address text box and **255.255.255.0** in the Subnet mask text box. Select the **Use the following DNS Server addresses** option button, and enter **192.168.54.1** in the Preferred DNS server text box.

11. Click the **Advanced** button. The Advanced TCP/IP Settings dialog box opens.

12. Click **Add** beneath the IP addresses list box. The TCP/IP Address dialog box opens.

13. Now you configure a secondary IP address. Enter **10.1.1.1** in the IP address text box and **255.255.255.0** in the Subnet mask text box.

14. Click **Add**. The dialog box closes, and the new IP address appears below "IP addresses" in the Advanced TCP/IP Settings dialog box.

15. Click **OK** three times to close the Local Area Connection Properties window. Click **Close** to close the Local Area Connection Status window.

16. Double-click **Local Area Connection 2**. The Local Area Connection 2 Status window opens.

17. Click **Properties**. The Local Area Connection 2 Properties window opens.

18. Double-click **Internet Protocol Version 4 (TCP/IPv4)**. The Internet Protocol (TCP/IP) Properties window opens.

19. Select the **Use the following IP address** option button. Enter **192.168.56.1** in the IP address text box and **255.255.255.0** in the Subnet mask text box. Select the **Use the following DNS Server addresses** option button, and enter **192.168.54.1** in the Preferred DNS server text box.

20. Click **OK** twice to close the Local Area Connection 2 Properties window. Click **Close** to close the Local Area Connection 2 Status window.

21. Click the **Start** button, point to **Administrative Tools**, and click **Routing and Remote Access**. The Routing and Remote Access window opens.

22. Right-click **SERVER1 (local)** in the left pane of the Routing and Remote Access window. Select **Configure and Enable Routing and Remote Access** from the shortcut menu. The Routing and Remote Access Server Setup Wizard opens.

23. Click **Next**.

24. Select the **Custom configuration** option. Click **Next**.

25. Click the **LAN routing** check box to select it. Click **Next**.

26. Click **Finish**. A dialog box opens, indicating that the service has been installed and asking if you would like to start the service. Click **Start service**. The service starts.

27. If necessary, click the **plus sign (+)** next to SERVER1 (local) to expand the tree. In the left pane of the Routing and Remote Access window, click the **plus sign (+)** to expand the tree below IPv4 if the tree is not already expanded. Right-click **General**, and then select **New Routing Protocol** from the shortcut menu. The New Routing Protocol dialog box opens.

28. Double-click **RIP Version 2 for Internet Protocol**. The dialog box closes, and RIP appears below IPv4 in the tree in the left pane of the Routing and Remote Access window.

29. Right-click **RIP** in the tree in the left pane. Select **New Interface** from the shortcut menu. The New Interface for RIP Version 2 for Internet Protocol dialog box opens.

30. Double-click **Local Area Connection**. The RIP Properties – Local Area Connection Properties window opens.

31. Click **OK**.

32. Repeat Steps 29 through 31 for Local Area Connection 2.

33. Right-click **SERVER1 (local)** in the left pane. A shortcut menu opens. Point to **All Tasks**, and then click **Restart**. The Routing and Remote Access service restarts.

34. On *SERVER2*, repeat Steps 6 through 10 and 15 through 33. (Note that when repeating Step 15, it is necessary to click **OK** only twice.) However, use **192.168.54.2** in the IP address text box and Preferred DNS server text box in Step 10, and use **192.168.56.2** in the IP address text box and **192.168.54.2** in the Preferred DNS server text box in Step 19.

35. On *SERVER2*, click the **Start** button, point to **All Programs**, click **Accessories**, and then click **Command Prompt**. A command prompt window opens.

36. Type `ping 10.1.1.1` and press **Enter**. You see a message indicating that the computer has received four replies from the remote computer. (If the `ping` command is unsuccessful, switch the cables attached to *SERVER2*'s NICs, and verify that the link light on each NIC and hub is illuminated as expected.)

37. Remove one of the cables attached to *SERVER2*. (However, leave all of the cables attached to *SERVER1*.)

38. Type `ping 10.1.1.1` and press **Enter**. You see a message indicating that the computer has received four replies from the remote computer despite the removal of the cable.

39. Log off both computers.

## Certification Objectives

Objectives for the Network+ Exam:

- 3.5 Describe different network topologies.
- 4.6 Explain different methods and rationales for network performance optimization.

## Review Questions

1. What is an advantage of using a parallel backbone over a collapsed backbone?

    a. A collapsed backbone requires too many connecting devices.

    b. A parallel backbone uses redundant connections and is more reliable.

    c. A collapsed backbone uses redundant connections, which costs more money.

    d. A parallel backbone uses fewer redundant connections, which costs less money.

2. What is the purpose of using the routing protocol in this lab?

    a. Each server can choose a different path when the current path fails.

    b. The network administrator does not have to configure static routes.

    c. It has no purpose.

    d. Each server saves the appropriate IP addresses in its ARP cache.

3. Which of the following is true about the use of parallel backbones in real-life networks?

    a. Parallel backbones are used when redundant connections are not possible.

    b. Parallel backbones are used whenever possible because they are so inexpensive.

    c. Parallel backbones only work in Ethernet networks.

    d. Parallel backbones are used for important servers and networks because they are more expensive to build.

4. In this lab, you configured the hubs and the two servers in a ring. How does the topology in this lab differ from a ring topology such as token ring? (Choose all that apply.)

    a. Each host transmits when necessary.

b. A single workstation or server in a simple ring topology could take down the entire ring.

c. Each host passes a token to the next host.

d. The topology in this lab is an example of an active topology.

5. Which of the following network technologies has built-in redundancies?

a. Token ring

b. Gigabit Ethernet

c. FDDI

d. 10Base-2 Ethernet

# Lab 5.2 Building a Daisy Chain

## Objectives

In this lab, you create a daisy chain, which is simply a linked series of devices. You would most likely have several workstations or servers connected to each hub in the daisy chain. Because the hubs are modular and only require Cat 5 (or better) cables, the sort of network built in this lab is inexpensive and quick.

In any daisy chain, however, you run the risk of expanding the network beyond its physical limitations. That is, your daisy chain might exceed the maximum length for the network technology used. For instance, on a 100Base-TX network, connecting more than three network segments with more than two hubs violates the standards. While on a Gigabit Ethernet network, you can use only one hub. Depending on the network devices involved, overextending a daisy chain can result in serious problems. On a network such as the one in this lab, for instance, overextension can result in high error rates, data transmission problems, or reduced throughput. These problems might also be intermittent and, hence, more difficult to identify and troubleshoot.

Ordinarily, you must use a crossover cable to connect two hubs or switches together. However, many switches and hubs have an uplink port. An uplink port allows you to use a straight-through cable instead. One end of the straight-through cable is attached to an uplink port, and the other end is attached to an ordinary switch or hub port. In other cases, the hub or switch might have a button that determines whether the uplink port functions as an uplink port or as an ordinary port.

After completing this lab, you will be able to:

• Identify common enterprise backbone topologies

• Build a simple version of a common enterprise backbone

## Materials Required

This lab requires the following:

• Four Ethernet hubs or switches set at a common speed

• Five straight-through Cat 5 (or better) UTP cables

• Three crossover Cat 5 (or better) UTP cables, if required, to connect the hubs

- A computer running Microsoft Windows 7 or Windows XP Professional named *WORKSTATION1*, with an RJ-45 NIC running at the same speed as the hubs or switches and with an IP address of 192.168.54.2 and a subnet mask of 255.255.255.0

- A computer running Microsoft Windows 7 or Windows XP Professional named *WORKSTATION2*, with an RJ-45 NIC running at the same speed as the hubs or switches and with an IP address of 192.168.54.3 and a subnet mask of 255.255.255.0

- Access as an administrator to both computers

Estimated completion time: **45 minutes**

## Activity

1. Power on each hub and each computer.

2. Plug one of the Cat 5 cables into a port in one of the switches. Plug the other end of this cable into the uplink port of one of the other switches. On both switches, a link light illuminates. If the switches do not have uplink ports or if the lights do not illuminate, use a crossover cable to connect the switches instead. The uplink port is designed to allow two switches to be connected with a straight-through cable, but not all hubs or switches have uplink ports.

3. Connect one of the remaining two switches to one of the two switches you connected in Step 2. Connect the remaining switch to the switch you just connected. Now you have a chain of four switches. Each connection on each switch should have an illuminated link light.

4. Plug the RJ-45 connector from one of the CAT 5 cables into a data port on one of the switches on the end. Plug the other end into the NIC in the back of one of the computers. A link light illuminates on both the switch and the NIC.

5. Repeat Step 4 by connecting the other computer into the switch at the other end of the chain. Figure 5-2 shows the network cabling for this lab.

WORKSTATION1     Hub     Hub     Hub     Hub     WORKSTATION2

© Cengage Learning 2013

**Figure 5-2**   Daisy chain network cabling

6. Log on to *WORKSTATION1* as an administrator. The Windows desktop appears.

7. Click the **Start** button, type **cmd** in the Search programs and files text box, and then press **Enter**. (In Windows XP, click the **Start** button, point to **All Programs**, point to **Accessories**, and click **Command Prompt**.) A command prompt window opens.

8. Type **ping 192.168.54.3** and press **Enter**. You see a message indicating that the computer has received four replies. (If you see an error message instead, go to the next step.)

9. Repeat the previous step, examining the lights on each switch for errors. (Typically, a light on a switch blinks red or does not blink at all if the switch is experiencing errors.) Do you see error lights on any of the switches?

10. Log off the computer.

## Certification Objective

Objective for the Network+ Exam:

- 3.5 Describe different network topologies.

## Review Questions

1. Does the network you built in this lab meet the requirements for the hubs that you used? Why or why not?

2. What type of port connects one hub to another in a daisy-chain fashion?

   a. Output port

   b. Patch panel port

   c. Uplink port

   d. External port

3. When connecting hubs in a daisy-chain fashion on a 100Base-T network, what is the maximum number of hubs you may connect?

   a. 2

   b. 3

   c. 4

   d. 5

4. When connectivity devices are connected in a daisy-chain fashion, what type of backbone do they create?

   a. Parallel

   b. Serial

   c. Collapsed

   d. Distributed

5. What type of network access method is used on a ring network?

   a. CSMA/CA

   b. CSMA/CD

   c. Demand priority

   d. Token passing

6. Which of the following is the most popular hybrid topology used on modern Ethernet networks?

   a. Star-wired bus

   b. Star-wired ring

   c. Ring-wired star

   d. Bus-wired star

7. What is risky about daisy-chaining hubs on a 100Base-T network? (Choose all that apply.)

   a. Too many hubs cause errors in addressing data for its proper destination.

   b. Too many hubs cause the network to exceed its maximum length.

   c. Too many hubs increase the attenuation of a data signal.

   d. Too many hubs increase the possibility for errors in data encryption and decryption.

# Lab 5.3 Examining Ethernet Frames

## Objectives

In this lab, you capture and examine the parts of an Ethernet frame using a software protocol analyzer called Wireshark. Every Ethernet frame contains a number of fields, including the 7-byte preamble (which tells the NIC that it is about to receive data), the 1-byte start-of-frame delimiter (which indicates that the frame is about to start), the 14-byte header (containing the destination MAC address, the source MAC address, and another field that depends on the frame type), 46 to 1500 bytes of data, and the 4-byte Frame Check Sequence (FCS) field, which uses a Cyclic Redundancy Check (CRC) to determine if the data in the frame has been corrupted. If the data field is not at least 46 bytes long, the sending host pads it until it is 46 bytes long. Only the header, the data and any padding, and the FCS field are used to determine the size of the frame.

The dominant Ethernet frame type in modern networks is Ethernet II. The most important difference between the Ethernet II frame and other types of Ethernet frames is the type field in the header. This field contains a code for the protocol used, such as IP, IPX, or ARP, and makes it possible for Ethernet II frames to carry multiple types of protocols. (The Ethernet SNAP frame type also has a type field. However, it also uses additional fields, resulting in extra overhead.)

Note that neither Wireshark nor most other software protocol analyzers can capture the preamble and the FCS field. On most operating systems, these fields are discarded before they reach the operating system. To see these fields, you might need to use a dedicated hardware protocol analyzer such as RADCOM's PrismLite Integrated WAN/LAN/ATM Protocol Analyzer.

After completing this lab, you will be able to:

- Distinguish among the parts of an Ethernet frame

## Materials Required

This lab requires the following:

- A computer running Windows Server 2008, Standard Edition with a NIC, configured with a name of *SERVER1,* an IP address of 192.168.54.1, and a subnet mask of 255.255.255.0
- The FTP service installed and configured from Lab 4.4

- A computer running Windows 7 or Windows XP Professional with a NIC, configured with a name of *WORKSTATION1*, an IP address of 192.168.54.2, and a subnet mask of 255.255.255.0

- The network protocol analyzer Wireshark (available from *www.wireshark.org*) installed on the Windows Server 2008 computer

- Access to both computers as an administrator

- Both computers connected to a hub or switch with straight-through Cat 5 (or better) UTP cables

Estimated completion time: **45 minutes**

## Activity

1. Log on to *SERVER1* as the administrator. The Windows Server 2008 desktop appears.

2. Click the **Start** button, point to **All Programs,** and click **Wireshark.** The Wireshark Network Protocol Analyzer opens.

3. Click **Capture,** and then click the **Start** button.

4. The Wireshark window opens, displaying the number of frames of each type captured.

5. Click the **Start** button, point to **All Programs,** click **Accessories,** and click **Command Prompt.** A command prompt window opens.

6. Type **ping -t 192.168.54.2** and press **Enter.** The computer begins pinging 192.168.54.2 and continues to do so until you stop it.

7. Now look at the Wireshark window. When the total number of frames captured is greater than 10, click **Stop.** A list of captured frames appears in the top pane, and details about the highlighted frame appear in the bottom two panes. Figure 5-3 shows an example of a captured frame.

**Figure 5-3** Captured frame

8. Click a frame listed as **ICMP** in the Protocol column to highlight it. Detailed information about the frame appears in the bottom two panes.

9. In the middle pane, click the **plus sign (+)** next to Ethernet II to expand the tree below it. Record the source and destination addresses.

10. Record the destination and source addresses in the Internet Protocol part of the frame. (This is part of the data field of the frame.) Was this frame sent from the Windows Server 2008 computer, or was it sent from the Windows 7 or XP computer?

11. In the command prompt window, press **Ctrl+C** to stop the `ping` command, and then type `ipconfig/all` and press **Enter**. What is the MAC address for this host? Does it match one of the addresses you recorded in Step 9?

12. Type `arp -a` and press **Enter**. Look for the IP address of the other computer. Does its associated MAC address match one of the addresses you recorded in Step 9?

13. Look at the type field below "Ethernet II." What is this frame's type? Does it match the protocol listed in Wireshark's protocol column? Why or why not?

14. Log off both computers.

## Certification Objectives

Objectives for the Network+ Exam:

- 1.2 Classify how applications, devices, and protocols relate to the OSI model layers.
- 1.6 Explain the function of common networking protocols.

## Review Questions

1. What is the purpose of the checksum?

   a. To ensure that data arrives in the proper sequence

   b. To ensure that data is properly encrypted and decrypted

   c. To ensure that data arrives at its intended destination

   d. To ensure that data arrives intact

2. How many times is a checksum calculated when a frame of data is sent from a source computer to a destination computer that resides on the same segment?

   a. 1

   b. 2

   c. 3

   d. 4

3. What type of address identifies the source of data in a frame?

   a. MAC

   b. Logical

   c. Network

   d. Host

4. What is the purpose of padding in an Ethernet frame?

   a. To ensure that the data in the frame is exactly 1500 bytes long

   b. To ensure that the data in the frame is no more than 46 bytes long

   c. To signal that the frame has ended

   d. To ensure that the data in the frame is at least 46 bytes long

5. What is the minimum size of an Ethernet frame?

   a. 56 bytes

   b. 64 bytes

   c. 128 bytes

   d. 256 bytes

6. Which parts of an Ethernet frame are Wireshark and other protocol analyzers unlikely to capture? (Choose all that apply.)

   a. The header

   b. The Frame Check Sequence

   c. The padding

   d. The preamble

# Lab 5.4 Capturing Network Data

## Objectives

Protocol analyzers such as Wireshark can also be used to look at the contents of a Frame. If the data is not securely encrypted, sensitive information such as usernames and passwords can be captured. In this lab, you use Wireshark to capture a frame from an FTP login attempt. Because FTP does not encrypt this information, it is readable.

After completing this lab, you will be able to:

- Read unsecured data from an Ethernet frame

## Materials Required

This lab requires the following:

- A computer running Windows Server 2008, Standard Edition with a NIC, configured with a name of *SERVER1,* an IP address of 192.168.54.1, and a subnet mask of 255.255.255.0

- A computer running Windows 7 or Windows XP Professional with a NIC, configured with a name of *WORKSTATION1*, an IP address of 192.168.54.2, and a subnet mask of 255.255.255.0

- The network protocol analyzer Wireshark (available from *www.wireshark.org*) installed on the Windows Server 2008 computer

- Access to both computers as an administrator

- Both computers connected to a hub or switch with straight-through Cat 5 (or better) UTP cables

Estimated completion time: **45 minutes**

## Activity

1. Log on to *SERVER1* as the administrator. The Windows Server 2008 desktop appears.

2. Click the **Start** button, point to **All Programs**, and then click **Wireshark**. The Wireshark Network Protocol Analyzer opens.

3. Click **Capture**, and then click the **Start** button.

4. The Wireshark window opens, displaying the number of frames of each type captured.

5. Now log on to *WORKSTATION1* as the administrator. The Windows desktop appears.

6. Click the **Start** button, type **cmd** in the Search Programs and files text box, and then press **Enter**. (In Windows XP, click the **Start** button, point to **All Programs**, point to **Accessories**, and click **Command Prompt**.) A command prompt window opens.

7. In the command prompt window, type **FTP 192.168.54.1** and press **Enter**. The computer indicates that you have connected to 192.168.54.1, and that the remote computer is running the Microsoft FTP service.

8. Attempt to log in with your first name as the username and **happy** as the password. Yes, the attempt fails.

9. Now look at the Wireshark window on SERVER1 and click **Stop**.

10. To find the login information, click **Edit**, and then click **Find Packet**.

11. Click **String**, and, under filter, enter your first name as you typed it when you attempted to log in.

12. Click **Find**.

13. Note that the frame contains both the username and password you used while attempting to log in to the FTP.

14. Close Wireshark and log off both computers.

## Certification Objectives

Objectives for the Network+ Exam:

- 1.2 Classify how applications, devices, and protocols relate to the OSI model layers.
- 1.6 Explain the function of common networking protocols.

## Review Questions

1. Which of the following is true about the major types of Ethernet frames?

   a. Each frame operates at the Network layer.

   b. Each frame contains the destination and source MAC addresses.

   c. Each frame has a different maximum size.

   d. Each frame uses a preamble at the end of the frame to signal the end of the frame.

2. This access method is used by all Ethernet networks.

   a. MPLS

   b. SDF

   c. PoE

   d. CSMA/CD

3. Which information is not included in an Ethernet Frame's 14-byte header?

   a. Frame check sequence

   b. Source address

   c. Destination address

   d. Ethernet type

4. The largest possible data field in an Ethernet frame is:

   a. 500 bytes

   b. 1000 bytes

   c. 1500 bytes

   d. 2000 bytes

5. This is the most common Ethernet Frame type used on modern networks.

   a. Ethernet II

   b. Ethernet 802.3

   c. Ethernet 802.2

   d. Ethernet SNAP

# NETWORK HARDWARE, SWITCHING, AND ROUTING

## Labs included in this chapter

- Lab 6.1 Configuring Transmission and Duplex Settings
- Lab 6.2 Creating a Multi-Homed Computer by Installing Two NICs
- Lab 6.3 Activating Routing and Remote Access in Windows Server 2008
- Lab 6.4 Activating a Routing Protocol in Windows Server 2008
- Lab 6.5 Configuring a Bridging Firewall

## Network+ Exam Objectives

| Objective | Lab |
| --- | --- |
| 1.2 Classify how applications, devices, and protocols relate to the OSI model layers. | 6.1, 6.2 |
| 1.4 Explain the purpose and properties of routing and switching. | 6.2, 6.3, 6.4 |
| 2.1 Given a scenario, install and configure routers and switches. | 6.4, 6.6 |
| 4.3 Given a scenario, use appropriate software tools to troubleshoot connectivity issues. | 6.3 |
| 5.5 Given a scenario, install and configure a basic firewall. | 6.5 |

# Lab 6.1 Configuring Transmission and Duplex Settings

## Objectives

On Ethernet networks, duplex and transmission settings are perhaps the most important settings for a NIC, aside from the network address. Ordinarily, these settings are configured automatically through the process of autonegotiation with attached switches. However, autonegotiation sometimes results in incorrect settings. A NIC whose transmission speed is set incorrectly does not operate at the correct speed. Duplex mismatches are a common source of errors on Ethernet networks and might force a computer to retransmit large numbers of frames because of collisions. Depending on traffic and the settings on the computer and the switch or hub, a duplex mismatch might or might not be easily noticed.

Typically, duplex and transmission settings are most important on servers. Compared with a workstation, a server is less likely to be moved, more likely to require high throughput, and more likely to be connected to a switch. In addition, checking duplex and transmission settings on workstations requires more work because an organization is likely to have fewer servers.

After completing this lab, you will be able to:

- Examine and configure transmission and duplex settings on a NIC

## Materials Required

This lab requires the following:

- A computer running Windows Server 2008, Standard Edition with at least one 10/100 NIC configured with an IP address of 192.168.54.1 and a subnet mask of 255.255.255.0
- Access to the computer as the administrator
- A computer running Windows 7 or Windows XP Professional configured with an IP address of 192.168.54.2 and a subnet mask of 255.255.255.0
- Drivers for the NIC installed on the Windows Server 2008 computer allowing configuration of speed and duplex settings, and knowledge of the settings for a 100-Mbps full duplex connection

To verify whether your NIC driver supports configuration of these settings, do the following: Click the **Start** button, click Control Panel, double-click Network and Sharing Center, click Manage network connections, and then double-click Local Area Connection. In the Local Area Connection Status dialog box, click Properties. In the Local Area Connection Properties window, click Configure, and then click the Advanced tab. Look for Connection Type, Media Type, Link Speed & Duplex, or similar options.

- An Ethernet switch or hub and the straight-through Cat 5 UTP cables (or better) required to connect the two computers

Estimated completion time: **45 minutes**

## Activity

1. Plug one end of each cable into the hub or switch. Plug the other end of each cable into one of the computers.

2. Log on to the Windows Server 2008 computer as the administrator. The Windows Server 2008 desktop appears.

3. Click the **Start** button, click **Control Panel,** double-click **Network and Sharing Center,** click **Manage network connections,** and then double-click **Local Area Connection.** The Local Area Connection Status dialog box opens.

4. Click **Properties.** The Local Area Connection Properties dialog box opens.

5. Click **Configure** under the name of the network card. The Properties dialog box for the NIC opens.

6. Click the **Advanced** tab. The Advanced tab opens. Figure 6-1 shows the Properties dialog box for a typical NIC.

7. The precise options might vary depending on the driver for the network card. Select **Connection Type, Media Type, Link Speed & Duplex** or the option indicated by your instructor in the Property list. Record the current value for this option. (Although it varies depending on the NIC driver used, typically it is *Auto Select* or *Auto Detect.*)

8. In the Value drop-down menu, select **100 Mbps Full Duplex** or the equivalent option, as indicated by your instructor. Click **OK.** The Properties dialog box closes. If the Local Area Connection Status dialog box also closes, go to Step 10.

9. Click **Close** to close the Local Area Connection Status dialog box.

**Figure 6-1**   Properties dialog box for a typical NIC

10. Click the **Start** button, point to **All Programs**, click **Accessories**, and then click **Command Prompt**. A command prompt window opens.

11. Type `ping 192.168.54.2` and press **Enter**. The computer indicates that it has received four replies from the remote computer. Do you see any red error lights on the switch (hub)? (You might not because this network does not have a lot of traffic.)

12. Repeat Steps 3 through 9. When you repeat Step 8, use the value that you recorded in Step 7 instead of 100 Mbps Full Duplex.

13. Log off the computer.

## Certification Objective

Objective for the Network+ Exam:

- 1.2 Classify how applications, devices, and protocols relate to the OSI model layers.

## Review Questions

1. What effect might an incorrect duplex setting have on a NIC? (Choose all that apply.)
   a. Errors
   b. Collisions
   c. Retransmitted frames
   d. Incorrect theoretical transmission speed

2. In the same dialog box in which you configured transmission speed and duplex settings, it is also possible to change the physical address of a NIC. What might happen if you were to do so?
   a. No devices could connect to that NIC because of its new physical address.
   b. TCP/IP communication would be normal immediately after the change.
   c. IPX/SPX communication would be normal after the ARP cache entries on other hosts timed out.
   d. TCP/IP communication would be normal after the ARP cache entries on other hosts timed out.

3. Changing the duplex setting on a NIC is the same as changing its physical address. True or False?

4. You have just attached a server to a new network. However, the server's throughput is lower than expected. Why might this be? (Choose all that apply.)
   a. The server is running the wrong routing protocol.
   b. The server's duplex setting is incorrect, and many frames are retransmitted.
   c. The server's transmission speed setting is incorrect.
   d. The server NIC's physical address is incorrectly configured.

5. What effect do duplex settings have on a server's routing protocols?
   a. None, the routing protocols operate at the Transport layer.
   b. None, the routing protocols operate at the Network layer.
   c. Mismatched duplex settings cause collisions and retransmissions.
   d. Mismatched duplex settings cause TCP/IP to fail altogether.

# Lab 6.2 Creating a Multi-Homed Computer by Installing Two NICs

## Objectives

Network adapters are connectivity devices that enable a workstation, server, printer, or other node to receive and transmit data over the network media. In most modern network devices, NICs contain the data transceiver, which is the device that transmits and receives data signals.

NICs operate at both the Physical layer and the Data Link layer of the OSI model because they apply data signals to the wire and assemble or disassemble data frames. They do not, however, analyze the data from higher layers. A router, on the other hand, operates at the Network layer of the OSI model and can interpret higher-layer logical addressing information.

In this lab, you perform the first step in creating a multi-homed computer consisting of a single computer with two NICs. A multi-homed computer has more than one NIC. Multi-homed computers function as a router and are used to interconnect dissimilar networks; the presence of two NICs in a computer allows it to connect to two different networks. Other types of networks may be connected by using different types of interfaces.

After completing this lab, you will be able to:

- Physically install NICs
- Make a multi-homed computer using two NICs
- Configure TCP/IP properties on NICs

## Materials Required

This lab requires the following:

- A computer named *SERVER1* running Windows Server 2008, Standard Edition without any NICs installed
- At least two PCI bus slots available on the Windows Server 2008 computer
- Access to the Windows Server 2008 computer as the administrator
- Two Ethernet PCI NICs with RJ-45 connectors listed on the Windows Server Catalog Hardware Compatibility List (HCL); at the time of this writing, you can find the Windows Server Catalog at *www.windowsservercatalog.com*
- Two Ethernet switches or hubs compatible with the NICs
- Two straight-through Cat 5 (or better) UTP cables
- A toolkit with a Phillips-head screwdriver, a ground mat, and a ground strap

Estimated completion time: **60 minutes**

## Activity

1. Power off the computer.

2. Unplug the power cord from the computer, and then place the computer on the ground mat.

3. Place the ground strap on your wrist and attach it to the ground mat underneath the computer.

4. Remove any screws from the computer's case.

5. Remove the computer case.

6. Choose a vacant PCI slot on the system board in which to insert the NIC. Remove the metal slot cover from the slot you chose.

7. Place the NIC in the slot, pushing it firmly and straight down into place.

8. Attach the NIC to the system unit with the Phillips-head screwdriver. This secures the NIC in place.

9. Replace the cover.

10. Reinsert the screws on the cover.

11. Connect one end of one cable to the NIC. Connect the other end of the same cable to one of the switches (hubs).

12. Plug in the computer and turn it on. Plug in the switch. Link lights on both the switch and the back of the NIC turn green. On some NICs, there might also be a yellow light or a flashing yellow light. If the link lights do not illuminate, verify that the cables are connected properly.

13. After the Windows Server 2008 computer is running, look at the lights on the NIC and at the port lights on the switch. They should be on. If they are not on, check the cabling. You might also need to turn off the computer, unplug it, and verify that the NIC is firmly seated inside the computer.

14. Log on to the server as the administrator. The Windows Server 2008 desktop appears, and a dialog box indicating that Windows Server 2008 has discovered new hardware opens briefly. A wizard might open, attempting to install new hardware. If so, click **Cancel** to close the wizard.

15. Click the **Start** button, click **Control Panel**, double-click **Network and Sharing Center**, click **Manage network connections**, and then double-click **Local Area Connection**. The Local Area Connection Status dialog box opens.

16. Click the **Properties** button. The Local Area Connection Properties dialog box opens.

17. Double-click **Internet Protocol Version 4 (TCP/IPv4)**. The Internet Protocol (TCP/IP) Properties dialog box opens.

18. Select the **Use the following IP address** option button. The IP address, Subnet mask, and Default gateway text boxes are enabled.

19. In the IP address text box, type **172.16.1.1**.

20. In the Subnet mask text box, type **255.255.255.0**.

21. Leave the Default gateway text box blank.

22. Click **OK**. A dialog box might open, indicating that the DNS server list is empty and that the computer will configure itself as the DNS server. If so, click **OK** again. You return to the Local Area Connection Properties dialog box.

23. Click **OK** again to close the Local Area Connection Properties dialog box. You return to the Local Area Connection Status dialog box.

24. Click **Close** to close the Local Area Connection Status dialog box.

25. Repeat Steps 1 through 24 with the second NIC. The second NIC should appear as Local Area Connection 2. When repeating Step 19, use an IP address of **192.168.54.1**. You have now built a multi-homed computer. You finish making this computer a router in Lab 6.3.

26. Log off the computer.

## Certification Objectives

Objectives for the Network+ Exam:

- 1.2 Classify how applications, devices, and protocols relate to the OSI model layers.
- 1.4 Explain the purpose and properties of routing and switching.

## Review Questions

1. Which of the following devices operates only at the Physical layer of the OSI model?

   a. NIC

   b. Hub

   c. Bridge

   d. Router

2. What type of address does a router interpret?

   a. Physical address

   b. MAC address

   c. Block ID

   d. Network address

3. Which of the following connectivity devices takes the most time to interpret the data frames it receives?

   a. Hub

   b. Bridge

   c. MAU

   d. Router

4. On a typical 100Base-T network, where would you find transceivers?

   a. In the NICs

   b. In the operating systems

   c. In the UPSs

   d. In the cabling

5. Which of the following is a difference between a router and a hub?

   a. A router is less sophisticated than a hub.

   b. A router operates at the Transport layer of the OSI model, whereas a hub operates at the Data Link layer of the OSI model.

   c. A router operates at the Network layer of the OSI model, whereas a hub operates at the Physical layer of the OSI model.

   d. A router regenerates signals, whereas a hub interprets addressing information to ensure that data is directed to the proper destination.

6. In which of the following networking scenarios would a router be the optimal connectivity device?

   a. A home network with five users who want to share documents that are stored on one of the five workstations

   b. A WAN that connects a college physics department with a classroom in a high school on the other side of town

   c. A LAN that connects 10 users, a server, and a printer at a small business

   d. A peer-to-peer LAN that connects eight users to provide a shared database

7. What is the most likely purpose of the hubs in this lab?

   a. To connect the computer to different networks

   b. To determine by checking the link lights whether the NIC was installed correctly

   c. To determine by checking the link lights whether you configured the IP addresses on the NICs correctly

   d. To allow the NICs to operate at the Network layer

# Lab 6.3 Activating Routing and Remote Access in Windows Server 2008

## Objectives

In this lab, you configure a multi-homed server to be a simple router and add a static route to its routing table. When a router receives a packet from a computer or another router, it looks in its routing table to see where it should send the packet. A routing table consists of a list of all the networks the router knows about and the next hop for each of these networks. Each route consists of a destination network and the next hop where the router should send packets to reach the destination. The next hop might be the IP address of the next router on the path to the destination or the network interface card closest to it. A router has separate routing tables for each routable protocol (such as TCP/IP or IPX/SPX) it runs.

For instance, suppose a router receives a packet with a destination address of 10.100.17.29. It looks in its routing table for a route that matches this address. It finds the route and sees that packets for 10.100.17.29 should be sent to the router at 10.100.17.1. Then it sends the packet to 10.100.17.1.

When the router at 10.100.17.1 receives the packet, it looks at its routing table for a matching route. The matching route tells the router to send the packet out its Ethernet NIC.

It sends the packet out its Ethernet NIC, where the destination computer receives it. In this manner, routers can send packets over long paths consisting of many hops.

To fill its routing table, a router must learn the routes it needs to use. One way routers learn routes is by looking at the addresses on their own interfaces. Network administrators can also add routes directly into a routing table. Routes configured by a network administrator are known as static routes.

Note that most network administrators use dedicated routing hardware whenever possible, rather than a software router such as the one you configure in this lab. Dedicated routing hardware typically is faster, more stable, and has more features than a software router.

After completing this lab, you will be able to:

- Activate and configure Routing and Remote Access Services on a Windows Server 2008 server
- Show the routing table of a Windows Server 2008 server configured as a network router
- Add a static route to a Windows Server 2008 server configured as a network router

## Materials Required

This lab requires the following:

- The network built at the end of Lab 6.2
- A computer named *SERVER1* running Windows Server 2008, Standard Edition with two NICs with Routing and Remote Access Service installed
- One NIC on the *SERVER1* computer configured with an IP address of 192.168.54.1 and a subnet mask of 255.255.255.0
- The other NIC on the *SERVER1* computer configured with an IP address of 172.16.1.1 and a subnet mask of 255.255.255.0
- Two computers running Windows 7 or Windows XP Professional with NICs compatible with the switches or hubs
- One of the Windows 7 or Windows XP Professional computers named *WORKSTATION1* and configured with an IP address of 192.168.54.2 and a default gateway of 192.168.54.1
- The other Windows 7 or Windows XP Professional computer named *WORKSTATION2* and configured with an IP address of 172.16.1.2 and a default gateway of 172.16.1.1
- Access to both Windows 7 or Windows XP computers as the local administrator
- Two straight-through Cat 5 (or better) UTP cables

Estimated completion time: **75 minutes**

## Activity

1. Plug in each NIC in *SERVER1* to one of the hubs. Log on to SERVER1 as the administrator. The Windows Server 2008 desktop appears.

2. On the Windows Server 2008 computer, click the **Start** button, point to **Administrative Tools**, and then click **Routing and Remote Access**.

3. In the left pane of the dialog box, click the name of the server to select it. Click **Action**, and, if necessary, click **Configure and Enable Routing and Remote Access**. The Routing and Remote Access Server Setup Wizard opens.

4. Click **Next**. The Configuration dialog box opens, listing several options for configuring this computer as a router.

5. Select the **Custom configuration** option, and then click **Next**. The Custom Configuration dialog box opens.

6. Click the **LAN routing** check box to place a check in it. Click **Next**.

7. Click **Finish**. The Routing and Remote Access Server Setup Wizard saves your settings and starts the Routing and Remote Access Service.

8. A dialog box opens, indicating that the Routing and Remote Access Service has been installed. Click **Start service** to start the service. A dialog box indicating that the service is initializing opens briefly. Close the Routing and Remote Access dialog box.

9. Plug the RJ-45 connector of one of the Cat 5 cables into one of the switches (hubs). Plug the other end of the cable into the NIC in the back of one of the workstation computers.

10. Repeat the previous step, connecting the other computer to the other switch. The workstation computers should each be plugged into different switches, while *SERVER1* should be plugged into both switches. This allows traffic from *WORKSTATION1* to travel through *SERVER1* to *WORKSTATION2*. Figure 6-2 shows the network cabling.

*WORKSTATION1*          *Hub*          *SERVER1*          *Hub*          *WORKSTATION2*

© Cengage Learning 2013

**Figure 6-2**    Network cabling for Lab 6.3

11. Log on to *WORKSTATION1* as an administrator. The Windows desktop appears.

12. Click the **Start** button, type **cmd** in the Start Search text box, and then press **Enter**. (In Windows XP, click the **Start** button, point to **All Programs**, point to **Accessories**, and then click **Command Prompt**.) A command prompt window opens.

13. Type **ping 172.16.1.2** and press **Enter**. If the output does not indicate that the computer has received four replies from 172.16.1.2, repeat Steps 9 and 10 before continuing, changing the switches to which each computer is attached.

14. Repeat Steps 11 and 12 with *WORKSTATION2*. The Windows Server 2008 computer is now acting as a router. This means that it accepts packets from *WORKSTATION1* and uses its routing table to determine where to send the packets so that they reach their destination, *WORKSTATION2*.

15. At the command prompt, type **ping 192.168.54.2** and press **Enter.** The output indicates that this computer has received four replies from the other computer. You have successfully used the Windows Server 2008 computer as a router.

16. Next, you configure a secondary IP address on *WORKSTATION2*. Click the **Start** button, right-click **Network,** and click **Properties.** Click **Change adapter settings.** (In Windows XP, click the **Start** button, point to **All Programs,** point to **Accessories,** point to **Communications,** and then click **Network Connections.**) The Network Connections dialog box opens.

17. Right-click the **Local Area Connection** icon, and then click **Properties** on the shortcut menu.

18. Double-click **Internet Protocol Version 4 (TCP/IPv4).** (In Windows XP, double-click **Internet Protocol (TCP/IP).**) The Internet Protocol (TCP/IPv4) Properties dialog box opens. Click **Advanced.** The Advanced TCP/IP Settings dialog box opens.

19. Click **Add** beneath the IP addresses heading at the top of the dialog box. The TCP/IP Address dialog box opens.

20. Type **10.1.1.1** in the IP address text box. Type **255.0.0.0** in the Subnet mask text box.

21. Click **Add.** You have just configured this computer with a second IP address, which it can also use to communicate with other computers. You return to the Advanced TCP/IP Settings dialog box.

22. Click **OK** to close the Advanced TCP/IP Settings dialog box, click **OK** to close the Internet Protocol Version 4 (TCP/IPv4) Properties dialog box, and then click **OK** to close the Local Area Connection Properties dialog box.

23. In the command prompt window for *WORKSTATION1*, type **ping 10.1.1.1** and press **Enter.** You see a reply (displayed four times on the screen) indicating that the destination host is unreachable.

24. Next, you check to see if a route exists on the Windows Server 2008 computer so that you can reach the secondary IP address on *WORKSTATION2* from *WORKSTATION1*. On the Windows Server 2008 computer, click the **Start** button, point to **All Programs,** click **Accessories,** and then click **Command Prompt.**

25. Type **route print** and press **Enter.** The computer displays a list of its interfaces and its routing table. Notice that no route to any IP address or network begins with 10. See Figure 6-3 for an example of a routing table on a Windows Server 2008 computer like *SERVER1* in this lab.

26. Recall that when you typed ping 10.1.1.1 in Step 23, the computer responded with "Destination host unreachable" four times. Now you configure a static route on *SERVER1* so that *WORKSTATION1* can reach 10.1.1.1. Type **route add 10.0.0.0 mask 255.0.0.0 172.16.1.2** and press **Enter.** This tells the router to add a route to any machine with a network number of 10.0.0.0 and a subnet mask of 255.0.0.0 through the computer with the IP address of 172.16.1.2.

27. Type **ping 10.1.1.1** and press **Enter.** The computer responds with "Reply from 10.1.1.1" four times.

**Figure 6-3**    Routing table

28. Type **route print** and press **Enter**. The computer displays its routing table. In the Network Destination column, you should see the route you added in Step 26, 10.0.0.0.

29. Return to the command prompt window you opened earlier on *WORKSTATION1*. Type **ping 10.1.1.1** and press **Enter**. The computer responds with "Reply from 10.1.1.1" four times. You have now successfully used the static route you configured on the Windows Server 2008 computer.

30. Finally, you look at the route used by packets to reach 10.1.1.1. Type **tracert 10.1.1.1** and press **Enter**. The computer displays the route that packets take to reach the address 10.1.1.1.

31. Log off all three computers.

## Certification Objectives

- 1.4 Explain the purpose and properties of routing and switching.
- 4.3 Given a scenario, use appropriate software tools to troubleshoot connectivity issues.

## Review Questions

1. What is the purpose of a routing table on a TCP/IP-based network?

    a. To associate the NetBIOS names of nodes with their IP addresses

    b. To associate the IP addresses of nodes with their host names

    c. To associate the IP addresses of nodes with their locations on the network

    d. To associate the host names of nodes with their MAC addresses

2. Which of the following most fully describes what a successful response from the ping command indicates?

   a. A node is powered on.

   b. A node is physically connected to the network.

   c. A node is running the Windows Server 2008 operating system.

   d. A node is connected to the network and is running TCP/IP successfully.

3. What does the tracert command show?

   a. The path taken by packets to the destination address

   b. The MAC address of the destination address

   c. Whether the remote host supports TCP/IP

   d. The operating system run by the host at the destination address

4. What command would you use to add a node's IP address, subnet mask, and network location interface to a routing table?

   a. Route add

   b. Add host

   c. Add node

   d. Route open

5. In the default ping command on a computer running Windows, how many replies do you receive if the test is successful?

   a. 1

   b. 2

   c. 3

   d. 4

6. What menu option sequence would you choose to set up Routing and Remote Access Services on a Windows Server 2008 computer?

   a. Start, Control Panel, Network Connections, Routing and Remote Access

   b. Start, Administrative Tools, Routing and Remote Access

   c. Start, All Programs, Accessories, Routing and Remote Access

   d. Start, Control Panel, Routing and Remote Access

# Lab 6.4 Activating a Routing Protocol in Windows Server 2008

## Objectives

Configuring more than a handful of static routes on a network is time consuming and error-prone. Many networks consist of hundreds or even thousands of routes. For instance, at the time of this writing, the Internet routing table consists of around 240,000 static routes. If you used static routes to maintain the routing tables on your routers, you would need to configure each static route on each router. Imagine configuring 500 or more routes on 50 routers! In addition, each time you added a new network, you would need to configure a new route on each router.

To simplify network administration, most networks of any size use a routing protocol to help routers learn routes. A router running a routing protocol tells connected routers, or neighbors, about the networks it knows about. In turn, it learns all the routes its neighbors know about. In this way, it can discover all the routes in the network. Routing protocols also allow routers to find the best routes to a destination. Finally, routing protocols allow routers to recover from outages. If a router fails, other routers learn this from information sent by the routing protocol. If another route to the destination is available, they will use it.

In this lab, you configure Routing Information Protocol (RIP) version 2 on a computer running Windows Server 2008. RIP is a relatively simple routing protocol that is supported on many network devices and servers. However, keep in mind that routing protocols can be quite complex and that mistakes with routing protocols can cause large outages.

After completing this lab, you will be able to:

- Explain the function of various routing protocols

- Install a routing protocol on a Windows Server 2008 computer

## Materials Required

This lab requires the following:

- A computer named *SERVER1* running Windows Server 2008, Standard Edition with two NICs

- One NIC on the *SERVER1* computer configured with an IP address of 192.168.54.1 and a subnet mask of 255.255.255.0

- The other NIC on the *SERVER1* computer configured with an IP address of 172.16.1.1 and a subnet mask of 255.255.255.0

- A computer named *SERVER2* running Windows Server 2008, with a NIC, an IP address of 192.168.54.2, a subnet mask of 255.255.255.0, and no default gateway

- Routing and Remote Access disabled on both computers

- Two Ethernet switches or hubs

- Three straight-through Cat 5 (or better) UTP cables

- Access as the administrator to both computers

Estimated completion time: **45 minutes**

## Activity

1. Connect each of the NICs in *SERVER1* to a separate switch (hub) with Cat 5 cables.

2. Connect the NIC in *SERVER2* to one of the switches with the remaining Cat 5 cable.

3. Log on to *SERVER2* as the administrator. The Windows Server 2008 desktop appears.

4. Click the **Start** button, point to **All Programs**, click **Accessories**, and click **Command Prompt**. A command prompt window opens.

5. Now you verify that you have network connectivity with *SERVER1*. Type **ping 192.168.54.1** and press **Enter**. The computer indicates that it has received four replies. If instead you see a timeout error (or other error), *SERVER2* is plugged into the wrong hub. Take the cable plugged into *SERVER2*'s NIC, remove the end attached to the switch, and plug it into the other switch. Repeat this step.

6. Now you attempt to reach the IP address of *SERVER1*'s other NIC. Type **ping 172.16.1.1** and press **Enter**. You see four messages indicating that the destination host is unreachable.

7. Type **route print** and press **Enter** to show the computer's routing table. Record the networks listed in the Network Destination column and the corresponding subnet masks in the Netmask column.

8. Log on to *SERVER1* as the administrator. The Windows Server 2008 desktop appears.

9. Click the **Start** button, point to **All Programs**, click **Accessories**, and click **Command Prompt**. A command prompt window opens.

10. Type **route print** and press **Enter**. The computer displays its routing table. Record the routes you see, as you did in Step 7.

11. Click the **Start** button, point to **Administrative Tools**, and click **Routing and Remote Access**. The Routing and Remote Access dialog box opens.

12. In the left pane, select **SERVER1**. Click **Action** on the menu bar, and then click **Configure and Enable Routing and Remote Access**. The Routing and Remote Access Server Setup Wizard appears.

13. Click **Next**. The Configuration dialog box opens, listing several options for configuring this computer as a router.

14. Select the **Custom configuration** option, and then click **Next**. The Custom Configuration dialog box opens.

15. Click the **LAN routing** check box to place a check in it. Click **Next**.

16. Click **Finish**. The Routing and Remote Access Server Setup Wizard saves your settings and starts the Routing and Remote Access Service.

17. A dialog box opens, indicating that the Routing and Remote Access Service has been installed. Click **Start service** to start the service. Dialog boxes indicating that the service is initializing open briefly.

18. In the left pane of the Routing and Remote Access dialog box, click the **plus sign (+)** next to the SERVER1 (local) icon, if necessary. A tree containing several nodes appears below the SERVER1 icon. Click the **plus sign (+)** next to the IPv4 node. More options appear underneath the IPv4 node, including an icon named General.

19. Right-click the **General** icon, and then click **New Routing Protocol** on the shortcut menu. The New Routing Protocol dialog box opens, as shown in Figure 6-4.

20. Click **RIP Version 2 for Internet Protocol**, and then click **OK**. An RIP icon appears in the left pane on the same tree as the General icon while the Windows Server 2008 computer installs the Routing Information Protocol.

**Figure 6-4**    Adding a new routing protocol

21. Right-click the new **RIP** icon in the tree in the left pane, and then click **New Interface**. The New Interface for RIP Version 2 for Internet Protocol dialog box opens.

22. Click **Local Area Connection**, if necessary, and then click **OK** to add the interface. The RIP Properties – Local Area Connection Properties dialog box opens.

23. Click **OK** to close the dialog box and finish adding the interface. If necessary, select RIP in the left pane. An icon for Local Area Connection appears in the right pane of the Routing and Remote Access dialog box.

24. Repeat Steps 21 through 23 for Local Area Connection 2.

25. Right-click the **SERVER1 (local)** icon. On the shortcut menu, point to **All Tasks**, and then click **Restart**. A dialog box opens briefly, indicating that the Routing and Remote Access Service is restarting.

26. Enable Routing and Remote Access on *SERVER2* by repeating Steps 11 through 23 and Step 25. After RIP for IP is installed on both computers, they dynamically share their routing tables within a minute.

27. Wait one minute. In the left pane of the Routing and Remote Access dialog box on *SERVER2*, right-click the **RIP** icon, and then click **Show Neighbors**. The SERVER2 – RIP Neighbors dialog box opens, showing the IP address of *SERVER1*. If you do not see the IP address of *SERVER1* in this dialog box, wait another minute and repeat this step.

28. In the command prompt window on *SERVER2*, type `ping 172.16.1.1` and press **Enter**.

29. Type `route print` and press **Enter**. What additional routes do you see now that you didn't see in Step 11?

30. Repeat the previous step on *SERVER1*.

## Certification Objectives

Objectives for the Network+ Exam:

- 1.4 Explain the purpose and properties of routing and switching.
- 2.1 Given a scenario, install and configure routers and switches.

## Review Questions

1. What does RIP stand for?

   a. Regulated Interaction Protocol

   b. Routing Information Protocol

   c. Response Interpretation Protocol

   d. Registered Installation Protocol

2. To determine the best path to transfer data, routers communicate using routing protocols such as TCP/IP. True or False?

3. What additional routes did you find in Step 29?

4. Which routing protocol is commonly used for Internet backbones?

   a. OSPF

   b. RIP for IP

   c. EIGRP

   d. BGP

5. When might the best path not equal the shortest distance between two nodes? (Choose all that apply.)

   a. A communications link has been recently added to the network.

   b. A communications link is suffering congestion.

   c. A router experiences routing protocol errors.

   d. The media on the shortest path is slower than the media on the best path.

6. Which protocol was developed by Cisco Systems and has a fast convergence time but is supported only on Cisco routers?

   a. OSPF

   b. RIP for IP

   c. EIGRP

   d. BGP

7. What does OSPF stand for?

   a. Open shortest path first

   b. Overhead system path forwarding

   c. Overlook system packet forwarding

   d. Open session peer first

# Lab 6.5 Configuring a Bridging Firewall

## Objectives

A firewall is a gateway used to connect two or more networks and to control the traffic allowed to cross a network. A firewall is often used to protect a network from potentially malicious traffic on the Internet. For example, the firewall is typically configured to allow users on the protected network, or inside the firewall, to use network resources on the Internet. Many firewalls can control traffic with varying degrees of ease anywhere from the Data Link layer up to the Application layer.

In many ways, the distinction between a firewall and a router is fuzzy. Many routers can also filter traffic. Like a router, a firewall can be a dedicated piece of hardware or software configured on a server. The function of a firewall also overlaps somewhat with that of a router. A firewall can use a handful of static routes, or it can run a routing protocol like a router.

However, a firewall does not need to be a router at all. In this lab, you configure a computer running Windows Server 2008 as both a bridge and a firewall. A bridge is a gateway device that operates at Layer 2 of the OSI model and does not require Layer 3 configuration. However, in the packets it receives, a bridging firewall can use information at Layer 3 and higher to decide whether to forward those packets.

In this lab, you configure the firewall to selectively prevent one computer from being able to ping the other. When one computer pings a second computer, it sends an ICMP echo request packet. The second computer sends an ICMP echo reply packet to acknowledge the ping. When the first computer receives the ICMP echo reply packet from the second computer, it knows that the ping has been successful. A firewall can prevent computers outside the firewall from pinging computers inside the firewall by filtering ICMP echo request packets. If the computers inside the firewall do not receive the ICMP echo request packets, they do not send ICMP echo reply packets. Thus, computers outside the firewall cannot successfully ping computers inside the firewall. At the same time, the firewall does not prevent computers inside it from pinging computers outside the firewall.

After completing this lab, you will be able to:

- Configure a computer running Windows Server 2008 as a simple firewall
- Configure the Windows Server 2008 firewall to filter ICMP echo request packets

## Materials Required

This lab requires the following:

- The network built at the end of Lab 6.2
- A computer named *SERVER1* running Windows Server 2008, Standard Edition with two NICs with Routing and Remote Access Service installed
- One NIC on the *SERVER1* computer configured with an IP address of 192.168.54.1 and a subnet mask of 255.255.255.0
- The other NIC on the *SERVER1* computer configured with an IP address of 172.16.1.1 and a subnet mask of 255.255.255.0
- Two computers running Windows 7 or Windows XP Professional with NICs compatible with the switches or hubs

- One of the Windows 7 or Windows XP computers named *WORKSTATION1* and configured with an IP address of 192.168.54.2 and a default gateway of 192.168.54.1
- The other Windows 7 or Windows XP computer named *WORKSTATION2* and configured with an IP address of 172.16.1.2 and a default gateway of 172.16.1.1
- Access to both Windows 7 or XP computers as the local administrator
- Two straight-through Cat 5 (or better) UTP cables

Estimated completion time: **30 minutes**

## Activity

1. Connect one end of a cable to one of the switches (hubs). Connect the other end of the cable to *WORKSTATION1*.
2. Repeat the previous step, connecting the other switch to *WORKSTATION2*.
3. Connect one end of a cable to one of the switches. Connect the other end of the cable to one of the NICs in *SERVER1*.
4. Repeat the previous step, connecting the other switch to *SERVER1*. Now both *WORKSTATION1* and *WORKSTATION2* are connected to different switches, and each switch is connected to one of the NICs on *SERVER1*.
5. Log on to *WORKSTATION1* as an administrator. The Windows desktop appears.
6. Click the **Start** button, type **cmd** in the Start Search text box, and then press **Enter**. (In Windows XP, click the **Start** button, point to **All Programs**, point to **Accessories**, and then click **Command Prompt**.) A command prompt window opens.
7. Type **ping 172.16.1.2** and press **Enter** to confirm that *WORKSTATION1* can successfully ping *WORKSTATION2*.
8. Now you configure *SERVER1* as a firewall.
9. Log on to *SERVER1* as the administrator. The Windows Server 2008 desktop appears.
10. On the Windows Server 2008 computer, click the **Start** button, point to **Administrative Tools,** and then click **Windows Firewall with Advanced Security**.
11. Right-click **Inbound Rules** and click **New Rule**.
12. Select **Custom** and click **Next**.
13. Select **All programs** and click **Next**.
14. Next to Protocol Type, select **ICMPv4** and click **Next**.
15. Confirm that this rule applies to any local and remote IP addresses and click **Next**.
16. Select **Block the connection**, click **Next**, and click **Next** again.
17. Name the rule **Ping Block** and click **Finish**.
18. The computer now drops ICMP echo request packets sent to *WORKSTATION2*.
19. In the command prompt window on *WORKSTATION1*, type **ping 172.16.1.2** and press **Enter**. The computer indicates four times that it is unable to reach the destination host.
20. Log off each computer.

## Certification Objective

Objective for the Network+ Exam:

- 5.5 Given a scenario, install and configure a basic firewall.

## Review Questions

1. Which of the following could serve as firewalls? (Choose all that apply.)

   a. A modem

   b. A Windows Server 2008 computer

   c. A hub

   d. A Linux server

2. A firewall can run a routing protocol like a router. True or False?

3. What is the highest level of the OSI model in which a firewall can operate?

   a. Data Link

   b. Network

   c. Transport

   d. Application

4. A gateway connects two different types of networks, two different types of communications protocols, or two different computer architectures. Which of the following is *not* considered a gateway?

   a. A router connecting a token ring

   b. A computer translating application data from TCP/IP to IPX/SPX

   c. A computer translating voice signals into data and transmitting it over a TCP/IP network

   d. A file and print server communicating with clients using both TCP/IP and IPX/SPX

5. You have configured a device that runs the OSPF routing protocol but whose primary purpose is to prevent unwanted Internet traffic from reaching your company's LAN. Which of the following is true about this device?

   a. It is a router because it runs a routing protocol.

   b. It is a router because its primary purpose is to control traffic.

   c. It is a firewall because it runs a routing protocol.

   d. It is a firewall because its primary purpose is to control traffic.

6. Which of the following statements about a bridge is false?

   a. Without IP addressing information, a bridge cannot be seen with the tracert command.

   b. Bridges require no Layer 3 addressing.

   c. Bridges decide which packets to forward based on their Layer 3 headers.

   d. Bridges operate at the Data Link layer.

# WIDE AREA NETWORKS

## Labs included in this chapter

- Lab 7.1 Pricing WAN Services
- Lab 7.2 Connecting to an Internet Service Provider in Windows Server 2008
- Lab 7.3 Connecting to a Cisco Router with Telnet
- Lab 7.4 Configuring a Cisco Router with HyperTerminal

## Network+ Exam Objectives

| Objective | Lab |
| --- | --- |
| 1.4 Explain the purpose and properties of routing and switching. | 7.3, 7.4 |
| 1.6 Explain the function of common networking protocols. | 7.3, 7.4 |
| 3.4 Categorize WAN technology types and properties. | 7.1, 7.2 |
| 4.3 Given a scenario, use appropriate software tools to troubleshoot connectivity issues. | 7.2, 7.3 |

# Lab 7.1 Pricing WAN Services

## Objectives

In this lab, you price several options for WAN services. Many organizations use multiple types of WAN links for redundancy and to eliminate single points of failure on the network. For example, an organization might use T1s to connect its two largest remote offices to its central office, and it might use ISDN lines as backups in case either T1 fails. To connect its smaller offices to the central office, an organization might use ISDN lines as the primary link and a dial-up modem as the backup link. Many organizations also have a backup link for their Internet connection.

You can use these services to connect an organization to the Internet as well as to connect offices in one location to offices in another location. The pricing of Internet services is often more complicated because you must purchase both a WAN link and Internet access. Depending on the type of WAN link, however, many WAN service providers offer both the WAN connection and the Internet access. Many telephone companies, for example, install a T1 and provide Internet access with the T1 service.

WAN topologies can also have a huge impact on price. The star, partial-mesh, and full-mesh WAN topologies are used most commonly. Independent of the cost of the actual WAN, the star topology is the least expensive. A star topology consists of one link from a central office to each satellite office. For each new office you add, you need to add only one new link. However, a star topology offers no redundancy in case of a link failure. In a partial-mesh topology, some (but not all) of the satellite offices are interconnected. If one link fails, there is often (but not always) a backup link. The price of adding an office rises depending on the number of satellite offices and on the degree to which they are linked. In a full-mesh topology, all offices are connected to each other. The price of adding an office increases with the number of offices. With a large number of offices, a full-mesh WAN topology costs many times what a star topology for the same number of offices would cost. Other WAN topologies, such as the bus and ring topologies, do not scale well and are rarely used for WANs with more than a handful of locations.

In this lab, you have the choice of calling a local company for information or doing research on the Web. You record information in Figure 7-1. If you choose to call a company, take time to review Figure 7-1 and the lab steps before calling so you can speak knowledgeably and efficiently with the customer service representative. In some cases, your instructor might want to minimize any disruption to local companies by making arrangements ahead of time. Take care to be polite and work as quickly as possible so as not to waste the representative's time. Remember to say "thank you" when you are finished. If you want, you can also follow up with a thank-you e-mail or letter after the call.

After completing this lab, you will be able to:

- Compare WAN links in terms of cost and speed
- Compare WAN topologies in terms of price and redundancy
- Identify WAN hardware components

## Materials Required

This lab requires the following:

- Pencil and paper
- If some of the services discussed in this lab are not offered in your area, use representative pricing provided by your instructor for those services

| | |
|---|---|
| Company name | |
| Phone call or Web research? | |
| Types of connections offered | |
| **T1 Service** | |
| Service available in your area? | |
| Geographic restrictions | |
| Bandwidth | |
| Does the company charge a monthly fee, or does the cost vary with usage? | |
| Monthly fee/usage charges | |
| Additional equipment required? | |
| If additional equipment is required, does the company provide it? | |
| If additional equipment is required, is the hardware charge a single flat fee or a monthly charge? | |
| Typical hardware cost | |
| Setup fees | |
| **DSL Service** | |
| Service available in your area? | |
| Geographic restrictions | |
| Bandwidth | |
| Does the company charge a monthly fee, or does the cost vary with usage? | |
| Monthly fee/usage charges | |
| Additional equipment required? | |
| If additional equipment is required, does the company provide it? | |
| If additional equipment is required, is the hardware charge a single flat fee or a monthly charge? | |
| Typical hardware cost | |
| Setup fees | |
| **128-Kbps Partial T1 or ISDN Service** | |
| Service available in your area? | |
| Geographic restrictions | |
| Bandwidth | |

© Cengage Learning 2013

(*Continues*)

| | |
|---|---|
| Does the company charge a monthly fee, or does the cost vary with usage? | |
| Monthly fee/usage charges | |
| Additional equipment required? | |
| If additional equipment is required, does the company provide it? | |
| If additional equipment is required, is the hardware charge a single flat fee or a monthly charge? | |
| Typical hardware cost | |
| Setup fees | |
| **Public Switched Telephone Network (PSTN) Connection Service** | |
| Service available in your area? | |
| Geographic restrictions | |
| Bandwidth | |
| Does the company charge a monthly fee, or does the cost vary with usage? | |
| Monthly fee/usage charges | |
| Additional equipment required? | |
| If additional equipment is required, does the company provide it? | |
| If additional equipment is required, is the hardware charge a single flat fee or a monthly charge? | |
| Typical hardware cost | |
| Setup fees | |
| Total setup, installation, and equipment costs | T1:<br><br>DSL:<br><br>128-Kbps partial T1 or ISDN:<br><br>PSTN:<br><br>Other: |
| Two years of service, excluding hardware | T1:<br><br>DSL:<br><br>128-Kbps partial T1 or ISDN:<br><br>PSTN:<br><br>Other: |

(*Continues*)

| | |
|---|---|
| Two years of service for star topology shown in Figure 7-2, excluding hardware | T1:<br><br>DSL:<br><br>128-Kbps partial T1 or ISDN:<br><br>PSTN:<br><br>Other: |
| Two years of service for the partial-mesh topology shown in Figure 7-3, excluding hardware | T1:<br><br>DSL:<br><br>128-Kbps partial T1 or ISDN:<br><br>PSTN:<br><br>Other: |
| Two years of service for the full-mesh topology shown in Figure 7-4, excluding hardware | T1:<br><br>DSL:<br><br>128-Kbps partial T1 or ISDN:<br><br>PSTN:<br><br>Other: |

© Cengage Learning 2013

**Figure 7-1**   Table for recording answers to Lab 7-1 (*Continued*)

Estimated completion time: **60–90 minutes**

## Activity

1. Go to the Web site of a local Internet service provider or telephone company and look for information about the cost and availability of high-speed Internet links for businesses. Alternatively, call and speak to a representative. Explain that you are doing research for a school project on the pricing of Internet links. Give your name, the name of the networking class you are taking, and the name of your school.

2. In Figure 7-1, write the name of the company, and indicate whether you did your research on the Web or called directly.

3. What types of WAN services do they offer (for example, T-Carrier, DSL, SONET, and so forth)? Record the answer in Figure 7-1.

4. Is T1 service available in your area? Record the answer in Figure 7-1. If the service is available, are there any geographic restrictions on the service? For instance, some services might not be available in all areas because the necessary infrastructure has not yet been built. Record the geographic availability of the service in Figure 7-1.

5. If the service is available, find out the bandwidth of the service and record it in Figure 7-1.

6. Does the company charge a monthly fee for T1 service, or does the charge vary depending on usage? Record this information in Figure 7-1.

7. If the company charges a monthly fee, record the amount in Figure 7-1; otherwise record the usage charges.

8. Is any additional equipment required for the service and, if so, does the company provide it?

9. Is the hardware charge a single fee or a monthly charge? If necessary, ask for the typical price of the additional equipment. In Figure 7-1, record the typical hardware charge.

10. What are the typical setup fees, such as fees for the installation of the T1 line itself? Record any setup fees in Figure 7-1.

11. Repeat Step 3 through Step 10, this time referencing digital subscriber line (DSL).

12. Repeat Step 3 through Step 10, this time referencing 128-Kbps partial T1 or ISDN.

13. Repeat Step 3 through Step 10, this time referencing a PSTN connection with a modem.

14. If you wish, repeat Step 3 through Step 10 for any other WAN services the carrier offers.

15. For each service, calculate the total setup and installation fees and the cost of equipment required (excluding monthly charges for hardware), and record this information in Figure 7-1.

16. For each service, calculate the cost of two years of service, including any monthly charges for hardware. If the service is billed based on usage, estimate the cost based on medium usage. Record the cost of two years of service.

17. For each service, compare the costs calculated in Step 15 and Step 16.

18. Now you examine the effects of different WAN topologies on WAN pricing. Calculate the cost of T1 service connecting each office in Figure 7-2 in the star topology shown. Use the two-year monthly service fees you calculated in Step 16.

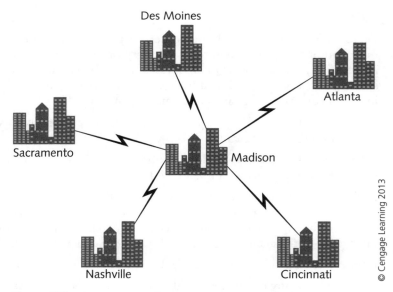

**Figure 7-2**  Star WAN topology

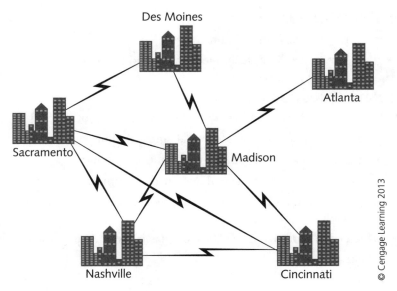

**Figure 7-3**    Partial-mesh WAN topology

© Cengage Learning 2013

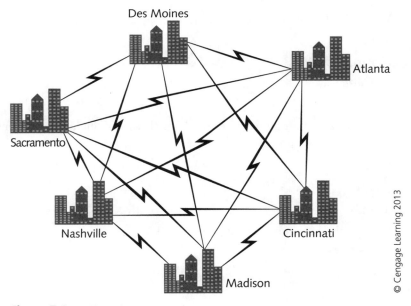

**Figure 7-4**    Full-mesh WAN topology

© Cengage Learning 2013

19. Calculate the cost of T1 service connecting each office in the partial-mesh topology shown in Figure 7-3 . Use the two-year monthly service fees you calculated in Step 16.

20. Calculate the cost of T1 service connecting each office in the full-mesh topology shown in Figure 7-4. Use the two-year monthly service fees you calculated in Step 16.

## Certification Objective

Objective for the Network+ Exam:

- 3.4 Categorize WAN technology types and properties.

## Review Questions

1. Which of the following best describes the function of a CSU?

    a. It transmits several signals over a single channel.

    b. It separates a single channel into multiple channels.

    c. It terminates a digital signal and ensures connection integrity.

    d. It converts the digital signal used by connectivity devices into the digital signal sent through the cabling.

2. Which of the following WAN topologies is the least expensive to build?

    a. Star-wired ring

    b. Full-mesh

    c. Partial-mesh

    d. Star

3. Which of the following WAN topologies gives the most redundancy?

    a. Bus

    b. Partial-mesh

    c. Full-mesh

    d. Star

4. What is the maximum number of channels that a single T1 can contain?

    a. 12

    b. 24

    c. 48

    d. 64

5. What is the maximum throughput of a T3 line?

    a. 1.544 Mbps

    b. 45 Mbps

    c. 672 Mbps

    d. 275 Mbps

6. What does DSL use to achieve higher throughput than PSTN over the same lines?

    a. Full duplexing

    b. Data modulation

    c. Message switching

    d. Framing

7. Which of the following WAN links is most reliable?

   a. DSL

   b. PSTN

   c. ISDN

   d. SONET

8. Which of the following is the most expensive type of connection to install and lease?

   a. DSL

   b. ISDN

   c. T1

   d. T3

# Lab 7.2 Connecting to an Internet Service Provider in Windows Server 2008

## Objectives

In this lab, you make a connection to an ISP. Although higher-speed connections such as DSL or cable allow many people to connect more quickly to the Internet, dial-up connections to the Internet are still common in some areas and are often used as a backup method to remotely connect to a server. Dial-up access using the Public Switched Telephone Network (PSTN), also known as the plain old telephone service (POTS), is still used in many rural areas that do not yet have access to high-speed alternatives. In your work as a networking professional, it is important that you understand how to configure and troubleshoot dial-up connections because some of your rural clients will rely on such connections for network access.

In many small networks, many or all users need at least occasional access to the Internet. Sharing a single Internet connection is more economical and easier to configure than giving users their own modems and ISP accounts. Using Internet Connection Sharing (ICS), you can configure one modem on one computer, and the rest of the office can connect through that computer. ICS automatically configures the server to give DHCP addresses to workstations. Furthermore, you can configure the ICS server to dial the ISP connection whenever a workstation requests information on the Internet. However, because a dial-up connection quickly becomes congested as you add users, most businesses choose a high-speed connection option, if possible.

In addition, ICS automatically configures Network Address Translation (NAT) for the ISP connection. NAT allows an ICS server and any workstation using the ICS server to connect to the Internet to appear to the ISP as one IP address. Otherwise, you would need to arrange with the ISP for each workstation to have its own IP address. This would require additional configuration as well as additional expense in many cases.

After completing this lab, you will be able to:

- Configure a dial-up connection to an ISP

- Share a dial-up Internet connection with a workstation

## Materials Required

This lab requires the following:

- A computer running Windows Server 2008, Standard Edition named *SERVER1* with a NIC configured with an IP address of 192.168.54.1 and a subnet mask of 255.255.255.0; no secondary IP addresses must be configured for this NIC

- Routing and Remote Access disabled on *SERVER1*

- A modem installed and configured on *SERVER1*, without any location or Internet connection information configured

- Access to an analog outside phone line, or a digital-to-analog converter (to prevent the digital phone lines from ruining the modems)

- Knowledge of an additional number, such as 9, if it is required to access the outside line

- The phone number of an ISP's dial-up pool and a username and password for a valid account that does not require any advanced settings

- A computer running Windows 7 or Windows XP Professional named *WORKSTATION1* with a NIC, and configured to receive an IP address through DHCP

- Administrative access to both computers

- Both computers connected to an Ethernet hub with straight-through Cat 5 (or better) UTP cables

---

Estimated completion time: **30 minutes**

---

## Activity

1. Plug the RJ-11 connector on one end of the phone cable into the modem attached to *SERVER1*. Plug the other end into the wall jack for the phone line.

2. Log on to *SERVER1* as the administrator. The Windows Server 2008 desktop appears.

3. Click the **Start** button, click **Control Panel**, click **Network and Internet,** then click **Network and Sharing Center**, and click **Set up a new Connection or Network**. The Set Up a Connection or Network window opens.

4. When you're asked to select a connection or network, make sure that the **Connect to the Internet** option is selected, and click **Next**.

5. Next, you are asked how you want to connect to the Internet. If necessary, click the **Dial-up** option.

6. Enter **Netplus Lab** in the Connection name text box, as shown in Figure 7-5.

7. Enter the phone number of the ISP in the Dial-up phone number text box. Include any additional digits needed, such as a 1, the area code, or any numbers (often a 9) required to use an outside phone line.

8. If necessary, select the **Allow other people to use this connection** option.

9. Enter the username in the User name text box, and enter the account's password in the Password text box.

10. Click **Create**. Click **Close**.

11. In the Network and Sharing Center, click **Manage network connections.**

12. Right-click **Netplus Lab,** and then click **Properties**. The Netplus Lab Properties dialog box opens.

13. Click the **Sharing** tab. The Sharing tab of the Netplus Lab Properties dialog box opens.

14. Click the **Allow other network users to connect through this computer's Internet connection** check box to place a check mark in it. If the **Establish a dial-up connection whenever a computer on my network attempts to access the Internet** check box is not checked, click it to insert a check.

15. If the Home networking connection drop-down box is present, select **Local Area Connection**. If not, go to the next step. (The Home networking connection drop-down box is available only if the computer has more than one network card.)

16. Click **OK**. A dialog box might open, indicating that when Internet Connection Sharing is enabled, the NIC is automatically configured with an IP address of 192.168.137.1 and that it might lose contact with other devices on the network.

17. Click **Yes**. If necessary, close The Netplus Lab Properties dialog box.

18. On *WORKSTATION1*, press **Ctrl+Alt+Del** to display the Log On to Windows dialog box, if necessary. Log on as an administrator. The Windows desktop appears.

**Figure 7-5**   Connect to the Internet dialog box

19. Click the **Start** button, type **cmd** in the Search programs and files text box, and then press **Enter**. (In Windows XP, click the **Start** button, point to **All Programs**, point to **Accessories**, and click **Command Prompt**.) A command prompt window opens.

20. Type **ipconfig /renew** and press **Enter**. The computer obtains a new IP address from the server. Record the new IP address.

21. Open Internet Explorer.

22. In the Address bar, type **www.microsoft.com** and press **Enter**. The modem attached to *SERVER1* dials the ISP connection, and the Microsoft home page opens.

23. Log off both computers.

## Certification Objectives

Objectives for the Network+ Exam:

- 3.4 Categorize WAN technology types and properties.
- 4.3 Given a scenario, use appropriate software tools to troubleshoot connectivity issues.

## Review Questions

1. What are two differences between PPP and SLIP?

   a. SLIP can handle only asynchronous transmission, whereas PPP can handle both asynchronous and synchronous transmission.

   b. SLIP encapsulates traffic according to its original Network layer protocol, whereas PPP masks SLIP traffic as IP-based data.

   c. SLIP cannot carry Network layer protocols other than TCP/IP, whereas PPP can carry any Network layer protocol.

   d. SLIP is compatible only with NetWare servers, whereas PPP is compatible with both NetWare and Windows computers.

2. Which of the following is one primary difference between PPP and PPTP?

   a. PPP can handle only asynchronous transmission, whereas PPTP can handle both asynchronous and synchronous transmission.

   b. PPP encapsulates traffic according to its original Network layer protocol, whereas PPTP masks PPP traffic as IP-based data.

   c. PPP cannot carry Network layer protocols other than TCP/IP, whereas PPTP can carry any Network layer protocol.

   d. PPP is compatible only with NetWare servers, whereas PPTP is compatible with both NetWare and Windows computers.

3. Which of the following is the most secure remote access protocol?

   a. SLIP

   b. PPP

   c. RAS

   d. PPTP

4. Which of the following best describes the asynchronous communications method?

    a. Data that is transmitted and received by nodes must conform to a timing scheme.

    b. Data that is transmitted and received by nodes does not have to conform to any timing scheme.

    c. Data that is transmitted and received by nodes is subject to resequencing by each connectivity device through which it passes.

    d. Data that is transmitted and received by nodes requires an additional sequencing bit to ensure that data is reassembled in the proper order.

5. If your ISP uses DHCP to assign TCP/IP information to a dial-up connection, which of the following must you still specify in your connection parameters?

    a. The type of server into which you are dialing

    b. Your workstation's IP address

    c. The network's DHCP server address

    d. The network's subnet mask

# Lab 7.3 Connecting to a Cisco Router with Telnet

## Objectives

Most small home and office routers can be set up through a network using a Web-based browser like Internet Explorer. Commercial routers and switches, on the other hand, are usually configured using a command-line interface (CLI). The CLI is typically accessed through a network using a virtual terminal program such as Telnet or SSH or through a direct serial connection called the console port.

After completing this lab, you will be able to:

- Connect to a Cisco router using Telnet

## Materials Required

This lab requires the following:

- An Ethernet switch or hub
- Two straight-through Cat 5 (or better) UTP cables
- A Cisco business class router such as the Catalyst 2600 series with a password set for Telnet
- Administrative access to a computer running Windows 7 or Windows XP Professional (with Telnet enabled) on the same network as the router

Estimated completion time: **20 minutes**

## Activity

1. Connect one end of the straight-through cable to the Windows computer and connect the other end to the hub or switch.

2. Connect the other cable between the hub or switch and the first Ethernet port on the router.

**Figure 7-6** Microsoft Telnet Client

3. Log on to the computer as the administrator. The Windows desktop appears.

4. Click the **Start** button, type **cmd** in the Search programs and files text box, and then press **Enter**. (In Windows XP, click the **Start** button, point to **All Programs**, point to **Accessories**, and then click **Command Prompt**.) A command prompt window opens.

5. At the command prompt, type **telnet**. The Telnet client opens, as pictured in Figure 7-6.

6. Connect to the router by typing **open  xx.xx.xx.xx**, where xx.xx.xx.xx is your router's IP address, and pressing **Enter**. A password prompt appears. Enter the router's password, and press **Enter**.

7. Next, enter privileged mode, which allows you to carry out administrative tasks, by typing **enable** and pressing **Enter**.

8. Next, type **show version** to display the IOS version running on the router. Examine the output to determine what types of interfaces are available on your router.

9. You can gather additional information on the router's interfaces by typing **show interfaces**. What is the Internet address of your first Ethernet port?

10. Type **show running-config** to examine the router's current running configuration file. This command can be used to determine information such as the IP addresses of the Ethernet ports or the DHCP configuration. How are the duplex and speed configured on your router's first Ethernet port?

11. Many networking commands are also available in the IOS. You can test a connection between the router and another device with the ping command. Type **ping xx.xx.xx.xx**, where xx.xx.xx.xx is your computer's IP address, and press **Enter**. What was the average round-trip time (in milliseconds) between your router and your computer?

12. Type **quit** and press **Enter** to log off the router.

13. Type **exit** to close the Command Prompt window, and log off the computer.

## Certification Objectives

Objectives for the Network+ Exam:

- 1.4 Explain the purpose and properties of routing and switching.
- 1.6 Explain the function of common networking protocols.

## Review Questions

1. What CLI command would you use to test a connection between a router and another device on the network?

   a. `enable`

   b. `ping`

   c. `show interfaces`

   d. `show version`

2. What direct serial connection can be used to access routers that are not already part of a network?

   a. Console port

   b. Telnet

   c. SSH

   d. Ethernet port

3. A router determines logical addressing information by interpreting the contents of an incoming _____.

   a. Datagram

   b. Segment

   c. Packet

   d. Frame

4. Routers operate at which layer of the OSI model?

   a. 2

   b. 3

   c. 4

   d. 5

5. Of the following tasks, which one are Routers incapable of performing?

   a. Connecting dissimilar networks

   b. Determining the best path to send data

   c. Rerouting traffic if the primary path is not available

   d. Interpreting MAC address information

# Lab 7.4 Configuring a Cisco Router with HyperTerminal

## Objectives

If a router is not already a member of your network, it can't be accessed through Telnet. In that case, you have to connect a computer directly to the console port of the router with a special cable, and then use terminal emulation software such as Windows HyperTerminal or Putty. This is often required to initially configure a router as part of your local network.

In this lab, you configure the router so it can be accessed through Telnet, as was done in Lab 7.3.

After completing this lab, you will be able to:

- Connect directly to a router through the console port
- Configure a router using the command-line interface

## Materials Required

This lab requires the following:

- A Cisco business-class router such as the Catalyst 2600 series
- A console management cable to connect a PC to the console port. The specifics of this cable might vary depending on your computer's configuration and might involve combining several devices such as a rollover cable, an RJ-45 to DB-9 adapter, and a serial-to-USB adapter.
- Administrative access to a computer running Windows 7 or Windows XP Professional
- Access to terminal emulation software such as HyperTerminal (included in Windows XP Professional) or Putty (free to download from http://www.putty.org.)

Estimated completion time: **20 minutes**

## Activity

1. Attach the console management cable to the console port of the router and the serial or USB port of the computer.
2. Log on to the computer as the administrator. The Windows desktop appears.
3. Open the terminal emulation client with the appropriate port settings for your router (for example, COM1, 9600 bps, 8 data bits, no parity, 1 stop bit, no flow control).
4. Press **Enter**. The router's prompt should appear.
5. Examine a list of available CLI commands by typing **?** and pressing **Enter**.
6. Enter privileged mode by typing **enable** and pressing **Enter**. How does the prompt change to let you know that you've enabled privileged mode?
7. Enter global configuration mode by typing **configure terminal**. How does the prompt change to let you know that you're in global configuration mode?
8. Type **interface fastethernet0/0** and press **Enter** to enter the configuration mode for the first Ethernet port.
9. Type **ip address 192.168.54.254 255.255.255.0** to set the IP address of the first Ethernet port.
10. Type **exit** and press **Enter** to move back into the global configuration mode.
11. Type **line vty 0 4** and press **Enter** to enter configuration mode for the virtual terminal on the router.

12. Type **login local** and press **Enter** to allow users to log in through Telnet, as was done in Lab 7.3.

13. Type **end** and press **Enter** to exit privileged mode

14. Close the terminal emulation software and log off the computer.

## Certification Objectives

Objectives for the Network+ Exam:

- 1.4 Explain the purpose and properties of routing and switching.
- 1.6 Explain the function of common networking protocols.

## Review Questions

1. What symbol does the CLI use to show privileged mode?

    a. >

    b. <

    c. #

    d. %

2. Why can't all routers just be configured through an Ethernet port?

    a. The Ethernet port must first be made a member of a local network.

    b. Telnet is no longer available in Windows 7.

    c. Most routers don't have Ethernet ports.

    d. The router bandwidth is too fast for most computer NICs to handle.

3. What kind of routers operate on the Internet backbone?

    a. Interior

    b. Exterior

    c. Border

    d. Gateway

4. What CLI command is used to enter privileged mode?

    a. **configure**

    b. **configure terminal**

    c. **reload**

    d. **enable**

5. Which CLI command shows a list of available commands?

    a. **?**

    b. **list**

    c. **line**

    d. **h**

# WIRELESS NETWORKING

## Labs included in this chapter

## Network+ Exam Objectives

| Objective | Lab |
|---|---|
| 2.1 Given a scenario, install and configure routers and switches | 8.4 |
| 2.2 Given a scenario, install and configure a wireless network | 8.1, 8.2, 8.3 |
| 2.4 Given a scenario, troubleshoot common wireless problems | 8.3 |
| 5.1 Given a scenario, implement appropriate wireless security measures | 8.4 |

# Lab 8.1 Adding a Windows Client to a Wireless Network

## Objectives

In this lab, you add a host to a wireless network. Wireless networks allow a user to connect to the network without cabling. This makes it possible to use a networked computer in a cafeteria, outdoors, in a coffee shop, and in many other places.

However, wireless networks come with a number of disadvantages. They do not have the throughput that some wired networks provide. Throughput also varies depending on reception, and good reception might not be possible from all locations. Wireless signals are affected by sources of electronic noise, including the weather, fluorescent lights, and microwave ovens. Finally, wireless networks might not be as secure as cabled networks. An unsecured wireless access point might mean that anyone with a wireless card in the next building or in the parking lot could gain access to your network resources.

After completing this lab, you will be able to:

- Add a Windows client to a wireless network

## Materials Required

This lab requires the following:

- A computer (ideally a laptop) named *WORKSTATION1* running Windows 7 or Windows XP Professional with a wireless network card configured so that Windows manages wireless settings (instead of using the network card's client software to manage wireless settings)

- A wireless access point named *netplus* (or another name supplied by your instructor) configured with an IP address of 192.168.1.1 and a subnet mask of 255.255.255.0

- The wireless access point configured to give out DHCP addresses between 192.168.1.2 and 192.168.1.254 (or some portion of that range) and a subnet mask of 255.255.255.0

- Any additional settings needed to connect the Windows 7 or Windows XP computer to this wireless access point

Estimated completion time: **25 minutes**

## Activity

In Windows 7:

1. Log on to *WORKSTATION1* as an administrator. The Windows desktop appears.

2. Click the **Start** button, click **Control Panel**, click **Network and Internet**, and click **Network and Sharing Center**. The Network and Sharing Center window opens.

3. Click **Connect to a network**. A list of available wireless networks appears.

4. If you see the name of the wireless network, select it and go to Step 7. If you do not see the name of the wireless network, go to Step 5.

5. Click **Set up a new connection or network**, click **Manually connect to a wireless network**, and click **Next**. The Manually connect to a wireless network dialog box opens as shown in Figure 8-1.

**Figure 8-1**    Manually connecting to a wireless network

6. Enter **netplus** (or the name of the wireless access point) in the Network name text box. Configure any additional settings as indicated by your instructor, and click **Next**.

7. After you've connected to the network, close any open windows.

In Windows XP:

1. Log on to *WORKSTATION1* as an administrator. The Windows desktop appears.

2. Click the **Start** button, point to **All Programs**, point to **Accessories**, point to **Communications**, and click **Network Connections**. The Network Connections window opens.

3. Right-click **Wireless Network Connection**, and then select **Properties** from the shortcut menu that appears. The Wireless Network Connection Properties window opens.

4. Click the **Wireless Networks** tab. If necessary, click the **View Wireless Networks** button. A list of available wireless networks appears under Available networks.

5. If you see the name of the wireless network, select it and go to Step 9. If you do not see the name of the wireless network, go to Step 6.

6. Click **Add** under Preferred networks. The Wireless network properties dialog box opens.

7. Enter **netplus** (or the name of the wireless access point) in the Network name (SSID) text box. Configure any additional settings as indicated by your instructor.

8. Click **OK**. The Wireless network properties dialog box closes, and the name of the wireless access point appears under Available networks.

9. Click **OK** to close the Wireless Network Connection Properties window.

In either version of Windows:

1. Now you can test your connectivity to the wireless network. Click the **Start** button, type **cmd** in the Search programs and files text box, and then press **Enter**. (In Windows XP, click the **Start** button, point to **All Programs**, point to **Accessories**, and then click **Command Prompt**.) A command prompt window opens.

2. Type **ping 192.168.1.1** and press **Enter**. The computer indicates that it has received four replies.

3. If the Windows computer is a laptop, type **ping –t 192.168.1.1** and press **Enter**. The **ping** command begins running continuously and does not stop until you end it. Pick up the laptop and walk away from the wireless access point. How far can you walk away from the wireless access point before the computer indicates that it is unable to reach 192.168.1.1?

4. Press **Ctrl+C** to stop the **ping** command.

5. Log off the computer.

## Certification Objective

Objective for the Network+ Exam:

- 2.2 Given a scenario, install and configure a wireless network.

## Review Questions

1. In which of the following ways does a wireless LAN differ from an Ethernet LAN?

   a. A wireless LAN requires additional protocols in the TCP/IP suite.

   b. A wireless LAN uses completely different protocols than an Ethernet LAN.

   c. A wireless LAN uses different techniques at the Physical layer to transmit data.

   d. A wireless LAN uses different techniques at the Data Link layer to transmit frames.

2. Which of the following are potential disadvantages of wireless LANs as compared with cabled LANs? (Choose all that apply.)

   a. Controlling access to a wireless LAN is more difficult.

   b. Issues such as the location of buildings and the weather can affect connectivity to a wireless LAN.

   c. The additional protocols required by wireless LANs create additional overhead.

   d. Signal strength can be affected by many sources of electronic noise.

3. How is a wireless NIC different from a NIC that requires a cable?

   a. A wireless NIC contains an antenna.

   b. A wireless NIC contains a chip, which does additional processing at higher levels of the OSI model.

   c. A wireless NIC requires an external power source.

   d. A wireless NIC requires an external antenna.

4. You have been hired as a network consultant by the East Coast Savings bank. East Coast Savings would like to implement a wireless LAN but with high standards of security. What sort of restrictions would you recommend placing on the wireless LAN?

    a. Wireless LAN users have the same access as users attached to the Ethernet network.

    b. Wireless LAN users may surf the Web, but may not access the rest of the bank's network.

    c. Wireless LAN users may surf the Web, but may not access the rest of the bank's network without special security software.

    d. Wireless LAN users must use their own wireless ISP.

5. Why is a wireless signal susceptible to noise?

    a. Wireless NICs are usually poorly made.

    b. Wireless transmissions cannot be shielded like transmissions along an Ethernet cable.

    c. Wireless NICs do not support the network protocols necessary for error correction.

    d. Wireless NICs rely on the upper levels of the OSI model for error correction.

# Lab 8.2 Adding a Linux Client to a Wireless Network

## Objectives

In this lab, you add a Linux host to a wireless network using the Network Manager tool. The Network Manager service can be accessed and configured through an applet in the GNOME environment. This makes connecting to a wireless network relatively easy, like in Windows, and involves only a small number of steps. Without the graphical network manager, the connection would have to be manually configured at the command line.

After completing this lab, you will be able to:

- Add a Linux client to a wireless network

## Materials Required

This lab requires the following:

- A computer (ideally a laptop) running a current version of Fedora Linux, with a wireless network card, the GNOME desktop environment, and Network Manager installed

- A wireless access point named "netplus" (or another name supplied by your instructor) configured with an IP address of 192.168.1.1 and a subnet mask of 255.255.255.0

- The wireless access point configured to give out DHCP addresses between 192.168.1.2 and 192.168.1.254 (or some portion of that range) and a subnet mask of 255.255.255.0

- Any additional settings needed to connect the Linux computer to this wireless access point

Estimated completion time: **30 minutes**

## Activity

1. Power on the computer and log on as root. The Fedora desktop appears.

2. If the Network Manager is not already active, you can start it by opening a terminal and typing **sudo systemctl enable NetworkManager.service** and then typing **sudo systemctl start NetworkManager.service.**

3. Once the system has had a few minutes to discover any available wireless networks, click the Network Manager applet in the system tray to view them.

4. Select the wireless network named **netplus** by clicking it. If netplus has been set up with a password, you can enter it now to connect.

5. Test your wireless connection by moving back to the terminal and typing **ping 192.168.1.1** and pressing **Enter**. The computer indicates that it has received four replies.

6. Close any open applications and log off the computer.

## Certification Objective

Objective for the Network+ Exam:

- 2.2 Given a scenario, install and configure a wireless network.

## Review Questions

1. What is the administrator's default account called in Linux?

    a. Admin

    b. Administrator

    c. Default

    d. Root

2. What command line utility is replaced with Network Manager?

    a. ipconfig

    b. iwconfig

    c. ifconfig

    d. inconfig

3. Describe how you could use Network Manager to switch between networks.

4. What Linux command is used to test network connections?

    a. root

    b. sudo

    c. ping

    d. start

5. What term is used to describe when a mobile user moves out of one access point's range and into the range of another?

    a. Reassociation

    b. Deassociation

    c. Reallocation

    d. Extending the service set

# Lab 8.3 Installing a Wireless Router

## Objectives

In this lab, you set up a basic unsecured wireless router. Later, in Lab 11.5, you also implement some essential security features on the router. A wireless router is often used at home or with small peer-to-peer networks to allow several computers to wirelessly connect to an ISP and share an Internet connection. The router can also provide additional features such as functioning as a firewall or a DHCP server.

After completing this lab, you will be able to:

- Set up a wireless router

## Materials Required

This lab requires the following:

- A computer (ideally a laptop) running Windows 7 or Windows XP Professional with a wireless network card
- An unconfigured wireless router with setup CD or user's manual
- A Cat 5 (or better) network cable

Estimated completion time: **30 minutes**

## Activity

1. If your router comes with a setup CD/DVD, run the setup program on your Windows 7 or Windows XP computer. Follow the instructions in the manual on how to disconnect the Internet connection from your Windows computer and connect it to the router.

2. Physically connect your computer to a network port on the router using a Cat 5 (or better) straight-through cable. (Be sure to connect to one of the LAN ports on the router, not the Internet port.)

3. Plug in the router and turn it on.

4. Firmware on the router contains a configuration program that can usually be accessed using a Web browser. Determine the IP address of the router either by consulting the manual or by asking your instructor.

5. In your browser's Address bar, enter the IP address of the router (e.g., 192.168.1.1) and press **Enter.**

6. You might be required to sign in to the utility using a default password.

7. The main router configuration page should appear. The page most likely has a drop-down menu with categories such as Setup, Wireless, and Security. Figure 8-2 shows the basic settings page for a Netgear wireless router.

8. For most situations, the default settings should work without any changes. However, the router should be secured by changing the default password, enabling wireless encryption (preferably WPA2), and so on. Securing a router is covered in Lab 11.5. The setup program should take you through the process of configuring your router.

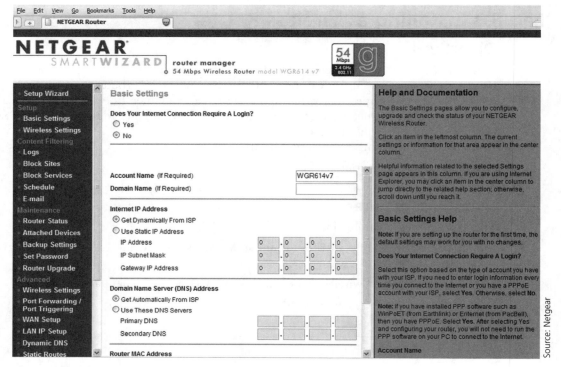

**Figure 8-2**   The Netgear router Basic Settings page

9. Even if you're choosing not to secure your router, it's always a good idea to change your router's default password so other people cannot change the settings.

10. Spend some time examining the basic features of your router, and then make the following changes:

   a. Enable DHCP.

   b. Set the range of assigned addresses to begin at 192.168.1.100.

   c. Change the Network Name (SSID) to "NETLAB."

   d. Set the Wireless Channel to "Auto."

11. After you've configured the router, you might have to reconnect your Internet connection so it correctly syncs up with the router.

12. Now shut down the Windows computer and disconnect the patch cable from the router.

13. Boot the Windows computer and use the steps in Lab 8.1 to wirelessly connect to the Internet.

14. When you're finished, close any open programs, and log off the computer.

## Certification Objectives

Objectives for the Network+ Exam:

- 2.2 Given a scenario, install and configure a wireless network.
- 2.4 Given a scenario, troubleshoot common wireless problems.

## Review Questions

1. How is a wireless router's configuration utility usually accessed?

   a. By flashing the RAM BIOS

   b. Through a Web browser

   c. With the Windows Cfgrtr utility

   d. From the command line

2. Why is it a good idea to change your wireless router's password?

   a. So other people cannot change the router's settings

   b. So you won't forget it

   c. To make it the same as your login password

   d. The default password is most likely too complex.

3. What type of connection is used to attach to the network port on a wireless router?

   a. None, it is wireless.

   b. USB

   c. Serial

   d. Straight-through patch cable

4. Which of the following Wi-Fi standards has the highest effective throughput?

   a. 802.11g

   b. 802.11a

   c. 802.11b

   d. 802.11n

5. Wireless access points are assigned a unique name or _____.

   a. FHSS

   b. DSSS

   c. CSMA

   d. SSID

# Lab 8.4 Investigating Wireless Access Points

## Objectives

In this lab, you compare several wireless access points and choose the solution that best meets your needs. A wireless local area network (WLAN) connects computers through a wireless NIC to a device called a wireless access point (WAP or AP). WLANs use a variety of standards that offer different features such as range and throughput.

After completing this lab, you will be able to:

- Compare wireless access points in terms of price and features
- Identify wireless access point hardware

## Materials Required

This lab requires the following:

- Pencil and paper
- A computer running Windows 7 or Windows XP Professional with Internet access
- An ordinary user account on the computer

Estimated completion time: **30 minutes**

## Activity

1. Log on to the computer as an ordinary user. The Windows desktop appears.

2. Perform whatever steps are necessary for the computer to access the Internet. Start Internet Explorer (or another browser) and browse the Web sites of several distributors that sell networking equipment, including wireless access points. Common manufacturers of wireless access points include Cisco/Linksys, D-Link, and 3Com.

3. Use these sites to find access points from at least two different manufacturers that meet the following criteria:

   - 802.11g and 802.11n support
   - Power over Ethernet (PoE)
   - Ceiling mounted
   - Plenum rated
   - WPA2 encryption

4. On a separate piece of paper, record the make, model number, price, and a brief list of distinguishing features for each of the access points that you found.

5. Which access point is the best value?

6. Did you have any trouble finding information on the equipment?

7. When you're finished, log off the computer.

## Certification Objectives

Objectives for the Network+ Exam:

- 2.1 Given a scenario, install and configure routers and switches.
- 5.1 Given a scenario, implement appropriate wireless security measures.

## Review Questions

1. Which wireless networking standard is fastest?

   a. 802.11a

   b. 802.11b

   c. 802.11g

   d. 802.11n

2. What feature eliminates the need for a separate electrical outlet for your WAP?

    a. PoE

    b. WPA

    c. WPA2

    d. 802.11n

3. Why is plenum-rated cable often a requirement for ceiling-mounted access points?

    a. Ceiling-mounted APs are more than seven feet off the ground.

    b. They work at higher speeds.

    c. They need to operate at higher temperatures.

    d. In the case of a fire, they do not give off toxic fumes.

4. In an enterprise-wide WLAN, coverage can be extended across multiple access points by joining them to the same _____.

    a. ESS

    b. WPA

    c. MAC

    d. MIMO

5. Some wireless access points can associate a client's MAC address with a port on a switch allowing a client to stay connected to a(n) _____ as they move throughout an area.

    a. DSSS

    b. FHSS

    c. RTS/CTS

    d. VLAN

# IN-DEPTH TCP/IP NETWORKING

## Labs included in this chapter

- Lab 9.1 Subnetting a Network
- Lab 9.2 Understanding the Purpose of the Default Gateway
- Lab 9.3 Understanding the TCP/IP Hosts File
- Lab 9.4 Setting Up an FTP Server
- Lab 9.5 Configuring a Mail Server

## Network+ Exam Objectives

| Objective | Lab |
|---|---|
| 1.3 Explain the purpose and properties of IP addressing. | 9.1 |
| 1.6 Explain the function of common networking protocols. | 9.4, 9.5 |
| 2.1 Given a scenario, install and configure routers and switches. | 9.2, 9.3 |
| 4.3 Given a scenario, use appropriate software tools to troubleshoot connectivity issues. | 9.2 |

# Lab 9.1 Subnetting a Network

## Objectives

Subnetting allows you to divide a single network into several smaller, separate networks. This might be done to enhance security, improve performance, or simplify network troubleshooting. Subnetting is accomplished by changing the subnet mask on each of the computers in a network. Because subnet masks are used to determine which part of an IP address corresponds to the network address, changing the subnet mask can also change the network address. In this lab, you subnet a network by changing the subnet mask on the host computers.

After completing this lab, you will be able to:

- Subnet a network into several smaller networks

## Materials Required

This lab requires the following:

- A computer running Windows 7 or Windows XP Professional named *WORKSTATION1* and configured with an IP address of 192.168.54.3, a subnet mask of 255.255.255.0, no default gateway, and the Windows firewall disabled
- A computer running Windows 7 or Windows XP Professional named *WORKSTATION2* and configured with an IP address of 192.168.54.132, a subnet mask of 255.255.255.0, no default gateway, and the Windows firewall disabled
- Administrative access to both computers
- Both computers connected to an Ethernet switch or hub (not a router) with straight-through Cat 5 (or better) UTP cables

Estimated completion time: **30 minutes**

## Activity

1. Log on to *WORKSTATION1* as an administrator. The Windows desktop appears.

2. Click the **Start** button, type **cmd** in the Search programs and files text box, and then press **Enter**. (In Windows XP, click the **Start** button, point to **All Programs**, point to **Accessories**, and then click **Command Prompt**.) A command prompt window opens.

3. At the command prompt, type `ping 192.168.54.132` and press **Enter**. The computer indicates that it has received four replies from the remote computer and is, therefore, on the same network.

4. Now you change the subnet mask on one of the computers. On *WORKSTATION1*, click the **Start** button, click **Control Panel**, click **Network and Internet**, click **Network and Sharing Center** and then click **Change adapter settings**. (In Windows XP, click the **Start** button, point to **All Programs**, point to **Accessories**, point to **Communications**, and then click **Network Connections**. The Network Connections window opens.)

5. Right-click **Local Area Connection**, and then click **Properties** in the shortcut menu. The Local Area Connection Properties window opens.

6. Double-click **Internet Protocol (TCP/IPv4)**. (In Windows XP, double-click **Internet Protocol (TCP/IP)**.) The Internet Protocol Version 4 (TCP/IPv4) Properties window opens.

7. Change the subnet mask from 255.255.255.0 to **255.255.255.240**. This creates 16 new networks from your original Class C network.

8. Repeat Steps 4 through 7 on *WORKSTATION2* to also change its subnet mask.

9. Now use Ping to test the connection between *WORKSTATION1* and *WORKSTATION2* (see Steps 2 and 3). The ping test is not successful because the computers are now on separate networks. *WORKSTATION1* is still on network 192.168.54.0, whereas *WORKSTATION2* has been moved to network 192.168.54.128.

10. Log off both computers.

## Certification Objective

Objective for the Network+ Exam:

- 1.3 Explain the purpose and properties of IP addressing.

## Review Questions

1. Why are *WORKSTATION1* and *WORKSTATION2* no longer able to communicate?

   a. They have different IP addresses.

   b. They are on different networks.

   c. TCP/IP was uninstalled on WORKSTATION2.

   d. The ping command can be used only once.

2. Which of the following is *not* an advantage of subnetting?

   a. Enhanced network security

   b. More hosts per network

   c. Improved network performance

   d. Simplified network troubleshooting

3. How is subnetting accomplished?

   a. By changing the subnet mask on the host computers

   b. By changing the IP address on the host computers

   c. By installing the subnet protocol

   d. By installing a router running DHCP

4. What is the default subnet mask for a Class C network?

   a. 255.0.0.0

   b. 255.255.0.0

   c. 255.255.255.0

   d. 255.255.255.255

# Lab 9.2 Understanding the Purpose of the Default Gateway

## Objectives

To ensure that a computer knows where to send packets outside its own network, you can configure a default gateway. The default gateway is a computer or router that knows where to send packets so that they reach their destination. Often, the default gateway appears in a computer's routing table as a route to 0.0.0.0 with a subnet mask of 0.0.0.0. The IP address 0.0.0.0 is a generic way to refer to all possible IP addresses.

For instance, suppose a small network has a single router that is attached to the Internet. Suppose also that each computer on the network has this Internet router configured as its default gateway. Each computer has a route in its routing table for the local network so it can send packets bound for local network resources to the appropriate computer. If the address of a network resource is not on the local network, each computer sends the packet to the Internet router. The Internet router knows where to send the packet so that it reaches its destination.

Often, the Internet router's routing table specifies just a few local routes and a default route to an ISP router. It sends any packet with a destination address that is not in its routing table to the ISP router. The ISP router usually has a large routing table containing information about destination networks on the Internet.

After completing this lab, you will be able to:

- Identify the purpose of a default gateway
- Configure a default gateway

## Materials Required

This lab requires the following:

- A computer running Windows 7 or Windows XP Professional named *WORKSTATION1* and configured with an IP address of 192.168.54.3, a subnet mask of 255.255.255.0, no default gateway, and the Windows firewall disabled
- A computer running Windows 7 or Windows XP Professional named *WORKSTATION2* and configured with an IP address of 192.168.54.4, a subnet mask of 255.255.255.0, no default gateway, and the Windows firewall disabled
- Administrative access to both computers
- Both computers connected to an Ethernet switch or hub with straight-through Cat 5 (or better) UTP cables

---

Estimated completion time: **30 minutes**

---

## Activity

1. Log on to *WORKSTATION1* as an administrator. The Windows desktop appears.

2. Click the **Start** button, type **cmd** in the Search programs and files text box, and then press **Enter**. (In Windows XP, click the **Start** button, point to **All Programs**, point to **Accessories**, and then click **Command Prompt**.) A command prompt window opens.

3. At the command prompt, type `ping 192.168.54.4` and press **Enter**. The computer indicates that it has received four replies from the remote computer.

4. Repeat Steps 1 through 3 on *WORKSTATION2*. However, ping the address **192.168.54.3** instead.

5. Now you add a secondary IP address to one of the computers. On *WORKSTATION1*, click the **Start** button, click **Control Panel**, click **Network and Internet**, and click **Network and Sharing Center** and then click **Change adapter settings**. (In Windows XP, click the **Start** button, point to **All Programs**, point to **Accessories**, point to **Communications**, and then click **Network Connections**. The Network Connections window opens.)

6. Right-click **Local Area Connection**, and then click **Properties** from the shortcut menu. The Local Area Connection Properties window opens.

7. Double-click **Internet Protocol Version 4 (TCP/IPv4)**. (In Windows XP, double-click **Internet Protocol (TCP/IP)**.) The Internet Protocol Version 4 (TCP/IPv4) Properties window opens.

8. Click **Advanced**. The Advanced TCP/IP Settings window opens, as shown in Figure 9-1.

9. Below the IP addresses text box, click **Add**. The TCP/IP Address window opens. In the IP address text box, type **172.16.1.1**. In the Subnet mask text box, type **255.255.255.0**.

10. Click **Add**. Click **OK** three times to finish configuring the secondary IP address.

11. In the command prompt window on *WORKSTATION2*, type `ping 172.16.1.1` and press **Enter**. The computer indicates that it is unable to reach the remote computer. *WORKSTATION2* does not know where to send packets destined for 172.16.1.1.

**Figure 9-1**  Advanced TCP/IP Settings window

12. Type **netstat -r** and press **Enter** to display the routing table on *WORKSTATION2*. Record the destination addresses listed in the routing table.

13. You now add a default gateway to *WORKSTATION2*. Repeat Steps 5 through 7 on *WORKSTATION2* to open the Internet Protocol Version 4 (TCP/IPv4) Properties window.

14. In the Default gateway text box, type **192.168.54.3.** This tells *WORKSTATION2* to send packets to 192.168.54.3 whenever it does not have another route for them. Click **OK** and then click **Close**.

15. At the command prompt on *WORKSTATION2*, type **ping 172.16.1.1.** The computer indicates that it has received four replies from *WORKSTATION1*.

16. Type **netstat -r** and press **Enter** to show the routing table again on *WORKSTATION2*. Compare this routing table with the one you saw in Step 12. Record the new destination addresses.

17. Log off both computers.

## Certification Objectives

Objectives for the Network+ Exam:

- 2.1 Given a scenario, install and configure routers and switches.
- 4.3 Given a scenario, use appropriate software tools to troubleshoot connectivity issues.

## Review Questions

1. What is the purpose of the default gateway?

   a. To assign IP addresses to clients as soon as they log on to the network

   b. To ensure that no two nodes on the same subnet have identical TCP/IP addresses

   c. To accept and relay packets from nodes on one network destined for nodes on another network

   d. To advertise the best, current routing paths between networks from one router to another

2. Which of the following is most likely to act as a default gateway?

   a. Modem

   b. Hub

   c. Switch

   d. Router

3. What type of information would the netstat -r command yield when typed at the command prompt of a networked client?

   a. A list of all routers to which that client might connect

   b. A list of the client's NIC adapter IP addresses

   c. The client's routing table

   d. The client's TCP/IP settings

4. What is the default subnet mask for a Class B network in the IP version 4 addressing scheme?

a. 255.255.0.0

b. 255.255.255.0

c. 255.255.255.255

d. 0.0.0.0

5. Which of the following utilities can show the route a packet traverses between its source node and destination node on a network?

a. Ping

b. Nbtstat

c. Netstat

d. Tracert

# Lab 9.3 Understanding the TCP/IP Hosts File

## Objectives

To use host names instead of IP addresses to reach remote computers, a computer must have some way to find the IP address that corresponds to each remote computer. One of the simplest ways to do this is to use the hosts file. The hosts file contains a list of IP addresses and the names of the computers at those addresses. When the computer recognizes the name of another computer in its hosts file, it uses the associated IP address when it tries to communicate with that computer.

Because it would be impossible to distribute hosts files to all the computers on the Internet, computers typically use the Domain Name System (DNS) to associate host names with IP addresses rather than use a copy of the hosts file. However, the hosts file is often useful as a temporary measure or when you cannot make a DNS entry. The hosts file can be useful, for example, when you want to make a DNS entry in a domain you do not control or when you are using Network Address Translation (NAT). An IP address translated by NAT might not match the actual IP address of a computer, but a hosts entry forces the computer to use the appropriate IP address.

After completing this lab, you will be able to:

- Identify the purpose of the hosts file
- Modify a computer's hosts file
- Connect to another computer using its host name

## Materials Required

This lab requires the following:

- A computer running Windows 7 or Windows XP Professional named *WORKSTATION1* with an IP address of 192.168.54.3 and a subnet mask of 255.255.255.0
- Administrative access to the Windows computer

- A computer running a current version of Fedora Linux named *LINUX1.NETPLUSLAB.NET,* installed as a server with no firewall, and the GNOME Desktop Environment

- *LINUX1.NETPLUSLAB.NET* configured with an IP address of 192.168.54.5 and a subnet mask of 255.255.255.0

- A user named netplus on *LINUX1.NETPLUSLAB.NET* and the root password for *LINUX1.NETPLUSLAB.NET*

- Each computer connected to a switch or hub with straight-through Cat 5 (or better) UTP cables

Estimated completion time: **25 minutes**

## Activity

1. Log on to *WORKSTATION1* as an administrator. The Windows desktop appears.

2. Click the **Start** button, type **cmd** in the Search programs and files box, right-click **cmd.exe** in the results list, and then click **Run as administrator**. (In Windows XP, click the **Start** button, point to **All Programs**, point to **Accessories**, right-click **Command Prompt**, click **Run as**, click **The following user** option button, select **Administrator** in the User name list box, type the password in the Password text box, and then click **OK**.) A command prompt window opens.

3. In the command prompt window, type **cd  C:\windows\system32\drivers\etc** and press **Enter**. On a Windows 7 or XP computer, this directory contains the hosts file.

4. To modify the hosts file, type **notepad  hosts** and press **Enter**. Notepad opens with the text of the hosts file. Note that many lines begin with a pound sign (#). These lines are comments and are ignored by the computer when it uses the hosts file.

5. At the bottom of the file, on a line by itself, type **192.168.54.5    linux1.netpluslab.net**. Click **File** on the menu bar, and then click **Save**. Figure 9-2 shows the Windows 7 hosts file.

6. Click **File** on the menu bar, and then click **Exit**. Notepad closes.

7. At the command prompt, type **ping  linux1.netpluslab.net** and press **Enter**. The computer indicates that it has received four replies from *LINUX1.NETPLUSLAB.NET*.

8. Log on to *LINUX1.NETPLUSLAB.NET* as the netplus user. The Fedora desktop appears.

9. Open a terminal window. At the prompt, type **su** – and press **Enter**. The Password prompt appears.

10. Type the root password for *LINUX1.NETPLUSLAB.NET*, and press **Enter**. The prompt changes to end in #, indicating that you are now logged on as the root user.

11. Type **cd  /etc** and press **Enter**.

12. Type **echo "192.168.54.3 workstation1.netpluslab.net" >> hosts** and press **Enter**. The computer appends the IP address and the host name between the quotation marks into the hosts file.

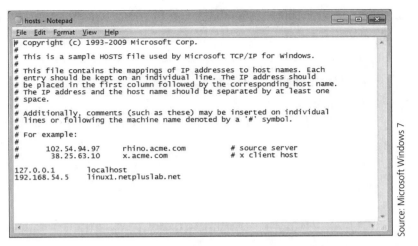

**Figure 9-2**    Windows 7 hosts file

13. To see what the hosts file contains, type **cat hosts** and press **Enter**. The computer displays the contents of the hosts file.

14. Type **ping workstation1.netpluslab.net** and press **Enter**. The computer indicates that it is receiving replies from *WORKSTATION1*. Press **Ctrl+C** to stop the Ping utility.

15. Log off both computers.

## Certification Objectives

Objective for the Network+ Exam:

- 2.1 Given a scenario, install and configure routers and switches.

## Review Questions

1. What is the purpose of a host name?

   a. To uniquely identify a node on a network

   b. To associate a node with a particular domain

   c. To indicate which domain a node belongs to

   d. To identify the IP address of a host

2. What is the purpose of a hosts file?

   a. To help determine the best route for packets between gateways

   b. To make it easier for network administrators to remember a computer's IP address

   c. To map IP addresses to host names

   d. To indicate which hosts on a network are available to a client

3. What file on a Linux system holds information about host names and their IP addresses?

   a. /etc/hosts

   b. /bin/hosts

   c. /lib/users/hostfile

   d. /root/hostfile

4. Which of the following symbols indicates a comment in the hosts file?

   a. >

   b. >>

   c. :

   d. #

5. What is the alias of the computer whose host name is "C2" in the following hosts file?

| | | |
|---|---|---|
| `160.12.122.13` | `C1C2.gameco.com` | `canasta` |
| `156.11.21.145` | `Comp2.gameco.com` | `chess` |
| `123.14.11.214` | `C2.gameco.com` | `checkers` |
| `44.112.133.15` | `CIC2.gameco.com` | `backgammon` |

   a. `canasta`

   b. `chess`

   c. `checkers`

   d. `backgammon`

---

# Lab 9.4 Setting Up an FTP Server

## Objectives

File Transfer Protocol (FTP) is an Application layer protocol used to send and receive files. The process requires both server and client software to function. In Lab 4.4, you learned how to use an FTP client to download files from an FTP server running on a remote host. In this lab, you learn how to install and configure the FTP service in Windows Server 2008.

After completing this lab, you will be able to:

- Install the FTP service in IIS
- Set permissions so that certain users can connect to the FTP server and download files

## Materials Required

This lab requires the following:

- A computer running Windows Server 2008, Standard Edition named *SERVER1*, configured as a domain controller for the netpluslab.net domain with an IP address of 192.168.54.1 and a subnet mask of 255.255.255.0
- Access to *SERVER1* as the administrator

- A user account named netplus in the Domain Users group in the netpluslab.net domain
- A computer running Windows 7 or Windows XP Professional named *WORKSTATION1*, configured with an IP address of 192.168.54.3 and a subnet mask of 255.255.255.0
- Both computers connected to a switch or hub with Cat 5 (or better) UTP cables

> Estimated completion time: **30 minutes**

## Activity

1. Log on to *SERVER1* as the administrator. The Windows Server 2008 desktop appears.

2. Click the **Start** button, and click **Server Manager**. The Server Manager window opens.

3. Click **Roles**. If IIS is not yet installed, click **Add Roles** from the Roles Summary section in the right pane. The Add Roles Wizard opens. If IIS is already installed, proceed to Step 8.

4. If the Before You Begin window opens, click **Next** to continue.

5. Place a check mark in the **Web Server (IIS)** check box, and click **Add Required Features** in the Add Roles Wizard dialog box that opens. Click **Next**, and click **Next** again after reading the description of IIS.

6. On the Select Role Services window, place a check mark in the **FTP Publishing Service** check box, and click **Add Required Role Services** in the Add Roles Wizard dialog box that opens. Click **Next** to continue.

7. Click **Install** to confirm your installation selections, and click **Close** after the installation is complete.

8. Click the **Start** button, point to **Administrative Tools**, click **Services**, right-click **FTP Publishing Service**, and click the **Start** button, if necessary.

9. Click the **Start** button, point to **Administrative Tools**, and click **Internet Information Services (IIS) 6.0 Manager**.

10. Double-click *SERVER1*, double-click **FTP Sites**, and right-click **Default FTP Site**. If necessary, click the **Start** button. If a message appears that says "Cannot change the state of this site," click **Yes**.

11. Right-click **Default FTP Site** and click **Properties**. The Default FTP Site Properties window opens, as shown in Figure 9-3.

12. Click the **Security Accounts** tab, and select the **netplus** user for anonymous access. Click the **Browse** button, enter **netplus** as the username, click **Check Names**, and click **OK**. Click the **Home Directory** tab and ensure that the local path to the ftproot directory is C:\inetpub\ftproot.

13. Click **OK** and close the Internet Information Services IIS (6.0) Manager.

14. Click the **Start** button, point to **All Programs**, click **Accessories**, and then click **Command Prompt**. A command prompt window opens.

**Figure 9-3** Default FTP Site Properties window

15. In the command prompt window, type **echo** *your name* **> C:\Inetpub\ftproot\** **netplus.txt** and press **Enter**. (Substitute your name for *your name*.) This creates a file named netplus.txt containing your name in the C:\Inetpub\ftproot directory.

16. Use the skills you learned in Lab 4.4 to connect to the FTP server from the Windows client.

17. When you're finished, close any open windows and log off both computers.

## Certification Objective

Objective for the Network+ Exam:

- 1.6 Explain the function of common networking protocols.

## Review Questions

1. What is the default FTP directory in Windows Server 2008?

   a. C:\ftp\root

   b. C:\root\dir\ftp

   c. C:\ftproot\ftproot

   d. C:\Inetpub\ftproot

2. The FTP protocol functions at which layer?

   a. Application

   b. Transport

   c. Internetwork

   d. Network Interface

3. Using FTP to upload or download data requires both server and _____ software.

   a. Session

   b. Client

   c. IIS

   d. Remote host

4. General access to an FTP server is referred to as what kind of access?

   a. Root

   b. Anonymous

   c. Limited

   d. Privileged

# Lab 9.5 Configuring a Mail Server

## Objectives

E-mail is one of the most important applications on the majority of business networks. E-mail is sent from a user's computer to its destination using the Simple Mail Transfer Protocol (SMTP). A wide variety of programs run SMTP. In this lab, you configure one such program, Sendmail. Sendmail is used primarily on Linux and UNIX computers.

A computer running SMTP looks at the domain name in the e-mail address and performs a DNS lookup to find the mail exchanger, or MX, record for the domain. The MX record is the domain name of the e-mail server where e-mail for that domain must be sent. For instance, the netpluslab.net domain might have an MX record of linux1.netpluslab.net. This tells other computers running SMTP that any e-mail sent to e-mail addresses in the netpluslab.net domain (such as netplus@netpluslab.net) should be sent to the server linux1.netpluslab.net. As you might expect, DNS must be properly configured for SMTP to work correctly and for e-mail to be delivered. A domain might have multiple MX records with different priorities, which allows for load balancing or for a backup server to collect e-mail in case the primary server fails.

After an e-mail has been delivered to its final destination, the user must collect it. E-mail programs employ a variety of methods to collect e-mail. Some popular protocols used for collecting e-mail include POP3 and IMAP. In this lab, you configure the Outlook Express program to use POP3 to collect e-mail. Typically, settings for receiving mail are given to users by their network administrators.

After completing this lab, you will be able to:

- Configure an e-mail server

## Materials Required

This lab requires the following:

- A computer running Windows Server 2008, Standard Edition named *SERVER1*, configured as a domain controller for the netpluslab.net domain and with an IP address of 192.168.54.1 and a subnet mask of 255.255.255.0

- A user named netplus configured in the netpluslab.net domain

- A computer running Windows 7 or Windows XP Professional named *WORKSTATION1* configured with an IP address of 192.168.54.3 and a subnet mask of 255.255.255.0

- A Windows Mail client installed on *WORKSTATION1* such as Windows Live Mail for Windows 7 or Outlook Express for Windows XP

Several different versions of Windows Live Mail for Windows 7 are currently available from Microsoft. This lab assumes you are using the version that is bundled with Windows Live Essentials 2011. If you choose a different version, the details of the steps may vary slightly.

- A computer running a current version of Fedora Linux named *LINUX1. NETPLUSLAB.NET,* installed as a server with no firewall, and the GNOME Desktop Environment; in addition to the Mail Server package, Dovecot IMAP needs to be installed

- *LINUX1.NETPLUSLAB.NET* configured with an IP address of 192.168.54.5 and a subnet mask of 255.255.255.0

- A user named netplus on *LINUX1.NETPLUSLAB.NET*

- *LINUX1.NETPLUSLAB.NET* configured to use 192.168.54.1 as its DNS server; the file /etc/resolv.conf should contain the line "nameserver 192.168.54.1"

- The DNS server on *SERVER1* configured and running, with a domain named netpluslab.net

- Forward and reverse DNS entries for *LINUX1.NETPLUSLAB.NET* at 192.168.54.5 and for *WORKSTATION1.NETPLUSLAB.NET* at 192.168.54.3

- All three computers configured to use 192.168.54.1 for DNS resolution

- A line in the /etc/hosts file on *LINUX1.NETPLUSLAB.NET* for 192.168.54.5 containing the text "192.168.54.5 linux1.netpluslab.net"

- The default /etc/mail/sendmail.mc and /etc/dovecot.conf files on *LINUX1. NETPLUSLAB.NET*

- No e-mail accounts already configured in Windows Live Mail or Outlook Express on *WORKSTATION1*

Estimated completion time: **90–120 minutes**

## Activity

1. Log on to *LINUX1.NETPLUSLAB.NET* as the netplus user. The Fedora desktop appears.

2. Open a terminal window, and, at the prompt, type **su** - and press **Enter**. The Password prompt appears. Type the root password, and press **Enter**. The prompt now ends in a pound sign (#), indicating that you are logged on as the root user.

3. Next, you configure the dovecot daemon to allow users to check for e-mail from this computer. Dovecot is one of a variety of programs that delivers e-mail to users using POP3, IMAP3, and other protocols. Type **vi /etc/dovecot.conf** and press **Enter**. The vi editor opens the file /etc/dovecot.conf in normal mode.

4. Press **G**. The cursor moves to the last line of the file.

5. Press **i**. The vi editor enters insert mode.

6. Type **protocols = pop3** and press **Esc**. The vi editor enters normal mode.

7. Type **:wq** and press **Enter**. The vi editor saves the file and exits.

8. Type **/etc/init.d/dovecot start** and press **Enter**. The computer starts the Dovecot IMAP server.

9. Now you configure the Sendmail program so that this computer can be used to send e-mail. Type **vi /etc/mail/sendmail.mc** and press **Enter**. The /etc/mail/sendmail.mc file opens.

10. Type **/127.0.0.1** and press **Enter**. The vi editor searches for the text 127.0.0.1. Type **/** and press **Enter**. The vi editor searches for the text from the previous search (127.0.0.1). Repeat until the vi editor places the cursor at the beginning of the IP address 127.0.0.1 in the line "DAEMON OPTIONS('Port=smtp, Addr=127.0.0.1, Name=MTA') dnl."

11. Press **0**. The cursor moves to the beginning of the line.

12. Press **i**. The vi editor goes into insert mode.

13. Type **dnl #** at the beginning of the line. This command tells the computer to ignore this line when the file is processed later in the lab. Press **Esc** to put the vi editor back into normal mode.

14. Type **/LOCAL_DOMAIN** and press **Enter**. The cursor moves to the start of a line containing the text LOCAL_DOMAIN.

15. Press **w** twice. The cursor moves to the beginning of the word "localhost.localdomain."

16. Type **d3w**. The computer deletes the text "localhost.localdomain."

17. Press **i**. The vi editor goes into insert mode. Type **netpluslab.net** and press **Esc**.

18. Type **:wq** and press **Enter**. The vi editor saves the file and then closes.

19. Type **cd /etc/mail** and press **Enter**. The computer changes your current working directory to /etc/mail.

20. Type **make** and press **Enter**. The computer processes the changes you made in the sendmail.mc file and places them in the sendmail.cf file.

21. Type **/etc/init.d/sendmail restart** and press **Enter**. The computer restarts the Sendmail daemon with the configuration changes you have made.

22. Now you configure DNS so that each computer on the network knows where to send e-mail. Log on to *SERVER1* as the administrator. The Windows Server 2008 desktop appears.

23. Press **Start**, point to **Administrative Tools**, and then click **DNS**. The DNS Manager window opens.

**Figure 9-4** The New Resource Record dialog box

24. In the left pane of the window, click **SERVER1**. Icons appear in the right pane.

25. Double-click the **Forward Lookup Zones** icon in the right pane of the window. A list of domains appears. Double-click the **netpluslab.net** icon in the right pane.

26. Right-click **netpluslab.net** in the left pane, and click **New Mail Exchanger (MX)**. The New Resource Record dialog box opens.

27. In the "Fully qualified domain name (FQDN) of mail server" text box, enter **linux1. netpluslab.net**. See Figure 9-4.

28. Click **OK**. The New Resource Record dialog box closes. Right-click the **netpluslab.net** icon, and click **Reload**. The DNS dialog box opens, asking if you want to reload the domain.

29. Click **Yes**. The computer reloads the netpluslab.net domain.

In Windows 7, follow these steps:

30. Log on to *WORKSTATION1* as the netplus user. The Windows desktop appears.

31. Click the **Start** button, type **windows live mail** in the Search programs and files text box, and then press **Enter**. The Windows Live Mail program opens or you are directed to go online and get Windows Live Essentials.

32. Click on the **Accounts** tab and then click **Email** button to add a new e-mail account. In the Email address text box, enter **netplus@netpluslab.net**.

33. In the Password text box, enter the password for the netplus account on *LINUX1. NETPLUSLAB.NET*.

34. Click the **Manually configure server settings** checkbox, and click **Next**.

35. In the Server address text box for the incoming server (left column), enter **linux1.netpluslab.net**. In the Server address text box for the outgoing server (right column), enter **linux1.netpluslab.net**. Click **Next**.

36. A window indicates that your e-mail account was added. Click **Finish**.

37. In the Windows Live Mail window, click the **Home** tab and then click **Email message**. The New Message window opens.

38. In the To... text box, enter **netplus@netpluslab.net**. In the Subject text box, enter **Test Message**. In the bottom window, enter your name. Click **Send**. Windows Mail sends the message.

39. In the tree in the left pane, click **Inbox**. In the upper-right pane, a message with the subject "Test Message" appears.

40. If the message does not appear, click the **Send/Receive** Button. The Windows Live Mail dialog box opens briefly as the program checks for e-mail.

41. Double-click the message with the subject "Test Message" to open it in a new window.

42. Close the Test Message window and exit from Windows Live Mail.

43. Log off all three computers.

In Windows XP, follow these steps:

44. Log on to *WORKSTATION1* as the netplus user. The Windows XP desktop appears.

45. Click the **Start** button, and then click **Outlook E-mail Express**. The Outlook Express window opens. If the Internet Connection Wizard does not open, click **Tools** on the menu bar, and then click **Accounts**. The Internet Accounts window opens. Click **Add**, and then click **Mail**.

46. In the Display name text box, enter **Net+ Lab**. Click **Next**. The next wizard window asks for an e-mail address.

47. In the E-mail address text box, enter **netplus@netpluslab.net**. Click **Next**. The next wizard window asks for information about the e-mail servers you will use.

48. In the Incoming mail (POP3, IMAP or HTTP) server text box, enter **linux1.netpluslab.net**. In the Outgoing mail (SMTP) server text box, enter **linux1.netpluslab.net**. Click **Next**. Now the wizard asks for information about the account you will use.

49. In the Account name text box, enter **netplus**. In the Password text box, enter the password for the netplus account on *LINUX1.NETPLUSLAB.NET*. If necessary, uncheck the **Log on using Secure Password Authentication (SPA)** check box. Click **Next**. The next wizard window indicates that you have finished.

50. Click **Finish**. The Internet Connection Wizard closes.

51. In the Outlook Express window, click **Create Mail**. The New Message dialog box opens.

52. In the To text box, enter **netplus@netpluslab.net**. In the Subject text box, enter **Test Message**. In the bottom window, enter your name. Click **Send**. Outlook Express sends the message.

53. Click **Send/Recv**. The Outlook Express dialog box opens briefly as the program checks for e-mail.

54. In the tree in the left pane, click **Inbox**. In the upper-right pane, a message with the subject "Test Message" appears.

55. Double-click the message with the subject "Test Message." The message opens in the Test Message dialog box.

56. Click **File** on the menu bar, and then click **Close** to close the Test Message dialog box.

57. Click **File** on the menu bar, and then click **Exit**. Outlook Express closes.

58. Log off all three computers.

## Certification Objective

Objective for the Network+ Exam:

- 1.6 Explain the function of common networking protocols.

## Review Questions

1. Which of the following protocols is used to send e-mail?

   a. POP3

   b. SMTP

   c. IMAP

   d. SNMP

2. You are sending e-mail to your friend Bob, whose e-mail address is bob@otherdomain.com. What information does your SMTP server need to deliver this e-mail to Bob?

   a. It needs to look up the IP address of otherdomain.com.

   b. It needs to look up the IP address of the otherdomain.com POP3 server.

   c. It needs to use the MX record for the otherdomain.com domain to find the IP address of the appropriate IMAP server.

   d. It needs to use the MX record for the otherdomain.com domain to find the IP address of the appropriate SMTP server.

3. The DNS server on your network is not functioning properly. Which of the following is *not* a possible consequence of this?

   a. User e-mail programs inside your network are unable to find the IP address of your SMTP server.

   b. SMTP servers outside your network are unable to make TCP connections to your mail server.

   c. Your SMTP server is unable to find the IP addresses of remote mail servers.

   d. User e-mail programs inside your network are unable to find the IP address of your IMAP server.

4. Why is it important to secure and configure a mail server properly?

   a. A misconfigured or improperly secured mail server might not be able to deliver e-mail.

   b. A misconfigured or improperly secured mail server might be hijacked to send large amounts of unsolicited commercial e-mail.

   c. A misconfigured or improperly secured mail server might not be able to run SMTP.

   d. A misconfigured or improperly secured mail server might not allow clients to download their e-mail.

5. A user has been given an e-mail address of sally@otherorg.net. How is this user most likely to determine the settings she needs to receive e-mail?

   a. From the MX record for the otherorg.net domain

   b. By finding the IP address of the otherorg.net domain

   c. From the network administrator

   d. From other SMTP servers on the Internet

# VIRTUAL NETWORKING AND REMOTE ACCESS

## Labs included in this chapter

- Lab 10.1 Configuring a Remote Access Server
- Lab 10.2 Creating a VPN with the Point-to-Point Tunneling Protocol
- Lab 10.3 Configuring Remote Desktop Services (Terminal Services) on Windows Server 2008
- Lab 10.4 Remotely Managing a Computer with Active Directory
- Lab 10.5 Remotely Managing a Linux Server

## Network+ Exam Objectives

| Objective | Lab |
|---|---|
| 2.6 Given a set of requirements, plan and implement a basic SOHO network. | 1.2, 1.3, 1.4 |
| 3.1 Categorize standard media types and associated properties. | 1.1 |
| 3.2 Categorize standard connector types based on network media. | 1.1 |
| 3.5 Describe different network topologies. | 1.1 |
| 3.7 Compare and contrast different LAN technologies. | 1.1 |
| 4.5 Describe the purpose of configuration management documentation. | 1.1 |
| 5.3 Explain methods of user authentication. | 1.3 |

# Lab 10.1 Configuring a Remote Access Server

## Objectives

In this lab, you create a remote access server (RAS) and connect to it from a client. With a remote access server, users may access network resources from home or on the road even if they don't have access to an Internet connection. A salesperson, for example, might be on the road a large percentage of the time and have no network access besides her dial-up connection. By dialing into a dial-up server with Routing and Remote Access Service (RRAS), a remote user can check e-mail, share files, and use the network just as if she were locally connected to the network.

In Windows Server 2008, keep in mind that you need to specifically enable a user to dial in remotely to a Windows Server 2008 computer. Even if the server has a modem and is configured to accept incoming calls, it may still reject a call for security reasons if a user does not have dial-in permission.

After completing this lab, you will be able to:

- Configure RRAS to allow a Windows Server 2008 computer to accept dial-up connections

## Materials Required

This lab requires the following:

- A computer running Windows Server 2008, Standard Edition named *SERVER1* in the NETPLUS workgroup, with ICS disabled and Routing and Remote Access installed but not activated
- Two NICs on *SERVER1,* one configured with an IP address of 192.168.54.1 and a subnet mask of 255.255.255.0 and the other configured with an IP address of 172.16.1.1 and a subnet mask of 255.255.255.0
- A shared folder on *SERVER1* named NETPLUS containing at least one text file
- A computer running Windows 7 or Windows XP Professional named *WORKSTATION1*
- Administrative access to both computers
- A user account named netplus configured on *SERVER1* with the rights needed to dial in to the server
- Modems installed and configured on both machines
- Access to two outside analog phone lines in the same or different locations or to two digital-to-analog converters (to prevent digital phone lines from ruining the modems)
- Knowledge of the telephone number of the phone line to which the Windows Server 2008 computer is attached
- Two phone cords with RJ-11 connectors on both ends that are long enough to reach the wall outlet

Estimated completion time: **60 minutes**

## Activity

1. Connect one end of a phone cord to the back of the modem installed on *SERVER1*, and connect the other end to the wall outlet.

2. Repeat the previous step with the Windows 7 or XP computer.

3. Log on to *SERVER1* as the administrator. The Windows Server 2008 desktop appears.

4. Click the **Start** button, point to **Administrative Tools,** and then click **Routing and Remote Access.** The Routing and Remote Access dialog box opens.

5. Right-click the **SERVER1 (local)** icon in the left pane of the dialog box. From the short-cut menu, click **Configure and Enable Routing and Remote Access.** The Routing and Remote Access Server Setup Wizard opens.

 If you have Internet Connection Sharing enabled on your network, you must disable it before you can configure Routing and Remote Access.

6. Click **Next.** The wizard asks you for information on how to configure the Routing and Remote Access Service.

7. If necessary, select the **Remote access (dial-up or VPN)** option. Click **Next.**

8. Click the **Dial-up** check box to select it. Click **Next.** The wizard shows you information about the interfaces to which dial-up users will connect.

9. Make sure that **Local Area Connection** is highlighted, and click **Next.** The wizard asks you to choose how IP addresses will be assigned to remote clients. Figure 10-1 shows you an example of this dialog box in the Routing and Remote Access Server Setup Wizard.

10. Make sure that the **Automatically** option button is selected, and click **Next.** The wizard asks you how you would like to configure authentication.

11. Make sure that the **No, use Routing and Remote Access to authenticate connection requests** option is selected, and click **Next.** The computer indicates that you have completed the wizard.

12. Click **Finish.** A dialog box opens, indicating that to support the relaying of DHCP messages from remote access clients, you must configure the DHCP Relay Agent.

13. Click **OK.** Message boxes appear, indicating that the service is initializing. The Routing and Remote Access Server Setup Wizard closes. Log on to *WORKSTATION1* as an administrator. The Windows desktop appears.

14. On *WORKSTATION1*, click the **Start** button, click **Control Panel,** click **Network and Internet,** click **Network and Sharing Center,** and click **Set up a new connection or network.** Select **Set up a dial-up connection,** and click **Next.** (In Windows XP, click the **Start** button, point to **All Programs,** point to **Accessories,** point to **Communications,** and click **New Connection Wizard.** The New Connection Wizard opens, and the Location Information dialog box opens on top of it.) If the Location Information dialog box does not open, go to Step 17 (if you are using Windows XP) or go to Step 23 (if you are using Windows 7).

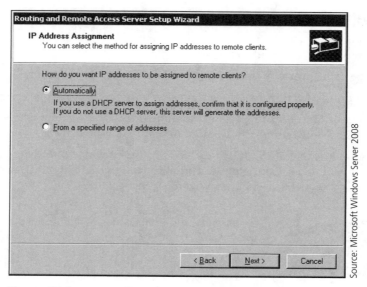

**Figure 10-1** Assigning IP addresses to remote clients

15. Select your country from the drop-down menu. Enter your area code in the "What area code (or city code) are you in now?" text box. If you need to enter a number to specify a carrier code or access an outside line, enter them in the appropriate text boxes. Click **OK**. The Location Information dialog box closes, and the Phone and Modem Options dialog box opens.

16. Click **OK**. The Phone and Modem Options dialog box closes, leaving the New Connection Wizard open.

If you are using Windows XP, follow these steps:

17. Click **Next**. The wizard asks what type of connection you would like to configure.

18. Select the **Connect to the network at my workplace** option. Click **Next**. The wizard asks how you would like to connect.

19. Select the **Dial-up connection** option, and click **Next**. The wizard asks you to specify a name for the connection. Enter **Netplus Lab** in the Company Name box. Click **Next**. The wizard asks you for the phone number for the connection.

20. Enter the phone number of *SERVER1* in the Phone number text box. Click **Next**. The wizard asks you whether the account should be configured for all accounts or only this account.

21. If necessary, select **Anyone's use** and click **Next**. The computer indicates that you have completed the wizard.

22. Click **Finish**. The New Connection Wizard closes. Proceed to Step 27.

If you are using Windows 7, follow these steps:

23. Enter the phone number of *SERVER1* in the Dial-up phone number text box.

24. Enter the appropriate username and password to connect to *SERVER1*.

25. Enter **Netplus Lab** in the Connection name text box.

26. Make sure that **Allow other people to use this connection** is selected, and click **Create**.

27. Click the **Start** button, right-click **Network,** and click **Properties.** Click **Change adapter settings** (In Windows XP, click the **Start** button, point to **All Programs,** point to **Accessories,** point to **Communications,** and click **Network Connections.**) The Network Connections dialog box opens.

28. Right-click the **Netplus Lab** icon, and select **Connect** from the shortcut menu.

29. In the User name text box, enter **netplus.** In the Password text box, enter the password your instructor gave you for this account. Click **Connect.** The modem connects to the remote access server.

30. A dialog box indicating that you have connected successfully opens. Click **OK.** You have successfully logged on to the remote access server.

31. Click the **Start** button, and then click **Computer** (or click **My Computer** in Windows XP).

32. On the menu bar, click **Map network drive.** (In Windows XP, on the menu bar, click **Tools,** and then click **Map Network Drive.**) The Map Network Drive dialog box opens.

If you are using Windows 7, follow these steps:
33. In the Folder text box, enter **\\192.168.54.1\NETPLUS.** Click **Connect using different credentials.**

34. Click **Finish.** The Enter Network Password dialog box opens.

35. Type **Administrator** in the User name text box, and enter the password for the administrator account on *SERVER1* in the Password text box. Click **OK.** The Enter Network Password dialog box closes. The Map Network Drive dialog box opens briefly, indicating that the computer is attempting to map the network drive. After it closes, an icon for the mapped network drive appears underneath Network Drives in the My Computer window. Proceed to Step 39.

If you are using Windows XP, follow these steps:
36. In the Folder text box, enter **\\192.168.54.1\NETPLUS.** Click **Connect using a different user name.** The Connect As dialog box opens.

37. Type **Administrator** in the User name text box, and enter the password for the administrator account on *SERVER1* in the Password text box. Click **OK.** The Connect As dialog box closes.

38. Click **Finish.** The Map Network Drive dialog box opens briefly, indicating that the computer is attempting to map the network drive. After it closes, an icon for the mapped network drive appears underneath Network Drives in the My Computer window.

39. Double-click the icon for the mapped network drive. A folder containing the name of at least one text file appears.

40. Double-click the text file. The text file opens.

41. Close the text file and log off both computers.

## Certification Objective

Objective for the Network+ Exam:

- This lab does not directly map to an objective on the exam; however, it does teach a skill that is valuable to networking professionals.

## Review Questions

1. Which of the following best describes a modem's function?

   a. To encapsulate Data Link layer protocols as Network layer protocols before transmitting data over the PSTN

   b. To separate data into frames as it is transmitted from the computer to the PSTN, and then strip data from frames as it is received from the PSTN

   c. To encrypt data as it is transmitted from the computer to the PSTN, and then decrypt data as it is received from the PSTN

   d. To convert a source computer's digital pulses into analog signals for the PSTN, and then convert analog signals back into digital pulses for the destination computer

2. What is another common term for *Public Switched Telephone Network?*

   a. Plain old telephone service

   b. Basic rate telephone service

   c. Limited access telephone service

   d. Transcontinental public telephone service

3. Which of the following types of dial-up connections would result in the best performance from the client's perspective?

   a. A PPP dial-up connection to an RRAS server that allowed the client to launch an application from the RRAS server

   b. A PPTP dial-up connection to an RRAS server that allowed the client to launch an application from another server on the LAN

   c. A SLIP dial-up connection to an RRAS server that allowed the client to log on to an application server on the LAN and run an application from that application server

   d. A PPTP dial-up connection to an RRAS server that allowed the client to log on to a Citrix terminal server and use ICA to run an application

4. What does RAS stand for?

   a. Remote authentication service

   b. Remote access server

   c. Remote accounting service

   d. Remote addressing server

5. Why do most remote clients (for example, those that dial in to an RRAS server) use DHCP and not static IP addressing?

   a. Using DHCP allows more efficient use of a limited number of IP addresses.

   b. Using DHCP ensures that the client is authorized to access the network.

   c. Using DHCP ensures that the client is assigned a valid IP address.

   d. Using DHCP allows the client to use the same IP address each time he or she dials in to the LAN.

# Lab 10.2 Creating a VPN with the Point-to-Point Tunneling Protocol

## Objectives

Although a remote access server allows users to dial in and use network resources, dialing in to a remote access server can be quite slow and expensive if many of the users have to dial long distance. One way to reduce the time and cost of using a remote access server is to create a virtual private network (VPN). In a VPN, users connect to the remote access server over an encrypted channel through a public network, typically the Internet. Remote users have the same access that they had when dialing in directly to the remote access server. However, instead of paying long-distance fees per minute, an organization pays for its users' Internet connections and the Internet connectivity of its remote access server.

A VPN can be thought of as an imaginary cable that is connected from one end of the VPN to the other end. In many types of VPNs, a virtual network interface is created on both ends of the VPN, just as if they were directly linked by the same cable even though the two endpoints might be across the Internet. Each virtual network interface has an IP address just as a normal interface does. However, this IP address is associated with a logical NIC and not a physical NIC. For this reason, an IP address like this is often called a virtual IP address.

In this lab, you create a VPN using the Point-to-Point Tunneling Protocol (PPTP). PPTP creates virtual NICs on the server and client. Traffic between each virtual NIC is encrypted so that a malicious user with a protocol analyzer cannot view the contents. Although there might be many network devices between the client and the server, the PPTP tunnel makes the client and server seem to be attached to the same hub.

Other protocols, including IPSec, can also be used to carry VPN traffic. VPNs run on a wide variety of hardware, including servers with several different operating systems, routers, firewalls, and dedicated VPN hardware such as Cisco's ASA 5500 Series devices. Because VPN traffic requires additional processing and can use a lot of CPU time, many devices offload processing of VPN traffic onto a special chip or module.

After completing this lab, you will be able to:

- Configure a VPN with PPTP between a client computer and a Windows Server 2008 computer

## Materials Required

This lab requires the following:

- A computer running Windows Server 2008, Standard Edition named *SERVER1* with two NICs, one configured with an IP address of 192.168.54.1 and a subnet mask of 255.255.255.0 and the other configured with an IP address of 172.16.1.1 and a subnet mask of 255.255.255.0
- Routing and Remote Access disabled on the Windows Server 2008 computer
- A shared folder on *SERVER1* containing at least one text file
- A computer running Windows 7 or XP Professional named *WORKSTATION1* with a NIC configured with an IP address of 192.168.54.2 and a subnet mask of 255.255.255.0

- Each NIC on both computers connected with straight-through Cat 5 (or better) UTP cables to a single switch or hub
- Administrative access to both computers
- An account on *SERVER1* with a known password and sufficient rights to connect to *SERVER1*

Estimated completion time: **30 minutes**

## Activity

1. Log on to *SERVER1* as the administrator. The Windows Server 2008 desktop appears.

2. Click the **Start** button, point to **Administrative Tools,** and then click **Routing and Remote Access.** The Routing and Remote Access dialog box opens.

3. In the left pane of the dialog box, right-click **SERVER1 (local).** From the shortcut menu, select **Configure and Enable Routing and Remote Access.** The Routing and Remote Access Server Setup Wizard opens.

4. Click **Next.** The wizard displays configuration options for the Routing and Remote Access Service.

5. Select the **Virtual private network (VPN) access and NAT** option. Click **Next.** The wizard asks you to select at least one interface that connects this server to the Internet.

6. Select **Local Area Connection** and click **Next.** The wizard asks you to select options for IP address assignment.

7. If necessary, select the **Automatically** option and click **Next.** The wizard asks you to select options for managing multiple remote access servers.

8. If necessary, select **No, use Routing and Remote Access to authenticate connection requests,** and click **Next.** The wizard indicates that you have finished.

9. Click **Finish.** A Routing and Remote Access dialog box might open, indicating that you must make further configuration changes to support the relay of DHCP messages. If not, go to Step 11.

10. Click **OK.** A dialog box opens, indicating that the Routing and Remote Access Service is starting. The dialog box closes, and the tree underneath SERVER1 (local) has expanded.

11. Right-click **Ports** on the tree underneath SERVER1 (local), and select **Properties** from the shortcut menu. The Ports Properties dialog box opens. See Figure 10-2.

12. Click **WAN Miniport (PPTP)** to select it. Click **Configure.** The Configure Device – WAN Miniport (PPTP) dialog box opens.

13. Click the **Demand-dial routing connections (inbound and outbound)** check box to remove the check mark. Click **OK** twice.

14. Right-click **SERVER1 (local).** From the shortcut menu, point to **All Tasks,** and then click **Restart.** The Routing and Remote Access Service restarts.

15. Log on to *WORKSTATION1* as an administrator. The Windows desktop appears.

16. Click the **Start** button, and then click **Control Panel.** The Control Panel window opens.

**Figure 10-2**   Ports Properties dialog box

If you're using Windows 7, do the following steps:

17. Click **Network and Internet** and then click **Network and Sharing Center**.

18. Click **Set up a new connection or network**. The Set Up a Connection or Network window opens.

19. Scroll down and select **Connect to a workplace** and click **Next**.

20. Select the **No, create a new connection option**, and then click **Next**.

21. Click **Use my Internet connection (VPN)**.

22. Enter **192.168.54.1** as the Internet address and **NetPlus** as the Destination name, and click **Next**.

23. Enter the username and password for the account that can connect to *SERVER1* in the User name and Password text boxes. Click **Connect**. The Connecting NetPlus dialog box opens, indicating that the computer is being registered on the network.

24. Skip to Step 39.

If you're using Windows XP, do the following steps:

25. Click the **Network and Internet Connections** category.

26. Click the **Set up or change your Internet connection** icon. The Internet Properties dialog box opens with the Connections tab displayed.

27. Click **Setup**. The New Connection Wizard opens. If no location information has been configured previously, the Location Information dialog box opens on top of it. If the Location Information dialog box does not open, go to Step 29.

28. Enter the area code. Click **OK** to close the Location Information dialog box.

29. In the New Connection Wizard, click **Next**. The wizard asks you to select network connection types.

30. Select **Connect to the network at my workplace**, and click **Next**. The wizard asks you to select the type of connection.

31. Select **Virtual Private Network connection**, and then click **Next**. The wizard asks you to enter a company name.

32. Enter **NetPlus** in the Company Name box. Click **Next**. The wizard asks you to configure settings for dialing the initial connection to the Internet or other public network. If the wizard instead asks for the name or IP address of the VPN server, go to Step 34.

33. Select the **Do not dial the initial connection** option button. Click **Next**. The wizard instead asks for the name or IP address of the VPN server.

34. Enter **192.168.54.1** in the Host name or IP address text box. Click **Next**. If the wizard asks who will be using the connection, select **Anyone's use** and click **Next**. The wizard indicates that you have finished.

35. Click **Finish**. The New Connection Wizard closes.

36. Click the **Network Connections** icon. The Network Connections window opens.

37. Double-click the **NetPlus** icon.

38. Enter the username and password for the account that can connect to *SERVER1* in the User name and Password text boxes. Click **Connect**. The Connecting NetPlus dialog box opens, indicating that the computer is being registered on the network.

39. Click the **Start** button, type **cmd** in the Start Search text box, and then press **Enter**. (In Windows XP, click the **Start** button, point to **All Programs**, point to **Accessories**, and then click **Command Prompt**.)

40. Type **ipconfig** and press **Enter**. The computer displays the IP address for each NIC on the computer, including the virtual NIC. (Note that the virtual NIC is named PPP adapter NetPlus.) What is the IP address of the virtual interface?

41. On *SERVER1*, click the **Start** button, point to **All Programs**, click **Accessories**, and then click **Command Prompt**. A command prompt window opens.

42. Type **ipconfig** and press **Enter**. The computer displays the IP address for each NIC on the computer, including the virtual NIC for the VPN. Note that the name of the virtual NIC is PPP Adapter RAS Server (Dial In) Interface. What is the IP address of the virtual interface on *SERVER1?*

43. On *WORKSTATION1*, click the **Start** button, and then click **Computer** (or **My Computer** in XP).

44. On the menu bar, click **Map network drive**. (In Windows XP, on the menu bar, click **Tools**, and then click **Map Network Drive**.) The Map Network Drive dialog box opens.

If you are using Windows 7, follow these steps:

45. In the Folder text box, enter **\\192.168.54.1\NETPLUS**. Click **Connect using different credentials**.

46. Click **Finish**. The Enter Network Password dialog box opens.

47. Type **Administrator** in the User name text box, and enter the password for the administrator account on *SERVER1* in the Password text box. Click **OK**. The Enter Network Password dialog box closes. The Map Network Drive dialog box opens briefly, indicating that the computer is attempting to map the network drive. After it closes, an icon for the mapped network drive appears underneath Network Drives in the My Computer window. Proceed to Step 51.

If you are using Windows XP, follow these steps:

48. In the Folder text box, enter **\\192.168.54.1\NETPLUS**. Click **Connect using a different user name**. The Connect As dialog box opens.

49. Type **Administrator** in the User name text box, and enter the password for the administrator account on *SERVER1* in the Password text box. Click **OK**. The Connect As dialog box closes.

50. Click **Finish**. The Map Network Drive dialog box opens briefly, indicating that the computer is attempting to map the network drive. After it closes, an icon for the mapped network drive appears underneath Network Drives in the My Computer window.

51. Double-click the icon for the mapped network drive. A folder containing the name of at least one text file appears.

52. Double-click the text file. The text file opens.

53. Close the text file and log off both computers.


## Certification Objective

Objective for the Network+ Exam:

- 5.2 Explain the methods of network access security.


## Review Questions

1. What is one reason an organization might employ a VPN rather than simply allow users to dial directly in to their remote access server?

    a. VPNs always provide better performance than direct-dial connections.

    b. VPNs allow more users to connect to the LAN simultaneously.

    c. VPNs are less expensive for connecting a large number of remote users.

    d. VPNs prevent the need for firewalls between access servers and the Internet.

2. In this lab, you connected a workstation to a server using a VPN. Which of the following is true about the VPN connection you created in this lab?

    a. It uses physical IP addresses.

    b. It uses virtual IP addresses on the workstation end.

    c. It uses virtual IP addresses on both ends.

    d. It requires a modem for connection.

3. Which of the following transmission methods are VPN clients most apt to use?

a. PSTN

b. T-1

c. Frame relay

d. SONET

4. What does the "T" in PPTP stand for?

a. Tunneling

b. Transmission

c. Transport

d. Telecommunications

5. Which of the following protocol suites could be used to transmit data over a VPN that relies on PPTP? (Choose all that apply.)

a. IPX/SPX

b. TCP/IP

c. NetBEUI

d. AppleTalk

# Lab 10.3 Configuring Remote Desktop Services (Terminal Services) on Windows Server 2008

## Objectives

The primary remote administration tool for Windows Server 2008 is Remote Desktop Services (Terminal Services). Terminal Services allows a network administrator or support personnel to log on to a remote Windows Server 2008 computer almost as if the network administrator were at the console. This can be invaluable for administration or troubleshooting. For instance, suppose that a problem with a particular server occurs while you are at home. Without some means of accessing the computer remotely, you must go to the computer to fix the problem. With Terminal Services, however, you can connect to the computer remotely and fix the problem without ever leaving home.

By default, Terminal Services on Windows Server 2008 is configured in Remote Administration mode. You can also configure it in Application Server mode. Application Server mode allows users to log on to the server and run applications. This has several advantages. First, network administrators can manage applications from one location. Otherwise, each application must be managed for each user's computer. Second, Terminal Services allows a network administrator to take over a particular user's session. This allows you to see exactly what the user sees. Finally, computers connecting to a computer running Terminal Services in Application Server mode, or a terminal server, may use a wide variety of hardware and operating systems. The terminal server does the bulk of the processing for applications run in Terminal Services. As a result, users may use older or less powerful computers.

One disadvantage of allowing users to connect to a terminal server is cost. Using Terminal Services in Application Server mode requires additional licensing, whereas running Terminal

Services in Remote Administration mode does not. In this lab, you activate temporary licensing for Terminal Services, which allows the use of Terminal Services for 120 days without the purchase of additional licensing. Also note that managing applications on a terminal server is more complicated than managing the same applications on a user's desktop.

Finally, Windows 7 or XP allows users to log on to their computers through Remote Desktop. However, you cannot have more than one user, local or remote, logged on to the same computer at the same time. Remote Desktop should not be confused with Remote Desktop Connection, the client used to connect to Terminal Services on remote Windows Server 2008 computers and Remote Desktop on remote Windows 7 or XP computers.

After completing this lab, you will be able to:

- Configure Terminal Services on Windows Server 2008

## Materials Required

This lab requires the following:

- A computer running Windows Server 2008, Standard Edition named *SERVER1*, with a NIC configured with an IP address of 192.168.54.1 and a subnet mask of 255.255.255.0
- The server can be a member of a domain or a workgroup, although the steps will vary depending on your configuration
- Access to the Internet for *SERVER1* for activation of Terminal Server Licensing (and knowledge of any steps required to connect to the Internet), or prior activation of Terminal Server Licensing
- A computer named *WORKSTATION1* running Windows 7 or XP Professional (updated with SP3), with a NIC configured with an IP address of 192.168.54.2 and a subnet mask of 255.255.255.0
- Administrative access to each computer
- Each computer connected to a hub with straight-through Cat 5 or better UTP cables
- Terminal Services and Terminal Services Licensing not installed on *SERVER1*
- Four ordinary user accounts with known passwords on *SERVER1*, each with sufficient permissions to log on interactively to *SERVER1* using Terminal Services

> Estimated completion time: **45 minutes**

## Activity

1. Log on to *SERVER1* as the administrator. The Windows Server 2008 desktop appears.
2. Click the **Start** button, point to **Administrative Tools**, and then click **Server Manager**. The Server Manager window opens.
3. Select **Roles**, and click **Add Roles**. The Add Roles Wizard opens. If the Before You Begin window opens, click **Next**.
4. On the Select Server Roles window, check the **Terminal Services** check box.

5. Click **Next**. The next window in the wizard provides some information on Terminal Server.

6. Click **Next** to open the Select Role Services window.

7. Check the **Terminal Server** and **TS Licensing** check boxes, and click **Next**. If the server is a domain controller, a message appears warning you that Terminal Services is not recommended. Click **Install Terminal Server anyway (not recommended)**. The next window in the wizard recommends that you reinstall any applications for them to work properly on a Terminal Server. Click **Next**.

8. If you're running a Windows 7 client, select **Require Network Level Authentication** and click **Next**. The next window in the wizard is used to select the kind of client access licenses that will be used. If you're running Windows XP, select **Do not require Network Level Authentication**, and then click **Next**.

9. Select **Configure later**, and click **Next**. Select the **Administrators** groups, and click **Next**.

10. If necessary, select **This workgroup** or **This domain**, and click **Next**. The next window summarizes your configuration choices.

11. Click **Install**. After several moments, the Add Roles Wizard indicates that you have successfully finished.

12. Click **Close**. The Add Roles Wizard dialog box opens, indicating that you must restart the computer.

13. Click **Yes**. The computer reboots. Log on as the administrator and, when the installation of Terminal Services completes, click **Close** in the Installation Results window.

14. Now you log on to *SERVER1* (from *WORKSTATION1*) while it is still configured in Remote Administration mode. Log on to *WORKSTATION1* as an administrator. The Windows desktop appears.

15. Click the **Start** button, click **All Programs**, click **Accessories**, and click **Remote Desktop Connection**. (In Windows XP, click the **Start** button, point to **All Programs**, point to **Accessories**, and click **Remote Desktop Connection**.) The Remote Desktop Connection dialog box opens, as shown in Figure 10-3.

16. Enter **192.168.54.1** in the Computer text box. Click **Connect**. The Windows Security dialog box (Log On to Windows dialog box in Windows XP) opens for *SERVER1*. Log on to the remote computer as the administrator. The Windows Server 2008 desktop appears.

**Figure 10-3**  Remote Desktop Connection dialog box

17. Minimize the Remote Desktop Connection dialog box by clicking the horizontal line on the bar at the top of the screen.

18. Repeat Steps 14 through 17. Did Remote Desktop Connection allow you to open two sessions at the same time? If not, how was it prevented?

19. On *SERVER1*, press **Ctrl+Alt+Del**, and log on to the computer as the administrator. The Windows Server 2008 desktop appears.

20. Perform any steps that are necessary to obtain Internet access for *SERVER1*.

21. Click the **Start** button, point to **Administrative Tools**, point to **Terminal Services**, and click **TS Licensing Manager**. The TS Licensing Manager window opens, with an icon for *SERVER1* in the right pane of the window. In the Activation Status column, the activation status of *SERVER1* is Not activated.

22. If a dialog box opens, indicating that no license servers can be found, click **OK**. Right-click **All servers** in the left pane of the window and click **Connect**. The Connect to License Server dialog box opens. Enter **SERVER1**, and click **Connect**.

23. Right-click the SERVER1 icon. From the shortcut menu, select **Activate Server**. The Activate Server Wizard opens.

24. Click **Next**. The wizard asks you to select a connection method.

25. Make sure that **Automatic connection** is selected, and click **Next**. The wizard asks you for company information.

26. Fill in your name in the First name and Last name text boxes. Enter the name of your school in the Company text box, and select your country from the Country or Region drop-down menu. Click **Next**. The wizard asks you to fill in optional information, including your e-mail address.

27. Click **Next**. A dialog box opens briefly, indicating that the computer is looking for the Microsoft activation server. Then the computer indicates that you have completed the Activate Server Wizard.

28. Click the **Start Install Licenses Wizard now** check box to remove the check mark from it. Click **Finish**. The wizard closes, and the activation status of the SERVER1 icon is now Activated. Close the TS Licensing Manager window.

29. If necessary, reattach *SERVER1* to the lab network.

30. Click the **Start** button, point to **Administrative Tools**, point to **Terminal Services**, and then click **Terminal Services Configuration**. The Terminal Services Configuration window opens.

31. In the left pane of the window, click the **Terminal Services Configuration** folder. Icons for server settings appear in the right pane of the window.

32. Now you configure the server so that users can log on to multiple sessions. Right-click the **Restrict each user to a single session** icon. From the shortcut menu, click **Properties**. Uncheck **Restrict each user to a single session**, and click **OK**. The shortcut menu closes.

33. On *WORKSTATION1*, repeat Steps 14 through 17. Repeat three more times, logging on each time as a different ordinary user.

34. On *SERVER1,* click the **Start** button, point to **Administrative Tools,** point to **Terminal Services,** and click **Terminal Services Manager.** The right pane of the window shows all the users currently logged on to the server and their sessions.

35. Right-click one of the sessions, and click **Disconnect** from the shortcut menu. A Terminal Services Manager dialog box opens, indicating that each selected session will be disconnected.

36. Click **OK.** The session is disconnected, and the text underneath the Session heading reads Disconnected.

37. Repeat Steps 35 and 36 for each of the remaining sessions.

38. On *WORKSTATION1,* check to see if any of the sessions are open.

39. Log off both computers.

## Certification Objective

Objective for the Network+ Exam:

- This lab does not directly map to an objective on the exam; however, it does teach a skill that is valuable to networking professionals

## Review Questions

1. Which of the following are reasons you might implement Terminal Services instead of a remote access server? (Choose all that apply.)

   a. No modems required with Terminal Services

   b. Central configuration and control of applications on the Terminal Server

   c. No modems required on clients

   d. No need to configure security on the Terminal Server

2. What is the difference between configuring a Windows Server 2008 computer to accept Remote Desktop Connection and configuring it to run Terminal Services?

   a. Remote Desktop Connection requires additional licensing.

   b. Terminal Services requires each client to have a modem.

   c. Terminal Services allows no more than two simultaneous connections.

   d. Terminal Services allows more than two simultaneous connections.

3. What is one way a network administrator can effectively troubleshoot a user's problem in a Terminal Services session that can't be done with a remote access server?

   a. By speaking with the user over the phone

   b. By examining the Terminal Server's error logs

   c. By taking over the user's session temporarily

   d. By rebooting the server

4. Which of the following is a potential disadvantage of Terminal Services?

   a. It requires additional licensing.

   b. It requires the client to be running Windows XP (SP3).

c. It requires the client to have a high-speed connection such as a T-1.

d. It requires the server to have a minimum of 1 GB of RAM.

5. You cannot log on to a Windows XP computer using a Remote Desktop connection. True or False?

# Lab 10.4 Remotely Managing a Computer with Active Directory

## Objectives

In addition to controlling users and groups, you can use Active Directory to help you manage remote computers. Through Active Directory, you can perform many of the functions on a remote computer that you can do when directly logged on to that computer. For example, you can start and stop services on the remote computer, look at system information, and browse the Event Viewer. The Event Viewer is where you can view information about error messages and other events that have occurred on the computer. If you need to administer a network with many users and many computers, this can save you significant time.

After completing this lab, you will be able to:

- Remotely manage Windows computers

## Materials Required

This lab requires the following:

- The network on the NETPLUSLAB.NET domain, such as the one built at the end of Lab 1.3

Estimated completion time: **40 minutes**

## Activity

1. Log on to *SERVER1* as the administrator for the netpluslab.net domain. The Windows Server 2008 desktop appears.

2. Click the **Start** button, point to **Administrative Tools**, and click **Computer Management**. The Computer Management window opens.

3. Click the **Disk Management** icon below Storage. How many hard disks are on the server, how large are they, and with what file system have they been configured?

4. Click the **Event Viewer** icon in the tree in the left pane of the window. A list of the event logs available appears in the right pane of the window.

5. In the left pane, expand **Event Viewer** and **Windows Logs**, and then double-click the **System** node. A list of events in the System event log appears in the center pane. Double-click the top event. The Event Properties window opens, showing detailed information about the event.

6. Click the down arrow on the right side of the window. The Event Viewer moves to the next event. Repeat a few times to see more events.

7. Close the Event Properties window by clicking **Close**.

8. Right-click **Computer Management (Local)** at the top of the tree in the left pane of the window. Select **Connect to another computer** from the shortcut menu. The Select Computer dialog box opens.

9. In the Another computer text box, type **WORKSTATION1** and click **OK**. The icon at the top of the left pane of the window changes to Computer Management (WORKSTATION1). Figure 10-4 shows the Computer Management dialog box for *WORKSTATION1* as you manage the computer remotely.

10. Click the **plus sign (+)** next to System Tools to expand the tree underneath it. Repeat this step with the Services and Applications icon.

11. Repeat Steps 4 through 7 to look at events on *WORKSTATION1*. Does *WORKSTATION1* have as many types of event logs as *SERVER1* ?

12. Log on to *WORKSTATION1* as the administrator of the NETPLUSLAB domain. The Windows desktop appears.

13. Click the **Start** button, and then click **Control Panel**. The Control Panel opens.

14. Click the **System and Security (Performance and Maintenance** in Windows XP) category.

15. Click the **Administrative Tools** icon.

16. Double-click the **Services** icon. The Services window opens.

17. Look for the Automatic Updates icon. Its status is "Started."

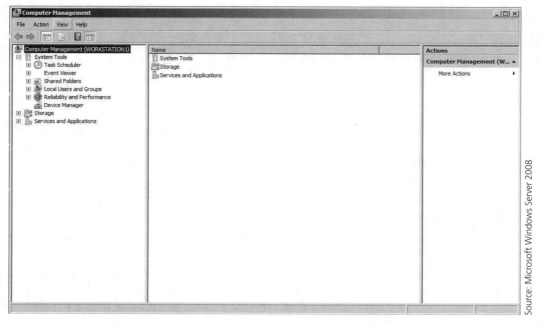

Source: Microsoft Windows Server 2008

**Figure 10-4** Managing *WORKSTATION1* remotely

18. On *SERVER1*, click the **Services** icon in the left pane of the Computer Management window. A list of the services running on *WORKSTATION1* appears in the right pane of the window.

19. Right-click the **Windows Update** icon (or **Automatic Updates** icon in Windows XP). From the shortcut menu, select **Stop**. A dialog box opens briefly, indicating that Windows is attempting to stop the service. The status disappears.

20. On *WORKSTATION1*, press **F5** to refresh the Services window. Look at the status of the Automatic Updates icon in the Services window. It is now blank, indicating that the service is not running.

21. Right-click the **Windows Update** icon (or the **Automatic Updates** icon in Windows XP) in the Services window. From the shortcut menu, select **Start**. A dialog box opens briefly, indicating that Windows is attempting to start the service. The status changes to "Started."

22. Log off both computers.

## Certification Objective

Objective for the Network+ Exam:

- 5.2 Explain the methods of network access security.

## Review Questions

1. Which of the following is a potential advantage of being able to manage computers remotely?

    a. You don't need to log on to each individual computer.

    b. It eliminates the need for authentications.

    c. It uses less CPU time.

    d. It prevents security problems.

2. Which Windows Server 2008 utility would you use to find events that have happened on a particular server?

    a. Device Manager

    b. Disk Defragmenter

    c. Command Prompt

    d. Event Viewer

3. Why are you able to log on to the remote computer without supplying a username and password?

    a. No username or password is necessary.

    b. Active Directory handles authentication on the remote computer for you.

    c. Active Directory does not require authentication for remote computers.

    d. Your computer automatically supplies the username and password without the help of Active Directory.

4. Only the domain administrator can manage remote computers. True or False?

5. When you select Services from the Administrative Tools menu on a Windows Server 2008 computer, what do you see?

   a. All services currently available on the Windows Server 2008 computer

   b. All services currently running on the Windows Server 2008 computer

   c. All services currently running on the Windows Server 2008 computer and its clients

   d. All services currently running on the Windows Server 2008 computer and other servers in the same domain

# Lab 10.5 Remotely Managing a Linux Server

## Objectives

Linux servers can be managed remotely much as they can be managed at the console, through a variety of tools. Almost all versions of Linux support Telnet servers. A Telnet server is a daemon that allows you to open a remote terminal session over a network. The Telnet client, usually just called Telnet, is available on most modern operating systems. However, the Telnet protocol does not use any encryption. As a result, Telnet is rapidly being replaced by the Secure Shell (SSH) protocol. The sshd daemon runs an SSH server, and the ssh program allows you to log on to an SSH server.

From a remote terminal window opened with the ssh program, you can do nearly anything that you can do on the system console. On a computer running the X Window software, you can also run any GUI program on the remote computer. X Window software is installed by default on most Linux computers, and can be installed on Windows computers as well. Remote terminal sessions run through either the ssh program or the Telnet program have only a few minor differences.

In this lab, you remotely connect to a Linux computer using a common ssh client called PuTTY. After completing this lab, you will be able to:

- Log on to a Linux computer remotely using SSH

## Materials Required

This lab requires the following:

- A computer running a current version of Fedora Linux named *LINUX1. NETPLUSLAB.NET,* configured with no firewall, and with the GNOME Desktop Environment installed

- *LINUX1.NETPLUSLAB.NET* configured with an IP address of 192.168.54.5 and a subnet mask of 255.255.255.0

- A user named netplus and knowledge of the root password

- A computer running Windows 7 or Windows XP Professional named *WORKSTATION1* and configured with an IP address of 192.168.54.3

- Access to the PuTTY SSH and telnet client (available at www.putty.org)

- Both computers connected to a switch or hub with straight-through Cat 5 (or better) UTP cables

Estimated completion time: **40 minutes**

## Activity

1. Log on to WORKSTATION1 as an administrator.

2. Open Internet Explorer.

3. In the Address bar, type **www.putty.org** and press **Enter**. The main Putty Web page opens.

4. Click **here** to download Putty.

5. Click **putty.exe** to download the latest release version of Putty.

6. Click **Run**. The PuTTY Configuration window opens, as pictured in Figure 10-5.

7. Specify the destination you want to connect to as **192.168.54.5** and click **Open**.

8. Log on to *LINUX1.NETPLUSLAB.NET* as the netplus user. The Fedora desktop appears.

9. Open a terminal window.

10. Type the password, and press **Enter**. The prompt changes to [netplus@192.168. 54.5]$, indicating that you are now logged on to *LINUX1.NETPLUSLAB.NET*.

11. Type **su** – and press **Enter**. The Password prompt appears. Type root's password, and press **Enter**. The prompt now ends in a pound sign (#), indicating that you are logged on as the root user.

**Figure 10-5**  The PuTTY Configuration window

12. Type **ifconfig** and press **Enter**. The computer displays information about the network card installed in it. In addition to the NIC in the computer (most likely named eth0 or eth1), the computer displays information about the local NIC, or the loopback. This is a virtual (or software-only) NIC, primarily used for testing. A loopback NIC is configured by default on most devices that use TCP/IP. What are the names and IP addresses of the NICs on the computer?

13. Type **ifconfig** and press **Enter**. The computer displays information about the NICs on the computer. What is the name of the new interface on the computer?

14. Type **exit** and press **Enter**. Type **exit** and press **Enter** again to exit from *LINUX1. NETPLUSLAB.NET*. The prompt in the terminal window changes back to indicate that you are on *LINUX2.NETPLUSLAB.NET*.

15. Type **ifconfig** and press **Enter**. The computer indicates that the command cannot be found.

16. Now you attempt to run the ifconfig command by typing the full path of the command. Type **/sbin/ifconfig** and press **Enter**. The computer displays information about the network cards on the computer. (The netplus user cannot find the ifconfig command without supplying the full pathname because the environment for the netplus user is different from that of the root user.)

17. Type **exit** and press **Enter**. Type **exit** and press **Enter** again to exit the SSH session on *LINUX1.NETPLUSLAB.NET*.

18. Log off both computers.

## Certification Objective

Objective for the Network+ Exam:

- 1.6 Explain the function of common networking protocols.

## Review Questions

1. What is the difference between the SSH protocol and the Telnet protocol?

   a. The Telnet protocol is encrypted.

   b. The Telnet protocol is faster than the SSH protocol.

   c. SSH is encrypted.

   d. SSH can be used only between Linux or UNIX servers.

2. Which of the following commands could you use to display a Linux computer's IP address?

   a. **ipconfig**

   b. **ssh**

   c. **ipdisplay**

   d. **ifconfig**

3. Why might a virtual NIC be configured on a Linux computer?

   a. Because an additional IP address is needed for a Web server

   b. For the computer to act as a router between two networks

   c. For redundancy

   d. For load balancing

4. The `ssh` command allows you to open a remote terminal window on another computer. What is the major difference between working in an SSH session on a remote computer in another city and working directly at the console of the remote computer?

   a. You cannot power cycle the remote computer.

   b. You cannot run GUI programs in the SSH session.

   c. You cannot run terminal programs such as top or ps while working in an SSH session.

   d. You cannot log on to other remote computers while working in an SSH session.

5. In this lab, how could you tell whether a terminal window was for the local computer or for an SSH session on a remote computer?

   a. The prompt indicated the name of the remote computer.

   b. There was no way to tell.

   c. The prompt indicated the name of the program being run.

   d. The computer beeped when you logged on to a remote computer.

10

# NETWORK SECURITY

## Labs included in this chapter

- Lab 11.1 Auditing
- Lab 11.2 Checking for Vulnerable Software
- Lab 11.3 Implementing Network Address Restrictions on a Linux Server
- Lab 11.4 Plaintext Versus Encrypted Protocols
- Lab 11.5 Securing a Wireless Network
- Lab 11.6 Delegating Administrative Rights

## Network+ Exam Objectives

| Objective | Lab |
| --- | --- |
| 4.3 Given a scenario, use appropriate software tools to troubleshoot connectivity issues. | 11.4 |
| 5.1 Given a scenario, implement appropriate wireless security measures. | 11.5 |
| 5.2 Explain the methods of network access security. | 11.4, 11.5 |
| 5.3 Explain methods of user authentication. | 11.1 |
| 5.4 Explain common threats, vulnerabilities, and mitigation techniques. | 11.1, 11.2, 11.3, 11.5, 11.6 |
| 5.6 Categorize different types of network security appliances and methods. | 11.2 |

# Lab 11.1 Auditing

## Objectives

Although preventing security problems should be the first goal of network administrators, security problems cannot always be prevented. That makes auditing essential. It can help you identify both security vulnerabilities and potential security breaches.

Auditing is the gathering and analysis of large amounts of network-related information, including data about logons, access attempts, system events, and so on. For instance, auditing can indicate when someone is repeatedly attempting and failing to log on to your domain controller, which could in turn indicate that someone is attempting to compromise your network. Auditing can also help you troubleshoot server problems, such as an unexpected failure.

Auditing is not limited to a network operating system; in most cases, you can configure firewalls, routers, and switches to compile, or log, information (on their own disks or to an external server) as well. Often, this information can be useful in determining whether intruders have attempted to access devices on your network.

In Windows Server 2008 (and in most other network operating systems), auditing is not enabled by default because it can affect performance and use a large amount of disk space. Thus, to view the failed logon attempts in a Windows Server 2008 domain, you must first activate auditing for the domain. Then, you must activate auditing on the domain controller so that it captures the logging.

After completing this lab, you will be able to:

- Enable auditing in Windows Server 2008 Standard Edition
- Review information on audited events

## Materials Required

This lab requires the following:

- A computer running Windows Server 2008, Standard Edition named *SERVER1*, with an IP address of 192.168.54.1 and a subnet mask of 255.255.255.0
- Access as the administrator to *SERVER1*
- A computer running Windows 7 or Windows XP Professional named *WORKSTATION1*, with an IP address of 192.168.54.3, a subnet mask of 255.255.255, and a preferred DNS server of 192.168.54.1
- Both computers connected to a switch or hub with straight-through Cat 5 (or better) UTP cables

Estimated completion time: **40 minutes**

## Activity

1. Log on to *SERVER1* as the administrator. The Windows Server 2008 desktop appears.
2. Click the **Start** button, and then click **Run**. The Run dialog box opens.

3. Type **dcpromo** and press **Enter**. If Terminal Services is installed on the computer, the Active Directory Domain Services Wizard dialog box opens. Click **OK** to close it. The Active Directory Domain Services Installation Wizard opens.

4. Click **Next**. The wizard describes some limitations that older versions of Windows have with Windows Server 2008.

5. Click **Next**. The wizard asks what sort of domain you would like to create.

6. Make sure the **Create a new domain in a new forest** option is selected, and click **Next**.

7. Type **Netpluslab.net** and click **Next**.

8. After several moments, the wizard asks you to select the forest functional level. Select **Windows Server 2008**, and click **Next**.

9. The wizard then asks you to select additional options for the domain controller. Make sure DNS server is selected, and click **Next**. If the Active Directory Domain Services Installation Wizard message box appears, click **Yes**.

10. The wizard asks you to specify the location of database and log files for Active Directory. Select the defaults by clicking **Next**.

11. The wizard asks you to select an administrator password for Directory Services Restore Mode. Enter the password **Passw0rd** and click **Next**.

12. The wizard summarizes the options you have selected. Click **Next**.

13. Click **Finish**, and click **Restart Now**.

14. Log on to *WORKSTATION1* as an administrator. The Windows desktop appears.

In Windows 7:

15. Click the **Start** button, right-click **Computer**, click **Properties**, and click **Change settings**.

16. Click **Network ID**, and click **Next**.

17. The wizard asks what sort of network you use. Make sure the **My company uses a network with a domain** option is selected, and click **Next**.

18. Click **Next**. The wizard asks for account information.

19. In the User name text box, enter **Administrator**. In the Password text box, enter the password for the administrator account of *SERVER1*. In the Domain name text box, enter **NETPLUSLAB.NET**. Click **Next**.

20. Click the **Do not add a domain user account** option, and click **Next**.

21. Click **Finish**, and then click **OK**.

22. Reboot the computer, and then log on to the NETPLUSLAB domain as the domain administrator. The Windows desktop appears.

23. Skip ahead to Step 33.

In Windows XP:

24. Click the **Start** button, right-click **My Computer**, and click **Properties**. The System Properties window opens. Click the **Computer Name** tab.

25. Click **Network ID**. The Network Identification Wizard opens.

26. Click **Next**. The Wizard asks how you want to use the computer. Make sure the **This computer is part of a business network, and I use it to connect to other computers at work** option is selected. Click **Next**.

27. The wizard asks what sort of network you use. Make sure the **My company uses a network with a domain** option is selected, and click **Next**.

28. Click **Next**. The wizard asks for account information.

29. In the User name text box, enter **Administrator**. In the Password text box, enter the password for the administrator account of *SERVER1*. In the Domain text box, enter **NETPLUSLAB.NET**. Click **OK**.

30. Click the **Do not add a user at this time** option button. Click **Next**.

31. Click **Finish,** and then click **Next**.

32. Reboot the computer, and then log on to the NETPLUSLAB domain as the domain administrator. The Windows desktop appears.

33. Now log on to *SERVER1* as the administrator. The Windows Server 2008 desktop appears.

34. Click the **Start** button, point to **Administrative Tools**, and click **Local Security Policy**. The Local Security Policy window opens.

35. Click **Local Policies** in the left pane. Icons for policies appear in the right pane.

36. In the right pane, double-click **Audit Policy**. Several icons whose names begin with "Audit" appear. As you'll see in the next few steps, you can double-click these icons to define and configure various policies.

37. Double-click **Audit account logon events**. The Audit account logon events Properties dialog box opens. This setting determines whether the computer will record every instance of a user logging on or off the domain.

38. If necessary, click to select the **Success** and **Failure** check boxes, and then click **OK**. Figure 11-1 shows the Audit account logon events Properties dialog box. You have now configured the computer to record every attempt by a user to log on, whether successful or unsuccessful.

39. Repeat Steps 37 and 38 for **Audit logon events**. (Note the distinction between "Audit account logon events" and "Audit logon events.") The Audit logon events settings determine whether the domain controller will record every instance of a user logging on or off a computer for which the domain controller performs authentication.

40. In the left pane, right-click **Security Settings**, and click **Reload** on the shortcut menu. The computer updates the security policy for the domain with the changes that you have made.

41. For auditing events to be captured, you must specifically enable logging on the domain controller itself. Otherwise, the domain controller does not know that it is supposed to capture audit events and will discard them. Click the **Start** button, point to **Administrative Tools**, and then click **Group Policy Management**. Double-click **Group Policy Management, Forest: netpluslab.net, Domains, netpluslab.net,** and **Domain Controllers,** right-click **Default Domain Controllers Policy,** and then click **Edit**. The Group Policy Management Editor window opens.

42. In the tree in the left pane, click **Local Policies**. A list of icons appears in the right pane. Double-click **Audit Policy**. Policies appear in the right pane.

**Figure 11-1**    Audit account logon events Properties dialog box

43. Double-click **Audit account logon events**. The Audit account logon events Properties dialog box opens.

44. Make sure that the **Define these policy settings, Success,** and **Failure** check boxes are all checked, and then click **OK**.

45. Repeat Steps 43 and 44 for **Audit logon events**.

46. Right-click **Security Settings,** and then click **Reload**. The computer reloads security policies for the domain controller.

47. Attempt to log on to *WORKSTATION1* using an invalid password. An error message appears, indicating that the logon attempt failed.

48. Click **OK**.

49. Repeat Steps 47 and 48.

50. Log on as the netplus user with the correct password. The Windows desktop appears.

51. On *SERVER1*, click the **Start** button, point to **Administrative Tools,** and click **Event Viewer**. The Event Viewer window opens.

52. In the left pane, expand **Windows Logs** (if necessary), and click **Security**. A list of security events appears in the middle pane, including all successful and failed logon attempts.

53. Double-click an **Audit Failure** icon. The Event Properties dialog box opens. The dialog box gives information about a failed logon attempt.

54. Repeat the previous step with an **Audit Success** icon.

55. Log off both computers.

## Certification Objectives

Objectives for the Network+ Exam:

- 5.3 Explain methods of user authentication.
- 5.4 Explain common threats, vulnerabilities, and mitigation techniques.

## Review Questions

1. Which of the following best describes authentication?

    a. The process of verifying the precise spelling of a username

    b. The process of accepting and matching a username with unique account information, such as a password

    c. The process of replicating user logon information from one domain controller to the others on a network

    d. The process of tracking a user's logon habits and collecting that information in an audit log

2. How does knowing about failed logon attempts help a network administrator's security efforts?

    a. The information could help her determine whether stricter password requirements need to be implemented.

    b. The information could help her refine the NOS schema.

    c. The information could help her determine whether an unauthorized user is attempting to log on with that username.

    d. The information could help her predict the likelihood of future security breaches.

3. Which of the following tools allows you to view security events that have occurred on a Windows Server 2008 computer?

    a. Event Viewer

    b. Authentication Log

    c. Domain Security Policy

    d. Domain Controller Security Policy

4. In the context of Windows networking, why must failed logon attempts be recorded by a domain controller instead of by any random server on the network?

    a. Only a domain controller has the resources necessary to record and hold the volume of information that auditing requires.

    b. Domain controllers contain a complete set of Windows Server 2008 computer administrative tools, whereas other servers do not.

    c. Domain controllers typically provide Web and remote access, enabling a network administrator to remotely audit events on a network.

    d. Domain controllers authenticate users.

5. As a network administrator, what should you do if you notice that a user account has experienced multiple failed logon attempts?

    a. Revoke the user's logon privileges.

    b. Change the user's password.

    c. Contact the user to find out whether she is having trouble logging on.

    d. Limit the times of day during which that user account may log on.

# Lab 11.2 Checking for Vulnerable Software

## Objectives

Software patches can reverse potentially dangerous vulnerabilities on a network. However, network administrators commonly compromise their networks' security by running unpatched software. For instance, in 2003 several worms, including the MSBlast and Sobig F worms, infected hundreds of thousands of computers even though software patches that could fix the vulnerabilities were available. Many administrators simply did not know that they needed to patch their software.

In this lab, you run a utility that can determine which service packs or hot fixes you need to apply to a Windows Server 2008 computer.

After completing this lab, you will be able to:

- Scan a Windows Server 2008 computer to identify whether it is operating with vulnerable software

## Materials Required

This lab requires the following:

- A computer running Windows Server 2008, Standard Edition with Internet access and with Internet Information Services (IIS) installed
- Microsoft Baseline Security Analyzer 2.2 (currently available from *www.microsoft. com/technet/security/tools*) installed on the Windows Server 2008 computer
- At least one missing security update for the computer; the missing security update should be minor, or the computer should be protected by a firewall
- Access as the administrator to the Windows Server 2008 computer

Estimated completion time: **30 minutes**

## Activity

1. Log on to the Windows Server 2008 computer as the administrator. The Windows Server 2008 desktop appears.

2. Establish a connection to the Internet.

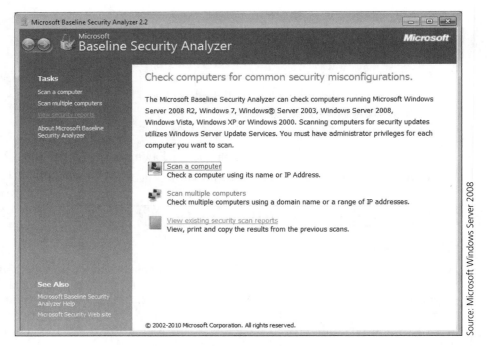

**Figure 11-2**    Microsoft Baseline Security Analyzer

3. Click the **Start** button, point to **All Programs**, and click **Microsoft Baseline Security Analyzer 2.2**. The Microsoft Baseline Security Analyzer opens, as shown in Figure 11-2.

4. Click **Scan a computer**. The computer asks you to choose a computer to scan for security vulnerabilities.

5. Make sure that the name of the local computer is selected in the Computer name drop-down box, and that the **Check for Windows administrative vulnerabilities, Check for weak passwords, Check for IIS administrative vulnerabilities**, and **Check for security updates** check boxes are checked. Uncheck the **Check for SQL administrative vulnerabilities** check box. Click **Start Scan**. The computer downloads security information from Microsoft and checks for security vulnerabilities. This might take several minutes. The computer then displays the results.

6. At the top of the report is a summary of the security status of the computer. What is the security assessment for your computer?

7. Scroll down to the Security Update Scan Results section. The program displays a red stop sign for any items that present a serious security risk, a green checkmark for any items that do not present a security vulnerability, a white i in a blue circle for any informational items, a yellow exclamation point (!) for any items that should be changed, and a blue star for any items that could be changed. Some types of items might not be present. Which critical security updates, if any, should you install on your computer?

8. Scroll down to the Vulnerabilities section under Windows Scan Results. What is the status of Automatic Updates on your computer? Do any items represent a serious security risk?

9. For one of the items with a red or yellow *icon*, click **Result details**. Internet Explorer opens to a page describing the security problem. Read the page, and close Internet Explorer.

10. For the item you selected in the previous step, click **How to correct this**. Internet Explorer opens with instructions on how to correct the problem. Read the page, and close Internet Explorer.

11. Log off the computer.

## Certification Objectives

Objectives for the Network+ Exam:

- 5.4 Explain common threats, vulnerabilities, and mitigation techniques.
- 5.6 Categorize different types of network security appliances and methods.

## Review Questions

1. Which of the following security risks can potentially be addressed by applying a new patch to a software program?

    a. Social engineering

    b. Insecure data transmissions between a Web client and Web server

    c. IP spoofing

    d. RF emission over a wireless network

2. Which of the following methods of accessing files over the Internet is the most secure?

    a. HTTP

    b. HTTPS

    c. TFTP

    d. FTP

3. Which of the following types of software can be patched to improve their security? (Choose all that apply.)

    a. Router OS

    b. Web browser

    c. E-mail client

    d. Workstation OS

4. Which of the following types of transmission media is the most secure?

    a. Fiber-optic cable

    b. Infrared wireless

    c. Shielded twisted-pair cable

    d. Coaxial cable

5. Which of the following network enhancements can introduce new security risks? (Choose all that apply.)

   a. Adding remote access for users who travel

   b. Adding time-of-day restrictions for logons

   c. Modifying a tape backup rotation scheme

   d. Providing Web access to a server's data files

# Lab 11.3 Implementing Network Address Restrictions on a Linux Server

## Objectives

Most NOSs have some mechanism that ensures that users can log on only from certain Network layer or Data Link layer addresses. The potential advantage to requiring users to log on from only certain machines is that you can prevent them from logging on to the network from any workstation but their own. This can help you keep a closer eye on users, as well as entirely prevent users from accessing certain networks. The disadvantage is that this requires more maintenance. If a user changes machines, you have to reconfigure the network address restrictions.

In addition, some network devices can restrict access by Network layer or Data Link layer addresses. For instance, some switches allow you to configure ports so that only certain MAC addresses can pass traffic through those ports. If a user attempts to plug another machine with another MAC address into the same port, the switch does not allow it to pass traffic and the computer will not be able to use the network.

On a Linux or UNIX server, the most common mechanism for configuring network address restrictions is the use of TCP Wrappers. TCP Wrappers are used by a variety of programs to determine whether they should accept network traffic from a particular address. Firewall software such as iptables on Linux is also commonly used.

A careful intruder can circumvent this sort of protection. For instance, an intruder can manually configure both IP addresses and MAC addresses on a computer, or he can attack a computer with packets containing bogus IP addresses. This is often called spoofing. However, good network security policies should make it difficult or impossible to use bogus addresses from outside a network. In this case, an intruder would need to place a machine physically on the network to circumvent address restrictions.

After completing this lab, you will be able to:

- Configure network address restrictions on a Linux server

## Materials Required

This lab requires the following:

- A computer running a current version of Fedora Linux named *LINUX1. NETPLUSLAB.NET,* configured with the firewall disabled, with SELinux disabled, and with the GNOME Desktop Environment

- *LINUX1.NETPLUSLAB.NET* configured with an IP address of 192.168.54.5 and a subnet mask of 255.255.255.0

- The default /etc/samba/smb.conf file in place
- A user named netplus on *LINUX1.NETPLUSLAB.NET* with a known password and a known password for the root account
- A computer running Windows 7 or Windows XP Professional named *WORKSTATION1*, configured with an IP address of 192.168.54.3 and a subnet mask of 255.255.255.0
- Cygwin 1.7.x (available at *www.cygwin.com*) installed on *WORKSTATION1*, with the openssh and openssl packages in the Net category installed in addition to the default packages
- Access to *WORKSTATION1* as an administrator
- Both computers connected to a switch or hub with straight-through Cat 5 (or better) UTP cables

---

Estimated completion time: **35 minutes**

---

## Activity

1. Log on to *LINUX1.NETPLUSLAB.NET* as the netplus user. The Fedora desktop appears.

2. Open a terminal window. The `netplus@LINUX1:~` prompt appears.

3. Type **su** **-** and press **Enter**. The Password prompt appears.

4. Enter the password for the root account, and press **Enter**. The prompt ends in a pound sign (**#**), indicating that you are logged on as the root user.

5. Type **echo "sshd: ALL" >>/etc/hosts.deny** and press **Enter**. The computer appends the text `sshd: ALL` to the file /etc/hosts.deny. This tells TCP Wrappers to prohibit computers from any IP address from logging on to *LINUX1.NETPLUSLAB.NET*.

6. Type **cat /var/run/sshd.pid** and press **Enter**. The computer displays the PID for the running sshd daemon. Record this number.

7. Type **kill -HUP** followed by the PID number you recorded in Step 6, and then press **Enter**. The computer restarts the sshd daemon.

8. Log on to *WORKSTATION1* as an administrator. The Windows desktop appears.

9. Click the **Start** button, click **All Programs**, click **Cygwin**, and then click **Cygwin Terminal**. (On Windows XP, click the **Start** button, point to **All Programs**, point to **Cygwin**, and then click **Cygwin Terminal**.) A terminal window opens.

10. In the terminal window, type **ssh netplus@192.168.54.5** and press **Enter**. As shown in Figure 11-3, the computer displays the error message `ssh_ exchange_ identification: Connection closed by remote host`.

11. Now you configure *LINUX1.NETPLUSLAB.NET* to accept SSH connections from *WORKSTATION1*. In the terminal window on *LINUX1.NETPLUSLAB.NET*, type **echo "sshd: 192.168.54.3" >>/etc/hosts.allow** and press **Enter**. The computer appends the text `sshd: 192.168.54.3` to the end of the file /etc/hosts.allow.

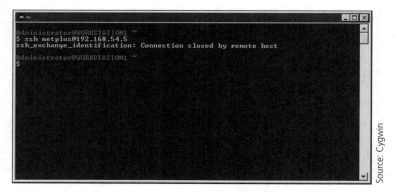

Source: Cygwin

**Figure 11-3** An SSH login prevented by TCP Wrappers

12. Repeat Steps 6 and 7 to restart the sshd daemon.

13. In the terminal window on *WORKSTATION1*, type **ssh netplus@192.168.54.5** and press **Enter**. If a message appears indicating that the authenticity of the connection cannot be confirmed, type **yes** and press **Enter**. The password prompt for netplus@192.168.54.5 appears.

14. Type the password for the netplus account, and press **Enter**. The prompt changes, indicating that you have logged on to the remote server.

15. Log off both computers.

## Certification Objective

Objective for the Network+ Exam:

- 5.4 Explain common threats, vulnerabilities, and mitigation techniques.

## Review Questions

1. Which of the following is a potential weakness in using restrictions on either Network layer addresses or Data Link layer addresses to control access to a network or server?

   a. For a machine on the same network, both Network and Data Link layer addresses may be configured manually.

   b. For a machine on an external network, both Network and Data Link layer addresses may be configured manually.

   c. Network address restrictions typically require more maintenance.

   d. Network layer addresses may be configured manually, whereas Data Link layer addresses may not.

2. Which files on a Linux server are used to configure TCP Wrappers? (Choose all that apply.)

   a. /etc/hosts

   b. /etc/hosts.allow

    c. /etc/hosts.deny

    d. /etc/tcpwrappers

3. Which of the following network security methods provides the greatest resistance to unauthorized external file access on a server?

    a. A central computer room that is accessible only to authorized personnel through hand scanning

    b. An NOS that is configured to allow logons only during the hours of 8:00 a.m. to 5:00 p.m.

    c. An NOS that requires users' computers to have an address that matches one belonging to their LAN segment to log on to the server

    d. A proxy server that disguises transmissions issued from clients on a private LAN

4. What is the best defense against social engineering?

    a. A strong security policy and educating users

    b. Employing Kerberos authentication for all users

    c. Configuring a firewall to accept transmissions only from certain IP addresses

    d. Limiting the ports on a server through which client communication may take place

5. In which of the following situations would it be most beneficial for a network administrator to employ network address restrictions on a TCP/IP-based network (that does not use DHCP) to improve security?

    a. A salesperson accesses a company's network via a dial-up connection to upload sales data every night.

    b. A corporate executive frequently travels to a company's various locations and requires access to confidential information on the server.

    c. A new employee is working on tutorials in temporary quarters until her office can be completely furnished.

    d. A contractor works on a project from a cubicle specially designated and furnished for use by consultants.

# Lab 11.4 Plaintext Versus Encrypted Protocols

## Objectives

Most of the older communications programs still in use, such as FTP or Telnet, use plaintext. Using such a program to administer a server or a network device can make it easy for an intruder to steal account information using a protocol analyzer.

In this lab, you use a protocol analyzer to examine the dangers of using plaintext protocols. An administrator who carelessly uses a plaintext protocol such as FTP or Telnet to manage a server might compromise its security. An intruder with a protocol analyzer can easily find the password and use it to log on to the server. Once intruders have compromised a server, they often install a protocol analyzer to find account names and passwords, which they can use to compromise other servers. Use of encrypted protocols such as SSH instead of FTP or Telnet makes compromise of account information more difficult.

It is important to keep in mind that, although a protocol analyzer is an important and valuable tool for network administrators, using a protocol analyzer to obtain the passwords of users or to eavesdrop on their communications without their consent is unethical and illegal. In addition, you should always have clear and specific consent before using a protocol analyzer. This is especially true on a network that is not yours, such as a customer network. On networks that you manage, you should determine whether use of a protocol analyzer is permissible before using one. In some high-security environments, such as a financial or military institution, you might be prohibited from using a protocol analyzer at all. In other environments, you should make sure that you have explicit permission to use a protocol analyzer when necessary.

After completing this lab, you will be able to:

- Describe the difference between encrypted and unencrypted network protocols

## Materials Required

This lab requires the following:

- A computer running Windows Server 2008, Standard Edition named *SERVER1*, configured with an IP address of 192.168.54.1 and a subnet mask of 255.255.255.0
- IIS and the File Transfer Protocol (FTP) Publishing Service installed and running on *SERVER1*
- A computer running Windows Server 2008, Standard Edition named *SERVER2*, configured with an IP address of 192.168.54.2 and a subnet mask of 255.255.255.0
- The Wireshark protocol analyzer (available from *www.wireshark.org)* and, if necessary, the WinPcap packet capture library (available from *winpcap.polito.it)* installed on *SERVER2*
- Access to *SERVER1* and *SERVER2* as the administrator
- A computer running a current version of Fedora Linux *LINUX1.NETPLUSLAB. NET,* configured with the firewall disabled, with SELinux disabled, and with the GNOME Desktop Environment
- *LINUX1.NETPLUSLAB.NET,* configured with an IP address of 192.168.54.5 and a subnet mask of 255.255.255.0
- A computer running Windows 7 or Windows XP Professional named *WORKSTATION1,* configured with an IP address of 192.168.54.3 and a subnet mask of 255.255.255.0
- A user named netplus on *LINUX1.NETPLUSLAB.NET* with a known password and a known password for the root account
- Cygwin 1.7.x (available at *www.cygwin.com)* installed on *WORKSTATION1*, with the openssh and openssl packages in the Net category installed in addition to the default packages
- Access to the Windows 7 or XP computer as the netplus user
- All four computers connected to a switch or hub with straight-through Cat 5 (or better) UTP cables

Estimated completion time:  **30 minutes**

## Activity

1. Log on to *SERVER1* as the administrator. The Windows Server 2008 desktop appears.

2. Click the **Start** button, point to **Administrative Tools**, and then click **Internet Information Services (IIS) 6.0 Manager**. The Internet Information Services (IIS) Manager window opens.

3. If necessary, click the **plus sign (+)** next to *SERVER1 (local computer)* to expand the tree in the left pane. In the left pane, right-click **FTP Sites**. On the shortcut menu, click **Properties**. The FTP Sites Properties dialog box opens.

4. Click the **Security Accounts** tab. Options appear for configuring access to the FTP sites on *SERVER1*.

5. If necessary, click the **Allow anonymous connections** check box to remove the check. The IIS6 Manager dialog box might open, indicating that the option you selected results in the transmission of cleartext passwords over the network.

6. If necessary, click **Yes** to close the IIS6 Manager dialog box. Click **OK** to close the FTP Sites Properties dialog box.

7. In the left pane, right-click **SERVER1 (local computer)**. On the shortcut menu, point to **All Tasks**, and then click **Restart IIS**. The Stop/Start/Restart dialog box opens.

8. Make sure that **Restart Internet Services on SERVER1** is selected, and click **OK**. A dialog box opens, indicating that Internet services are being shut down, and after a short wait, the Stop/Start/Restart dialog box closes.

9. Log on to *SERVER2* as the administrator. The Windows Server 2008 desktop appears.

10. Click the **Start** button, point to **All Programs**, and click **Wireshark**. The Wireshark Network Analyzer window opens.

11. On the menu bar, click **Capture**, click **Interfaces**, and then click the **Options** button that corresponds to your network adapter. The Wireshark: Capture Options window opens.

12. In the Capture Filter text box, enter **host 192.168.54.3**. This configures Wireshark to capture only packets being sent from or to IP address 192.168.54.3.

13. Click the **Start** button. Wireshark begins to capture any packets sent to or from 192.168.54.3.

14. Log on to *WORKSTATION1* as an administrator. The Windows desktop appears.

15. Click the **Start** button, type **cmd** in the Start Search text box, and then press **Enter**. (In Windows XP, click the **Start** button, point to **All Programs**, point to **Accessories**, and then click **Command Prompt**.) A command prompt window opens.

16. Type **ftp 192.168.54.1** and press **Enter**. The FTP program prompts for the username.

17. Type **netplus** and press **Enter**. The FTP program displays the Password prompt.

18. Type the password for the netplus account. The FTP program indicates that the netplus user has logged on.

19. Type **dir**. The computer displays any files that might be present in the root directory of the FTP server.

20. Type **quit** to exit the FTP program.

21. On *SERVER2*, click **Stop** in the Wireshark dialog box. Wireshark displays the captured packets.

22. In the Filter text box, type **ftp** and press **Enter**. The computer displays only those packets that have FTP in the Protocol field.

23. In the top pane, click the first packet. In the middle pane, click the plus sign next to File Transfer Protocol (FTP). Detailed information about the FTP portion of the packet appears. (You might need to scroll down to see it all.) Click any plus signs you see beneath File Transfer Protocol (FTP) so that more information appears beneath them.

24. In the top frame, click the first packet again. Using the ↓ key, scroll down through the list of packets. Look for a packet containing the text *Request: PASS* and a password. Figure 11-4 shows this packet. Does this password match the password you typed in Step 18?

25. Scroll through the remaining packets. Do you see everything that you typed when you were logged onto the FTP server?

26. Now you use a protocol analyzer to view an encrypted SFTP session. In the Wireshark window on *SERVER2*, click **Capture**, and then click the **Start** button. The Wireshark dialog box opens, asking if you would like to save the capture file.

27. Click **Continue without Saving**. The Wireshark: Capture Options dialog box opens. Notice that the Capture Filter text box still contains the text *host 192.168.54.3*. Wireshark begins capturing packets again.

28. On *WORKSTATION1*, click the **Start** button, click **All Programs**, click **Cygwin**, and then click **Cygwin Terminal**. (On Windows XP, click the **Start** button, point to **All Programs**, point to **Cygwin**, and then click **Cygwin Terminal**.) A terminal window named ~ opens.

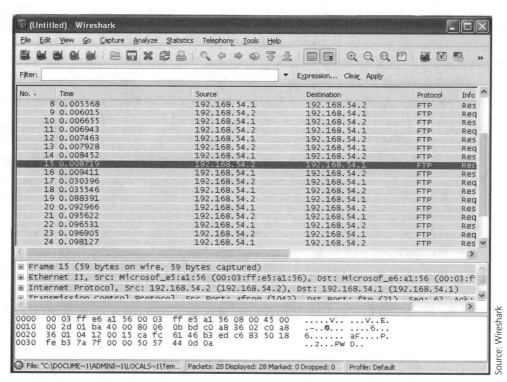

**Figure 11-4** A successful FTP login

29. Type **sftp netplus@192.168.54.5** and press **Enter.** The computer might indicate that the authenticity of the host cannot be established and ask if you would like to continue connecting. If so, type **yes.** The computer prompts for the netplus user's password.

30. Type the password for the netplus user account on *LINUX1.NETPLUSLAB.NET*, and press **Enter.** The computer displays the sftp> prompt.

31. Type **dir** and press **Enter.** The computer displays the names of any files in the home directory of the netplus user on *LINUX1.NETPLUSLAB.NET*.

32. Type **quit** and press **Enter.** The computer closes the SFTP connection.

33. On *SERVER2,* click **Stop** in the Wireshark dialog box. Wireshark displays the captured packets.

34. In the Filter text box, type **ssh** and press **Enter.** The computer displays only those packets that have SSHv2 in the Protocol field. (You type *ssh* instead of *sftp* in the Filter text box because the SFTP program uses the SSH protocol.)

35. In the top pane, click the first packet. In the middle pane, click the plus sign next to SSH Protocol. Detailed information about the SSH portion of the packet appears. (You might need to scroll down to see it all.) Click any plus signs you see beneath SSH Protocol so that more information appears beneath them.

36. In the top frame, click the first packet again. Scroll down through the list of packets. As you scroll through the packets, click any plus signs you see beneath SSH Protocol. Do you see any of the text you typed when connected to *LINUX1.NETPLUSLAB.NET?*

37. Log off all the computers.

## Certification Objectives

Objectives for the Network+ Exam:

- 4.3 Given a scenario, use appropriate software tools to troubleshoot connectivity issues.
- 5.2 Explain the methods of network access security.

## Review Questions

1. Encrypted protocols such as SSH do not send passwords over the network. True or False?

2. In which of the following situations would it be most beneficial for a network administrator to restrict the time of day during which the users can log on to the network to improve security?

   a. A salesperson accesses a company's network via a dial-up connection to upload sales data every night.

   b. Groups of customer service representatives access customer financial data during regular business hours.

   c. A corporate executive frequently travels to a company's various locations and requires access to confidential information on the server.

   d. A group of engineers is establishing an international office in a country several time zones away from the server's location.

3. What is the practice of falsifying an IP address called?

    a. Spoofing

    b. Faking

    c. Impersonating

    d. Configuring a secondary IP address

4. Which of the following encryption methods is commonly used to secure transmissions over virtual private networks (VPNs)?

    a. Kerberos

    b. RAS

    c. PGP

    d. IPSec

5. If someone floods your gateway with so much traffic that it cannot respond to or accept valid traffic, what type of security breach has she caused?

    a. IP spoofing

    b. Social engineering

    c. Denial of service

    d. Trojan horse

# Lab 11.5 Securing a Wireless Network

## Objectives

Wireless routers are often used to connect a laptop to a small peer-to-peer or home network. Without adequate security, a wireless router can leave your network open to a wide range of threats. In this lab, you learn how to implement some of the more common security features often found on wireless routers.

After completing this lab, you will be able to:

- Secure a wireless router

## Materials Required

This lab requires the following:

- A computer (ideally a laptop) running Windows 7 or Windows XP Professional with a wireless network card
- An unconfigured wireless router with the included setup CD or user's manual

Estimated completion time: **30 minutes**

## Activity

1. Begin by installing an unsecured wireless router (see Lab 8.3).

2. Most wireless routers can be configured through a Web browser. Use a browser to open your router's configuration program; typically, this is done by accessing the router's configuration page at, for example, http://192.168.1.1.

3. Although configuration programs can vary from router to router, they are usually menu-driven and fairly easy to navigate. Use the router's configuration pages to implement the changes in the following steps. When in doubt, consult the documentation included with the router.

4. Begin by updating the router's firmware either through the configuration program or from the manufacturer's Web site. This helps address any known security flaws with the router.

5. Set a strong password for the router itself. The default passwords for all common router models are available on the Internet; for example, the default password of many Linksys routers is "admin." With this information, an attacker can easily access the router's configuration program and disable any security features.

6. Change the name of the wireless network, or SSID (service set identifier), from the default name. The default SSID on most Linksys routers is "Linksys."

7. Turn off SSID broadcasting so your network does not show up in a list of available networks. This will not stop determined attackers, but it does prevent the network from appearing as available to casual wireless users in your area.

8. Disable remote administration so your router can be configured only by a computer that is physically attached.

9. Enable some form of encryption such as WEP, WPA, or WPA2. WPA and especially WPA2 are strongly preferred because knowledgeable attackers can easily break WEP encryption. However, using WEP encryption is preferable to using no encryption at all.

10. Use MAC filtering to create a list of computers that are allowed access to the network. This, too, prevents casual users from accessing your network, but can be overcome by an advanced user employing a wireless sniffer.

11. Now connect to the router with your wireless computer and test your wireless connection by opening your browser and navigating to a site on the Internet.

12. When you're finished, reset the router to its factory defaults and log off your computer.

## Certification Objectives

Objectives for the Network+ Exam:

- 5.1 Given a scenario, implement appropriate wireless security measures.
- 5.2 Explain the methods of network access security.
- 5.4 Explain common threats, vulnerabilities, and mitigation techniques.

## Review Questions

1. What does SSID stand for?

   a. Service set identifier

   b. Security service Internet domain

   c. Security station identification

   d. Simple security Internet device

2. WEP, WPA, and WPA2 are all forms of wireless _____.

   a. Access

   b. Routers

   c. Services

   d. Encryption

3. What can you use to limit access to certain computers?

   a. Encryption

   b. MAC filtering

   c. Remote administration

   d. A strong password

# Lab 11.6 Delegating Administrative Rights

## Objectives

One of the advantages of a directory service such as Microsoft Active Directory is that it allows the network administrator granular control over users and network resources. The administrator can make sure that users can access the network resources they need, while at the same time preventing them from accessing network resources they should not be able to access. This also allows the network administrator to delegate specific tasks to certain users without delegating any more authority than is needed.

For instance, in large organizations, resetting passwords, creating user accounts, and other relatively straightforward parts of network administration can take up a lot of time. This can prevent the network administrator from concentrating on larger issues of network design and maintenance. In some cases, it's more efficient to have a user in each department reset passwords and create user accounts specifically for that department, but only for that department. The network administrator is then free to spend time on more important issues. A department might also prefer to have control over its own resources. In large organizations, network administration might be divided between two or more groups.

One tool you can use to subdivide a domain is the organizational unit. An organizational unit is a group of users or network resources, such as printers. Organizational units can be used to enforce policies, including the delegation of administrative rights. For instance, a company might have a different organizational unit for each department. Dividing a domain into organizational units is simpler and usually more convenient than dividing a domain into multiple child domains.

Keep in mind that Active Directory can be quite complex, and it is often possible to find multiple ways to solve a particular problem. Although the simplest way to solve a problem might not be the best way, keeping your Active Directory installation as simple as possible makes it easier to administer over the long term.

After completing this lab, you will be able to:

- Create user accounts in Windows Server 2008
- Create organizational units in Windows Server 2008
- Delegate network administration roles as needed in Windows Server 2008

## Materials Required

This lab requires the following:

- The network configured at the end of Lab 11.1
- No organizational units named Accounting or Manufacturing in Active Directory
- Access to *SERVER1* as the administrator for the netpluslab.net domain
- Local logon for all users configured in the Domain Controller Security Policy (configured by an instructor, if necessary)

> Estimated completion time: **40 minutes**

## Activity

1. Log on to *SERVER1* as administrator in the netpluslab.net domain. The Windows Server 2008 desktop appears.

2. Click the **Start** button, point to **Administrative Tools**, click **Active Directory Users and Computers**. The Active Directory Users and Computers window opens. If necessary, click the **plus sign (+)** next to netpluslab.net to expand the tree below it.

3. Right-click **netpluslab.net** in the tree in the left pane. In the shortcut menu, point to **New**, and then click **Organizational Unit**. The New Object – Organizational Unit dialog box opens.

4. Type **Accounting** in the Name text box, and click **OK**. An Accounting icon appears below netpluslab.net in the tree.

5. Repeat Steps 3 and 4, creating an organizational unit named **Manufacturing**. Figure 11-5 shows the addition of a new organizational unit.

6. Right-click the icon for the **Accounting** object. From the shortcut menu, point to **New**, and then click **User**. The New Object – User dialog box opens.

7. In the Full name and User logon name text boxes, enter **accounting-admin**. Click **Next**.

8. In both the Password and the Confirm password text boxes, type a password at least eight characters long that contains at least one number and a mixture of uppercase and lowercase letters. Record or memorize this password.

Source: Microsoft Windows Server 2008

**Figure 11-5**    Adding an organizational unit

9. Click the **User must change password at next logon** check box to remove the checkmark. Click **Next**. The dialog box summarizes the account information.

10. Click **Finish** to close the dialog box. Click **Accounting** in the left pane and note that an icon for the accounting-admin account appears in the right pane. (If an Active Directory dialog box opens, indicating that Windows cannot set the password because it does not meet the minimum password policy requirements, click **OK**. Then click **Back**. Change the password, click **Next**, and then click **Finish**.)

11. Right-click the **accounting-admin** object, and select **Add to a group** from the shortcut menu.

12. Now you add the accounting-admin user to the Server Operators group. By default, users in the Server Operators group are able to log on to the domain controller, but ordinary users are not. In the "Enter the object names to select" text box, type **Server Operators**. Click **OK**. The Active Directory dialog box opens, indicating that the addition was successful. Click **OK**.

13. Repeat Steps 6 through 12 to create a user named **accountant** and add it to the Server Operators group. Record the password for this account.

14. Right-click the **Manufacturing** object. On the shortcut menu, point to **New**, and then click **User**. The New Object – User dialog box opens. Repeat Steps 6 through 10, creating a user account named **manufacturer**.

15. Right-click the **Accounting** object and select **Delegate Control** from the shortcut menu. The Delegation of Control Wizard opens.

16. Click **Next**. The wizard offers you the option of selecting users or groups.

17. Click **Add**. The Select Users, Computers, or Groups window opens. In the "Enter the object names to select" text box, type **accounting-admin** and click **OK**. The name of the user appears in the Selected users and groups box.

18. Click **Next**. The wizard lists a series of tasks you could delegate.

19. Place a check in the **Create, delete, and manage user accounts** check box. Click **Next**. The wizard summarizes the options you have chosen.

20. Click **Finish**. The wizard closes. You have now delegated control over user accounts in the Accounting organizational unit to the accounting-admin user. This user will not have rights over other parts of Active Directory, including the Manufacturing organizational unit.

21. Log off *SERVER1*.

22. Log on to *SERVER1* as the **accounting-admin** user. The Windows Server 2008 desktop appears.

23. Click the **Start** button, point to **Administrative Tools**, and then click **Active Directory Users and Computers**. If a UAC dialog box opens, enter the password for the accounting-admin user, and click **OK**. The Active Directory Users and Computers window opens.

24. If the tree below netpluslab.net (in the left pane of the window) has not been expanded already, click the **plus sign (+)** next to netpluslab.net. Then click the icon for the **Accounting** object. Icons for usernames appear in the right pane of the window.

25. Right-click the **accountant** user icon, and select **Reset Password**. The Reset Password dialog box opens.

26. Enter a new password in the New password and Confirm password text boxes. Click **OK**. A dialog box opens, indicating that the password for the accountant account has been changed.

27. Click **OK**.

28. Repeat Steps 6 through 10 for the Accounting object, creating a user named **bills**. Make sure to record the password.

29. Now you verify that the accounting-admin account has no rights to other parts of Active Directory. Click the icon for the **Manufacturing** object. The icon for the manufacturer user appears.

30. Right-click the icon for the **manufacturer** user in the right pane of the window. From the shortcut menu, select **Reset Password**. The Reset Password dialog box opens.

31. Enter the new password in the New password and Confirm password text boxes. Click **OK**. A dialog box opens, indicating that Windows could not complete the password change and that access is denied. Click **OK**.

32. Right-click the **Manufacturing** icon in the left pane of the window. From the shortcut menu, note that you do not have the option to create a new user. Select **Delegate Control**. A dialog box opens, indicating that you do not have permission to write security information for this object.

33. Click **OK**. The dialog box closes.

34. On *WORKSTATION1*, log on to the netpluslab.net domain as the **bills** user you created in Step 28. The Windows desktop appears.

35. Log off both computers.

## Certification Objective

Objective for the Network+ Exam:

- 5.4 Explain common threats, vulnerabilities, and mitigation techniques.

## Review Questions

1. What is an organizational unit?

   a. A department or division within an organization

   b. A container used to group users with similar permissions and rights

   c. A container used to group similar objects such as users or groups

   d. An organization

2. If a user is assigned Read permissions to a folder, what may he do with the folder's contents? (Choose all that apply.)

   a. View the listing of files in the folder.

   b. Launch executable files in the folder.

   c. Delete files in the folder.

   d. View the contents of files in the folder.

3. If a user is assigned Modify permissions to a folder, what may she do with the folder's contents? (Choose all that apply.)

   a. View the list of files in the folder.

   b. Launch executable files in the folder.

   c. Delete files in the folder.

   d. View the contents of files in the folder.

4. Which of the following is a potential advantage of delegating user administration to another user? (Choose all that apply.)

   a. The network administrator can concentrate on more important network maintenance issues.

   b. One or more users in each department can handle user administration for their department.

   c. It allows large network administration departments to delegate tasks.

   d. It allows each user in a department to handle the administration of his own account.

5. By default, what permissions do users in the Everyone group have to a newly shared Windows Server 2008 folder?

   a. Read and Execute only

   b. List Folder Contents only

   c. Full Access

   d. By default, users have no rights to newly shared folders.

6. In this lab, you grouped users in the same department into organizational units and then used the organizational units to delegate permissions within them. What is another approach you could have used to perform the same task?

a. Group each department into separate forests.

b. Group each department into separate domains in the same tree.

c. Create a new forest for each department.

d. Group each department into separate workgroups within the same tree.

# VOICE AND VIDEO OVER IP

## Labs included in this chapter

- Lab 12.1 Setting Up a Video Streaming Server
- Lab 12.2 Installing an SIP Proxy
- Lab 12.3 Installing an SIP Client
- Lab 12.4 Researching Open Source VoIP Solutions

## Network+ Exam Objective

| Objective | Lab |
| --- | --- |
| 1.6 Explain the function of common networking protocols. | 12.2, 12.3 |
| 1.9 Identify virtual network components. | 12.4 |
| 4.6 Explain different methods and rationales for network performance optimization. | 12.1, 12.2, 12.3 |

# Lab 12.1 Setting Up a Video Streaming Server

## Objectives

Streaming video is one of the more common applications of Video over IP. A video streaming server hosts a number of videos as stored files that can be viewed remotely from a client machine. Videos sent when requested are referred to as video-on-demand, whereas live streaming videos are those sent continuously regardless of whether they're requested. In this lab, you set up a popular open source program (VLC) that is capable of functioning as both a video streaming server and a media player. After completing this lab, you will be able to:

- Set up and configure a video streaming server
- Connect to a streaming video with a media player

## Materials Required

This lab requires the following:

- A computer running Windows Server 2008, Standard Edition named *SERVER1*, configured with an IP address of 192.168.54.1 and a subnet mask of 255.255.255.0
- A computer running Windows 7 or Windows XP Professional named *WORKSTATION1*, configured with an IP address of 192.168.54.2 and a subnet mask of 255.255.255.0
- VLC media player (*www.videolan.org*) downloaded and installed on both computers
- A video file suitable for streaming, such as DIVX or WMV, on *SERVER1*
- Portable media such as a USB drive to transfer VLC installation and video files if the computers do not have a direct connection to the Internet
- Both computers connected to a switch or hub with straight-through Cat 5 (or better) UTP cables
- Administrative access to both computers

Estimated completion time: **30 minutes**

## Activity

1. Log on to *SERVER1* as the administrator. The Windows desktop appears.
2. Click the **Start** button, click **All Programs**, click **VideoLAN**, and click **VLC media player**. If the Privacy and Network Access Policy dialog box opens, click **Save** and Continue.
3. Click **Media** on the menu bar, and click **Stream**. The Open Media window opens.
4. Click **Add**, choose the file you want to stream, and click **Open** to continue.
5. Select the **Network** tab.
6. If necessary, select **UDP** as the protocol, and enter **192.168.54.2** as the address of the computer that will receive the video stream.
7. Note the port being used, and then click **Stream**.

8. Click **Stream** again to begin streaming.

9. Now run VLC on *WORKSTATION1*.

10. Click **Media** in the menu bar, and then select **Open Network Stream**.

11. Make sure that the same port is being used. Click **Play**.

12. After a short pause, the video should start streaming. When you're finished, exit all programs, and log off both computers.

## Certification Objective

Objective for the Network+ Exam:

- 4.6 Explain different methods and rationales for network performance optimization.

## Review Questions

1. A computer that is sending a video stream is referred to as a video streaming _____.

    a. Hub

    b. Server

    c. Switch

    d. Proxy

2. Which protocol is typically used to stream video?

    a. UDP

    b. TCP

    c. HTTP

    d. FTP

3. For a client to receive a video stream, both the server and client applications must use the same _____.

    a. Gateway

    b. IP address

    c. Port

    d. SIP

# Lab 12.2 Installing an SIP Proxy

## Objectives

SIP and H.323 are the two most common protocols used by VoIP communications. Although SIP does not have as many features as H.323, it is more popular with most VoIP vendors because of its simplicity and lower overhead. SIP is an Application layer signaling protocol modeled on the HTTP protocol. In this lab, you install and configure part of an IP PBX called an SIP Proxy or Proxy Server.

After completing this lab, you will be able to:

- Set up and install an SIP Proxy Server

## Materials Required

This lab requires the following:

- A computer running Windows Server 2008, Standard Edition named *SERVER1*, configured with an IP address of 192.168.54.1 and a subnet mask of 255.255.255.0, with Internet access
- Access to the computer as the administrator
- The latest .NET Framework downloaded from *www.microsoft.com* and installed on *SERVER1*
- The Windows Server 2008 installation CD/DVD (if necessary)

Estimated completion time: **25 minutes**

## Activity

1. Log on to *SERVER1* as the administrator. The Windows desktop appears.
2. Perform whatever steps are necessary for the computer to access the Internet.
3. Start Internet Explorer.
4. Go to **www.officesip.com**.
5. Select the **SIP SERVER** tab on the top menu, and download OfficeSIP Server 3.1 to your desktop. Open the OfficeSIP-Server-3.1.zip file, and extract all files to your desktop.
6. Double-click **Setup-3.1.exe**. If an Open File Security Warning dialog box opens, click **Run** to continue. The OfficeSIP Server Setup Wizard window opens.
7. Click **Next** to continue to the License Agreement.
8. Click the **I Agree** option button, and click **Next**.
9. If necessary, keep the default officesip.local as a domain name, and click **Next**.
10. Click **Next** after selecting the installation folder, and click **Next** again to confirm your choices.
11. When the installation is complete, click **Close**.
12. To run OfficeSIP Server 2.5, click the **Start** button, click **All Programs**, click **OfficeSIP Server**, and click **Control Panel**.
13. Click **Connect** to log in, and the OfficeSIP Server Control Panel should open, as shown in Figure 12-1.
14. Select the **.csv File** tab, and click **Add** to add a new user.
15. Add the necessary user credentials to add a user named **User1** and click **OK**.

**Figure 12-1**    OfficeSIP Server Control Panel

16. Add a second user named **User2** and click **OK**.

17. Log off the computer unless you are progressing directly to Lab 12.3.

## Certification Objectives

Objectives for the Network+ Exam:

- 1.6 Explain the function of common networking protocols.
- 4.6 Explain different methods and rationales for network performance optimization.

## Review Questions

1. Why is SIP a popular choice with VoIP vendors?

    a. It has lower licensing costs.

    b. It is simpler with lower overhead.

    c. It is more fault tolerant and robust.

    d. It was the first standard developed.

2. SIP and H.323 are both examples of _____.

   a. Protocols

   b. Soft phones

   c. Media gateways

   d. End devices

3. At what layer does SIP function?

   a. Transport

   b. Data Link

   c. Network

   d. Application

# Lab 12.3 Installing an SIP Client

## Objectives

An SIP client is any end-user device that initiates an SIP connection. This could include physical devices, such as IP telephones or PDAs, or software applications, such as soft phones or messaging programs. An SIP client can use the SIP protocol to send text, voice, or video to another client. In this lab, you install an SIP client on two machines and have them communicate through the SIP server you set up in Lab 12.2. After completing this lab, you will be able to:

- Set up an SIP client application
- Communicate by voice with an SIP-based messaging application

## Materials Required

This lab requires the following:

- A computer running Windows Server 2008, Standard Edition named *SERVER1*, configured with an IP address of 192.168.54.1 and a subnet mask of 255.255.255.0
- The installation of OfficeSIP Server 3.1 running on *SERVER1* from Lab 12.2
- A computer running Windows 7 or Windows XP Professional named *WORKSTATION1*, configured with an IP address of 192.168.54.2 and a subnet mask of 255.255.255.0
- A second computer running Windows 7 or Windows XP Professional named *WORKSTATION2*, configured with an IP address of 192.168.54.3 and a subnet mask of 255.255.255.0
- Working speakers and a microphone on both *WORKSTATION1* and *WORKSTATION2*
- The latest .NET Framework downloaded from *www.microsoft.com* and installed on *WORKSTATION1* and *WORKSTATION2*
- All three computers connected to a switch or hub with straight-through Cat 5 (or better) UTP cables
- Administrative access to all three computers

Estimated completion time: | 30 minutes

## Activity

1. Log on to *WORKSTATION1* as an administrator. The Windows desktop appears.

2. Perform whatever steps are necessary for the computer to access the Internet.

3. Start Internet Explorer.

4. Go to **www.officesip.com**.

5. Select the **SIP MESSENGER** tab, download OfficeSIP Messenger 2.2.4 to your desktop, and double-click the setup icon to begin installing the program.

6. The OfficeSIP Messenger Setup Wizard opens. Click **Next** to continue.

7. Select an installation folder, and click **Next**.

8. Click **Next** to confirm the installation. If a User Account Control dialog box opens, click **Yes** to continue.

9. When the installation is complete, click **Close**.

10. Click the **Start** button, point to **All Programs**, and click **OfficeSIP Messenger** to run the program.

11. Log in with the credentials you created for User1 in Lab 12.2.

12. Repeat Steps 1 through 11 on *WORKSTATION2* and log in as User2.

13. Click **Contacts** on the menu bar, and then click **Add Contact**.

14. Add User1 as a contact, as shown in Figure 12-2.

Source: OfficeSIP Messenger 2.2.4

**Figure 12-2**  OfficeSIP Messenger Contacts

15. Click **Contacts** on the menu bar, and then select **Start Audio Conversation**. If a Windows Security Alert warns you that the Windows firewall has blocked some features of this program, click **Unblock**.

16. If possible, have a partner answer the call from *WORKSTATION1*; otherwise, terminate the session and close any windows.

17. Log off all three computers.

## Certification Objectives

Objectives for the Network+ Exam:

- 1.6 Explain the function of common networking protocols.
- 4.6 Explain different methods and rationales for network performance optimization.

## Review Questions

1. What are SIP clients?

    a. Daemons that run on an SIP server

    b. End-user devices

    c. Clients that never initiate an SIP connection

    d. Clients that are used to redirect requests from user agents

2. Hardware devices and software applications can both be SIP clients. True or False?

3. What does SIP stand for?

    a. Service Initialization Protocol

    b. Session Initialization Protocol

    c. Service Initiation Protocol

    d. Session Initiation Protocol

# Lab 12.4 Researching Open Source VoIP Solutions

## Objectives

VoIP (Voice over IP) is quickly becoming common in the workplace because of its lower cost, enhanced features, and centralized management. The infrastructure for voice and data is often integrated to avoid the redundancy of having separate networks and private branch exchange (PBX) systems.

To access VoIP, users can run client applications called soft phones and place calls through their computers or, with specialized hardware, place calls through either analog or digital telephone handsets. These devices are often connected through an IP PBX, which may be a hardware system, an application running on a server, or a remote host or virtual service offered by an Internet provider.

One of the more common open source IP PBX applications is called Asterisk. In this lab, you investigate some of the features available for a Windows version of Asterisk called AsteriskWin32.

After completing this lab, you will be able to:

- Identify some of the features available on an open source IP PBX

## Materials Required

This lab requires the following:

- Pencil and paper
- A computer running Windows 7 or Windows XP Professional with Internet access
- An ordinary user account on the computer

Estimated completion time: **20 minutes**

## Activity

1. Log on to the computer as an ordinary user. The Windows desktop appears.
2. Perform whatever steps are necessary for the computer to access the Internet.
3. Start Internet Explorer.
4. Go to **www.asterisk.org**, and click **Learn More**.
5. Record some of the protocols supported by Asterisk.
6. Explain the four key applications of Asterisk.
7. Record some of the operating systems that can run Asterisk.
8. There is also a Windows-based version of Asterisk called AsteriskWin32. Go to **http: // asteriskwin32.com/**, and click the **About** tab.
9. Does Asterisk require any additional hardware to connect soft phones?
10. Click the **Install & Notes** tab.
11. View the AsteriskWin32 Install videos on Installing, Configuring, Running, and SoftPhone Setup.
12. Close any open windows and log off both computers.

## Certification Objective

Objective for the Network+ Exam:

- 1.9 Identify virtual network components.

## Review Questions

1. Why is the infrastructure for voice and data often integrated into a single system?

    a. To improve security

    b. To adhere to local regulations

    c. To filter outgoing communications

    d. To avoid redundancy

2. What are client applications for placing VoIP called?

   a. Soft phones

   b. Digital phones

   c. Analog phones

   d. IP phones

3. Analog telephones require additional hardware to be used with VoIP. True or False?

# TROUBLESHOOTING NETWORK PROBLEMS

## Labs included in this chapter

- Lab 13.1 Using the Ping Utility to Troubleshoot a TCP/IP Network
- Lab 13.2 Using the Traceroute Utility to Troubleshoot a TCP/IP Network
- Lab 13.3 Troubleshooting Client Logon Problems
- Lab 13.4 Troubleshooting Web Client Problems

## Network+ Exam Objectives

| Objective | Lab |
| --- | --- |
| 1.8 Given a scenario, implement the following network troubleshooting methodology. | 13.3, 13.4 |
| 2.5 Given a scenario, troubleshoot common router and switch problems. | 13.4 |
| 4.3 Given a scenario, use appropriate software tools to troubleshoot connectivity issues. | 13.1, 13.2, 13.3 |

# Lab 13.1 Using the Ping Utility to Troubleshoot a TCP/IP Network

## Objectives

The Ping utility (also known as the `ping` command) is one of the basic tools used to check network connectivity in a TCP/IP network. Every operating system that supports the TCP/IP protocol suite also supports the Ping utility.

The `ping` command works by sending a message using the ICMP protocol to the target asking for a reply. If the message reaches the target, it sends an ICMP reply. This indicates that you have network connectivity between the computer where you used the `ping` command and the computer you are trying to reach. Keep in mind, however, that the Ping utility does not tell you anything about network services running on the remote computer, nor does the Ping utility tell you anything about the type or number of hops that the ICMP messages took to reach a host.

When you use the `ping` command to troubleshoot a connectivity problem, you should first verify that TCP/IP is working properly by pinging the loopback address (127.0.0.1) and the computer's own IP address. Then, you should ping each stop along the way to the unreachable remote host to verify that you can reach each intermediate stop. For instance, if you cannot ping a router along the way to a remote host, this might indicate that the router is down and might explain why you cannot reach the remote host. (Note that some routers or firewalls might block ICMP packets and prevent the Ping utility from working properly.)

After completing this lab, you will be able to:

- Use the `ping` command to determine the source of problems in a TCP/IP network
- Isolate a problem by following a logical methodology

## Materials Required

This lab requires the following:

- A computer running Windows Server 2008, Standard Edition named *SERVER1* with two NICs
- One NIC configured with an IP address of 192.168.54.1 and a subnet mask of 255.255.255.0, and the other NIC configured with an IP address of 172.16.1.1 and a subnet mask of 255.255.255.0
- Routing and Remote Access configured on *SERVER1* so that it acts as a router
- A switch or hub named *SWITCH1* connected (with a straight-through Cat 5 or better UTP cable) to the NIC on *SERVER1* that was configured with an IP address of 192.168.54.1
- A switch or hub named *SWITCH2* connected (with a straight-through Cat 5 or better UTP cable) to the NIC on *SERVER1* that was configured with an IP address of 172.16.1.1

- A computer running Windows 7 or Windows XP Professional named *WORKSTATION1*, configured with an IP address of 192.168.54.2 and a subnet mask of 255.255.255.0, connected to *SWITCH1* with a straight-through Cat 5 (or better) UTP cable

- A computer running Windows 7 or Windows XP Professional named *WORKSTATION2*, configured with an IP address of 172.16.1.2 and a subnet mask of 255.255.255.0, connected to *SWITCH2* with a straight-through Cat 5 (or better) UTP cable

- Administrative access to all three computers

Estimated completion time: **45 minutes**

## Activity

1. Review the layout and IP addresses of the network in Figure 13-1.

2. Now you can determine if *WORKSTATION2* (which has an IP address of 172.16.1.2) is up and running. Review the following problem-isolation methodology. (Do not perform the steps yet; simply review them so that you have an overall view of how you will troubleshoot the network.)

   - Log on to the *WORKSTATION1* computer. Ping the local computer's loopback address, 127.0.0.1, to ensure that TCP/IP is installed.

   - Ping the local computer's IP address to ensure that the local computer's NIC is addressed and functioning properly.

   - Ping the near side of the router to ensure that the connection between 192.168.54.2 and 192.168.54.1 is operating properly. The term *near side* refers to the router's NIC with an IP address on the same network as the local computer.

   - Ping the far side of the router to ensure that the connection through the router is operating properly; specifically, this test ensures that the connection between 192.168.54.2 and 172.16.1.1 is functional. The term *far side* refers to the router's NIC that is on the path to a destination host with an IP address on a different network than the local computer.

   - Ping a computer on the network segment on the far side of the router; in this situation, the computer on the far side of the router is the *WORKSTATION2* computer. This ensures connectivity all the way from *WORKSTATION1* at 192.168.54.2 to *WORKSTATION2* at 172.16.1.2.

If you are working from home, you could modify the following steps to ping either side of your home Internet router.

**Figure 13-1** Network layout of Lab 13.1

The following steps walk you through the procedure outlined in Step 2. For each ping test, the `ping` command issues a message indicating either success or failure. If the `ping` command returns an error at any step, you can assume that the problem lies with the connection at the particular step that produced the error.

3. Log on to *WORKSTATION1* as an administrator. The Windows desktop appears.

4. Click the **Start** button, type **cmd** in the Search programs and files text box, and then press **Enter**. (In Windows XP, click the **Start** button, point to **All Programs**, point to **Accessories**, and then click **Command Prompt**.) A command prompt window opens.

5. To determine if TCP/IP is operating properly, type **ping 127.0.0.1** and then press **Enter**. Was the `ping` command successful?

6. To determine if the local computer's NIC is operating correctly, type **ping 192.168.54.2** and then press **Enter**. Was the `ping` command successful?

7. To determine if the connection to the near side of the router is operating properly, type **ping 192.168.54.1** and then press **Enter**. Was the `ping` command successful?

8. To determine if the router is operating properly, type **ping 172.16.1.1** and then press **Enter**. Was the `ping` command successful?

9. To determine if a computer on the network segment on the far side of the router is operating properly, type **ping 172.16.1.2** and then press **Enter**. Was the `ping` command successful?

10. Cover the link lights on each switch with a piece of paper or another obstruction. If the link lights on each computer's NICs are visible, place a box or another obstruction in front of each NIC.

11. Have your instructor or lab partner unplug one of the cables from one of the NICs in the back of the router. This should be done so that you cannot identify which cable has been removed.

12. Without looking at the link lights on the NICs or the switches, repeat Steps 7 through 9. Record the step that failed, and record the cable you think failed.

13. Remove the obstructions added in Step 10, and examine the link lights on the switches and on the NICs. Which cable was unplugged?

14. Plug in the cable that was unplugged in Step 11.

15. If you have a lab partner, repeat Steps 10 through 14 with your lab partner.

16. Log off *WORKSTATION1*.

## Certification Objective

Objective for the Network+ Exam:

- 4.3 Given a scenario, use appropriate software tools to troubleshoot connectivity issues.

## Review Questions

1. What would you ping to determine whether TCP/IP was functioning properly on your computer?

    a. The gateway address

    b. The near side of the router

    c. The loopback address

    d. The far side of the router

2. Which of the following responses to a `ping` command issued on a Windows-based computer indicates that the ping test was successful?

    a. `Packets: Sent = 4, Received = 4, Lost = 0 (0%)`

    b. `Packets: Sent = 0, Received = 0, Lost = 0 (0%)`

    c. `Packets: Sent = 0, Received = 0, Lost = 4 (100%)`

    d. `Packets: Sent = 4, Received = 4, Lost = 4 (100%)`

3. When you issue a `ping` command, what Application layer protocol sends a message to the destination host?

    a. ARP

    b. RARP

    c. SNMP

    d. ICMP

4. Suppose you were troubleshooting a network connectivity problem between a workstation on a private LAN and a server on the Internet. As part of a logical troubleshooting methodology, what address would you ping after determining that the TCP/IP stack on the workstation was functioning properly?

    a. The workstation's loopback address

    b. The workstation's default gateway

    c. The private LAN's Internet name server

    d. The Internet server you're trying to reach

5. In the scenario described in question 4, as part of a logical troubleshooting methodology, what address would you ping second?

    a. The workstation's loopback address

    b. The workstation's default gateway

    c. The private LAN's Internet name server

    d. The Internet server

6. Which of the following is the loopback address in IP version 4 addressing?

   a. 127.0.0.1

   b. 1.1.1.1

   c. 127.0.0.0

   d. 10.0.0.0

7. What type of message would you receive if you were trying to ping *www.comptia.org* from a Windows XP computer and misspelled the host's name as *www.conptia.org* in the `ping` command syntax?

   a. `Host www.conptia.org not responding`

   b. `Ping request could not find host www.contia.org. Please check the name and try again.`

   c. `Reply from www.conptia.org: bytes=0`

   d. `Unknown host www.conptia.org`

# Lab 13.2 Using the Traceroute Utility to Troubleshoot a TCP/IP Network

## Objectives

Another useful troubleshooting command in a TCP/IP network is the `traceroute` command. The `traceroute` command traces the path a packet travels as it goes over the network from a source to a destination node. This is particularly useful on large networks (including the Internet) because it can indicate at which hop along the route between two computers a problem exists. In smaller networks where you already know the network path, you can use the `ping` command instead. Note that on the Internet, firewalls and packet filtering can restrict the usefulness of the `traceroute` command (as well as the `ping` command).

On Windows machines, the `traceroute` command is known as `tracert`. Both the `tracert` command and the `traceroute` command begin by sending a packet to the destination host with a TTL (Time to Live) value of one. When the packet reaches the first router along the way, the TTL expires and the router sends an ICMP message back to the computer running the command. The command uses this ICMP message to identify the first router along the path. The computer increases the TTL value by one and sends another packet to the destination host. When the packet reaches the next router, the TTL expires and the next router sends an ICMP message. The command continues to increase the TTL value until it either reaches the destination or until a maximum number of routers have been tested (usually 30 by default). Although each program uses the same basic technique, the implementation varies slightly. The UNIX `traceroute` command sends UDP packets as test packets, whereas the Windows `tracert` command sends ICMP packets.

After completing this lab, you will be able to:

- Use the `traceroute` and `tracert` commands to trace the path to a destination

- Interpret both successful and unsuccessful `traceroute` responses

## Materials Required

This lab requires the following:

- The lab setup built for Lab 13.1
- A computer running a current version of Fedora Linux named *LINUX1. NETPLUSLAB.NET*, configured with the firewall disabled and with the GNOME Desktop Environment
- *LINUX1.NETPLUSLAB.NET*, configured with an IP address of 192.168.54.5 and a subnet mask of 255.255.255.0, connected to *SWITCH1* with a straight-through Cat 5 (or better) UTP cable
- Access to *LINUX1.NETPLUSLAB.NET* as the NetPlus user
- A computer running Windows 7, Windows XP Professional, or Windows Server 2008 that is connected to the Internet

Estimated completion time: **35 minutes**

## Activity

1. Log on to *WORKSTATION1* as an administrator. The Windows desktop appears.

2. Click the **Start** button, type **cmd** in the Search programs and files text box, and then press **Enter**. (In Windows XP, click the **Start** button, point to **All Programs**, point to **Accessories**, and then click **Command Prompt**.) A command prompt window opens.

3. At the command prompt, type **tracert 172.16.1.2** and press **Enter**. The tracert command traces the path from *WORKSTATION1* to *WORKSTATION2*, showing the number of each hop, three round-trip response times, and the name or IP address for each hop. (Note that you can also use a domain name, such as microsoft.com.) Figure 13-2 shows an example of the output of the tracert command.

4. Remove the cable from the NIC attached to *WORKSTATION2*.

5. Type **tracert 172.16.1.2** and press **Enter**. Instead of recording two hops and stopping, the tracert command continues. However, after the first hop, the response times are replaced by asterisks and the IP address is replaced by "Request timed out." This indicates that the tracert command could not determine the path to the destination address after the first hop.

6. Replace the cable you removed from *WORKSTATION2* in Step 4.

7. Remove the cable from the NIC on *SERVER1* attached to *SWITCH1*.

8. Repeat Step 3. This time, the tracert command exits with the message "Destination host unreachable."

9. Replace the cable you removed in Step 7.

10. Log on to *LINUX1.NETPLUSLAB.NET* as the NetPlus user. The Fedora desktop appears.

```
Command Prompt                                              _ □ ×
Microsoft Windows XP [Version 5.1.2600]
(C) Copyright 1985-2001 Microsoft Corp.

C:\Documents and Settings\Administrator>tracert 172.16.1.2

Tracing route to 172.16.1.2 over a maximum of 30 hops

  1   <1 ms   <1 ms   <1 ms  server1.netpluslab.net [192.168.54.1]
  2   <1 ms   <1 ms   <1 ms  172.16.1.2

Trace complete.

C:\Documents and Settings\Administrator>
```

© Cengage Learning 2013

**Figure 13-2**  Output of the `tracert` command

11. Open a terminal window. Type **traceroute 172.16.1.2** and press **Enter**. The `tracert` command traces the path to *WORKSTATION2*, showing the number of each hop, three response times, and the name or IP address for each hop.

12. Remove the cable from the NIC attached to *WORKSTATION2*.

13. Repeat Step 11. How do the results differ from those in Step 11?

14. Replace the cable you removed in Step 12, and log off both computers.

15. On the Windows 7, Windows XP Professional, or Windows Server 2008 computer connected to the Internet, repeat Steps 1 through 3. However, substitute the name of a Web site such as *www.cisco.com* or *www.google.com* for the IP address in Step 3. Note that firewalls and other security measures between this computer and the Web site, as well as the security configuration of the Web site itself, might prevent the `tracert` command from working as expected. Repeat with several different Web sites.

## Certification Objective

Objective for the Network+ Exam:

- 4.3 Given a scenario, use appropriate software tools to troubleshoot connectivity issues.

## Review Questions

1. Which of the following commands can reveal the number of hops a packet takes between a source and target node?

    a. `ipconfig`

    b. `ping`

    c. `tracert`

    d. `ifconfig`

2. Which of the following commands can indicate whether a host is unreachable?

   a. `ping`

   b. `ipconfig`

   c. `ifconfig`

   d. `winipcfg`

3. Which of the following commands would you use to determine the relative location of network congestion between your Windows workstation and an Internet host?

   a. `netstat`

   b. `nbtstat`

   c. `tracert`

   d. `ipconfig`

4. If you attempted the `tracert` command on an Internet host and that host was not connected to the network, which of the following would the `tracert` command's response contain?

   a. Destination host unreachable

   b. Unknown host

   c. Host not responding

   d. Request timed out

5. What does a hop represent in the context of a `tracert` command?

   a. An Internet client

   b. A modem, hub, switch, or router

   c. A router

   d. A carrier's POP

# Lab 13.3 Troubleshooting Client Logon Problems

## Objectives

In this lab, you troubleshoot a scenario in which a user cannot log on to the server. From a user's perspective, when he cannot log on to the server, the network is unavailable, no matter what the reason. However, the ultimate cause of the problem might be anything from a hardware failure on the server to an expired password.

When troubleshooting problems, you should attempt to be as methodical as possible. You can start by determining the scope of the problem. Is only one user affected, or are all users affected? Then determine if the user's computer (or the users' computers, if multiple users are affected) and the server have physical connectivity. Do all the NICs seem to be working properly? Is the hub or switch functioning, and is the network cabled properly? After establishing that physical connectivity is not the problem, determine whether the user's computer has network connectivity. Can you ping the server from the user's computer? After you have determined that network connectivity is not the problem, try to determine if the application is functioning properly.

Keep in mind that being able to log on to a computer does not necessarily indicate that the network is functioning properly. Windows computers cache passwords for usernames so that a user can still log on to a computer during a network outage.

In this lab, you first verify that the network, the client computers, and the server are all functioning properly by logging on to two client computers. Then your instructor or another set of lab partners do something to prevent at least one of the computers from logging on to the server. Your assignment is to identify and solve the problem.

After completing this lab, you will be able to:

- Follow a logical troubleshooting methodology to determine the nature of client connectivity problems

- Identify a network problem by interpreting the results of diagnostic utilities such as Ping and Ipconfig

## Materials Required

This lab requires the following:

- A computer named *SERVER1* running Windows Server 2008, Standard Edition, configured as a domain controller for the netpluslab.net domain, with an IP address of 192.168.54.1 and a subnet mask of 255.255.255.0

- The DHCP server running on *SERVER1* and configured to assign DHCP addresses in the range from 192.168.54.50 to 192.168.54.100, with a subnet mask of 255.255.255.0

- Access as the administrator to the netpluslab.net domain and user accounts named *client1* and *client2* in the Domain Users group

- A shared folder named *NETPLUS* on *SERVER1*, configured so that the users in the Domain Users group have full control over the shared folder on the network

- Two computers running Windows 7 or Windows XP Professional named *WORKSTATION1* and *WORKSTATION2*, each configured to receive DHCP addresses

- Both *WORKSTATION1* and *WORKSTATION2* configured as members of the netpluslab.net domain

- All three computers configured to use *SERVER1* as their DNS server

- No network protocols besides TCP/IP configured on any of the computers

- Each computer connected to a switch or hub with straight-through Cat 5 (or better) UTP cables, as shown in Figure 13-3

- A faulty straight-through cable that is the same color of at least one of the working Cat 5 (or better) cables; a crossover cable may be substituted

- An instructor or classmate assigned to cause a problem in the network

Server 192.168.54.1

WORKSTATION1                                                    WORKSTATION2

SWITCH

**Figure 13-3**    Network layout of Lab 13.3

© Cengage Learning 2013

Estimated completion time:    **60–90 minutes**

## Activity

1. Log on to *WORKSTATION1* as client1. The Windows desktop appears.

2. Click the **Start** button, and then click **Computer** (**My Computer** in Windows XP). The My Computer window opens.

3. Click **Map network drive** on the toolbar. (In Windows XP, click **Tools** on the menu bar, and then click **Map Network Drive**.) The Map Network Drive dialog box opens.

4. Accept the default setting for the Drive drop-down menu, Z:. In the Folder text box, type **\\192.168.54.1\netplus** and click **Finish**. If necessary, enter the administrator username and password. The computer maps the NETPLUS shared folder.

5. Return to Computer or My Computer. The NetPlus (\\192.168.54.1) icon appears in the Network Location section. (In Windows XP, the NetPlus on '192.168.54.1' (Z:) icon now appears below the heading "Network Drives.")

6. Repeat Steps 1 through 5 on *WORKSTATION2*, logging on as the client2 user. You have now verified that you can log on to *SERVER1* with both client computers.

7. Leave the room while your instructor or classmate causes a network problem by performing one of the actions listed in Table 13-1. After performing one of the actions, your instructor or classmate should log off all three computers.

8. When you return to the room, reboot both client computers.

9. Attempt to repeat Steps 1 through 5 on *WORKSTATION1*. You should be unable to browse to the NETPLUS folder. Attempt to solve the problem using the following steps. If you identify the problem before completing all the steps, proceed to Step 16.

**Table 13-1   Possible actions to be performed by a classmate or instructor**

| Action | Instruction |
| --- | --- |
| Install faulty cable on *WORKSTATION1*. | Replace the network cable connecting *WORKSTATION1* to the switch with the faulty network cable. |
| Install faulty cable on server. | Replace the network cable connecting the Windows Server 2008 computer to the switch with the faulty network cable. |
| Disrupt cable Connection. | Pull the cable far enough out of *WORKSTATION1*'s NIC so that the link light turns off but not so far that it falls completely out of the NIC. |
| Reconfigure the IP address on *WORKSTATION1*. | a. Log off *WORKSTATION1*, and then log back on as an administrator. The Windows desktop appears.<br><br>b. Open the Network Connections window.<br><br>c. Right-click **Local Area Connection** and click **Properties**. The Local Area Connection Properties window opens.<br><br>d. Double-click **Internet Protocol Version 4 (TCP/IPv4)**. (In Windows XP, double-click **Internet Protocol (TCP/IP)**.) The Internet Protocol Version 4 (TCP/IPv4) Properties window opens.<br><br>e. Click the **Use the following IP address** option button, if necessary. In the IP address text box, type **192.168.154.50**. In the Subnet mask text box, type **255.255.255.0**.<br><br>f. Click **OK** twice (or click **OK**, and then click **Close**), and then close all open dialog boxes. |
| Reconfigure the IP address on *SERVER1*. | a. Log off *SERVER1*, and then log back on as an administrator. The Windows Server 2008 desktop appears.<br><br>b. Click the **Start** button, right-click **Network**, click **Properties**, and then click **Manage network connections**.<br><br>c. Right-click **Local Area Connection** and click **Properties**. The Local Area Connection Properties window opens.<br><br>d. Double-click **Internet Protocol Version 4 (TCP/IPv4)**. The Internet Protocol Version 4 (TCP/IPv4) Properties window opens. |

*(Continued)*

e. Click the **Use the following IP address** option button. In the IP address text box, type **192.168.54.11**. In the Subnet mask text box, type **255.255.255.0**.

f. Click **OK** twice, and then close all open dialog boxes or windows.

| | |
|---|---|
| Reconfigure the IP address on *WORKSTATION2*. | a. Log off *WORKSTATION2*, and then log back on as an administrator. The Windows desktop appears. |
| | b. Open the Network Connections window. |
| | c. Right-click **Local Area Connection** and click **Properties**. The Local Area Connection Properties window opens. |
| | d. Double-click **Internet Protocol Version 4 (TCP/IPv4)**. (In Windows XP, double-click **Internet Protocol (TCP/IP)**.) The Internet Protocol Version 4 (TCP/IPv4) Properties window opens. |
| | e. Click the **Use the following IP address** option button, if necessary. In the IP address text box, type **192.168.154.50**. In the Subnet mask text box, type **255.255.255.248**. |
| | f. Click **OK** twice (or click **OK**, and then click **Close**), and then close all open dialog boxes. |

© Cengage Learning 2013

10. Begin to determine the scope of the problem by attempting to log on to *WORKSTATION2*. Repeat Steps 1 through 5. If you are able to log on and browse the NETPLUS folder, the problem is local to the *WORKSTATION1* computer and you may concentrate on potential problems that affect only *WORKSTATION1*. Otherwise, the problem is common to all clients and you should concentrate on potential problems that affect all clients.

11. To determine the state of physical connectivity in the network, check the status of the link lights on the switch and in the NICs for each computer.

12. To determine the state of network connectivity in the network, on *WORKSTATION1*, click the **Start** button, type **cmd** in the Search programs and files text box, and then press **Enter**. (In Windows XP, click the **Start** button, point to **All Programs**, point to **Accessories**, and click **Command Prompt**.) A command prompt window opens. Type **ping 127.0.0.1** and then press **Enter**. Success indicates that the TCP/IP stack on *WORKSTATION1* is working. Depending on the scope of the problem, repeat this step for *WORKSTATION2*.

13. At the command prompt on *WORKSTATION1*, type **ping 192.168.54.1** and then press **Enter**. If the output indicates success, network connectivity exists between *WORKSTATION1* and the server. Depending on the scope of the problem, repeat this step for *WORKSTATION2*.

14. If there is no network connectivity, at the command prompt on *WORKSTATION1*, type **ipconfig** and then press **Enter**. IP addressing information is displayed on the computer. If this is correct, there might be a problem with the network configuration on the server. Depending on the scope of the problem, repeat for *WORKSTATION2*.

15. On *SERVER1*, repeat Steps 12 through 14. However, in Step 13, ping the IP addresses of the client computers.

16. By this time, you should have identified the problem. Fix it and repeat Steps 7 through 15, asking your instructor or classmate to perform another action listed in Table 13-1.

## Certification Objectives

Objectives for the Network+ Exam:

- 1.8 Given a scenario, implement the following network troubleshooting methodology: Identify the problem, establish a theory of probable cause, test the theory to determine cause, establish a plan of action to resolve the problem and identify potential effects, implement the solution or escalate as necessary, verify full system functionality, and, if applicable, implement preventive measures and document findings, actions, and outcomes.

- 4.3 Given a scenario, use appropriate software tools to troubleshoot connectivity issues.

## Review Questions

1. Which of the following comes first in the series of steps recommended for a logical approach to network troubleshooting?

    a. Establish what has changed on the network.

    b. Implement a solution.

    c. Establish the symptoms.

    d. Identify the affected area.

2. If a client workstation has been assigned the wrong IP address, which of the following will be true?

    a. The client can connect to other nodes on the LAN, but it cannot connect through its default gateway to the Internet.

    b. The client can ping the loopback address successfully, but it cannot connect to other nodes on the LAN.

    c. The client cannot ping the loopback address successfully, nor can it connect to other nodes on the LAN.

    d. The client can connect to other nodes on its LAN segment, but it cannot connect to nodes on other segments.

3. Which of the following commands reveal TCP/IP addressing information on a Windows Server 2008 computer?

    a. `ipconfig`

    b. `winipcfg`

    c. `ifconfig`

    d. `netipcfg`

4. If the LED on a workstation's NIC is blinking green, which of the following is true?

   a. The workstation is connected to the network and successfully exchanging data over its connection.

   b. The workstation is connected to the network but is not currently exchanging data over its connection.

   c. The workstation is connected to the network but is experiencing errors when attempting to exchange data over the network.

   d. The workstation is not successfully connected to the network.

5. Of the following troubleshooting actions, which one would come first in a logical troubleshooting methodology?

   a. Replace a faulty memory chip on a server.

   b. Determine whether a problem is limited to a segment or affects the whole network.

   c. Summarize your solution in a troubleshooting database.

   d. Determine whether your solution results in any other problems.

# Lab 13.4 Troubleshooting Web Client Problems

## Objectives

In this lab, you troubleshoot a problem with a Web client. Because the connection between a client and a host on the Internet usually relies on a great number and type of connections, problems might be difficult to identify and fix. Even if the nature of a problem is clear, you might not have any control over the network resources causing that problem. Coordination with other network administrators and other organizations is often essential to solving problems on the Internet.

In addition to basic physical and logical network connectivity, you must also make sure that DNS is working properly. Issues involving DNS are a common source of problems with Web servers and Web browsers. If the Web server is operating correctly but the client is unable to use DNS to find its address, the client also is unable to reach the Web server. The effect is the same as if the Web server were not functioning properly. However, the Web server typically is reachable through its IP address (if its IP address is known at all). DNS problems can occur for a variety of reasons, including incorrect DNS entries, misconfigured DNS servers, or even failure to pay domain name registration fees.

After completing this lab, you will be able to:

- Use a methodical troubleshooting approach to identify and solve a problem involving a Web client

- Investigate potential problems caused by DNS errors

## Materials Required

This lab requires the following:

- A computer running Windows Server 2008 named *SERVER1* with two NICs

**Figure 13-4** Network layout of Lab 13.4

- One NIC configured with an IP address of 192.168.54.1 and a subnet mask of 255.255.255.0 and the other NIC configured with an IP address of 172.16.1.1 and a subnet mask of 255.255.255.0

- Routing and Remote Access configured on *SERVER1* so that it acts as a router

- A switch or hub named *SWITCH1* connected to the NIC on *SERVER1* that was configured with an IP address of 192.168.54.1 with a straight-through Cat 5 (or better) UTP cable

- A switch or hub named *SWITCH2* connected to the NIC on *SERVER1* that was configured with an IP address of 172.16.1.1 with a straight-through Cat 5 (or better) UTP cable, as shown in Figure 13-4

- A computer running Windows 7 or Windows XP Professional named *WORKSTATION1*, configured with an IP address of 192.168.54.2 and a subnet mask of 255.255.255.0, connected to *SWITCH1* with a straight-through Cat 5 (or better) UTP cable

- A computer running Windows Server 2008, Standard Edition named *SERVER2*, configured with an IP address of 172.16.1.2 and a subnet mask of 255.255.255.0, connected to *SWITCH2* with a straight-through Cat 5 (or better) UTP cable

- IIS installed and running on *SERVER2*, with a file named default.htm containing the text "This is a test page" in C:\Inetpub\wwwroot

- The DNS server running on *SERVER1*, with an entry for *www.netpluslab.net* pointing to 172.16.1.2

- *WORKSTATION1* configured to use *SERVER1* as its DNS server

- Administrative access to all three computers

- A faulty network cable that is the same color as the network cables used in the other labs

- An instructor or classmate assigned to cause a problem in the network

Estimated completion time:  **60–90 minutes**

## Activity

1. Log on to *WORKSTATION1* as an administrator. The Windows desktop appears.
2. Open Internet Explorer.

3. In the Address bar, type **www.netpluslab.net** and then press **Enter**. A Web page opens with the text "This is a test page."

4. Close Internet Explorer.

5. Leave the room and ask your instructor or classmate to cause a network problem by performing one of the actions listed in Table 13-2.

6. After you return to the room, attempt to repeat Steps 1 through 3 on *WORKSTATION1*. You are unable to open the Web page. Attempt to solve the problem using the following steps. If you solve the problem before completing all the steps, proceed to Step 17.

7. Attempt to determine the state of physical connectivity in the network. Check the status of the link lights on both switches and the NICs in *WORKSTATION1*, the router, and the Web server.

8. Attempt to determine the state of network connectivity. On *WORKSTATION1*, click the **Start** button, type **cmd** in the Search programs and files text box, and then press **Enter**. (In Windows XP, click the **Start** button, point to **All Programs**, point to **Accessories**, and then click **Command Prompt**.) A command prompt window opens. Type **ping 127.0.0.1** and then press **Enter**. Success indicates that the TCP/IP stack on *WORKSTATION1* is working.

9. At the command prompt on *WORKSTATION1*, type **ping 192.168.54.1** and then press **Enter**. Success indicates that you can connect to the near NIC on the router.

10. Type **ping 172.16.1.1** and then press **Enter**. Success indicates that you can connect to the far NIC on the router.

11. Type **ping 172.16.1.2** and then press **Enter**. Success indicates that you can connect to the Web server.

**Table 13-2    Possible actions to be performed by an instructor or classmate**

| Action | Instruction |
| --- | --- |
| Install faulty cable on server. | Replace the network cable connecting the Web server to the switch with the faulty network cable. |
| Reconfigure the IP address on the Web server. | a. Log on to *SERVER2* as the administrator. The Windows Server 2008 desktop appears. |
| | b. Click the **Start** button, right-click **Network**, click **Properties**, and then click **Manage network connections**. |
| | c. Right-click **Local Area Connection**, and click **Properties**. The Local Area Connection Properties window opens. |
| | d. Double-click **Internet Protocol Version 4 (TCP/IPv4)**. The Internet Protocol Version 4 (TCP/IPv4) Properties window opens. |
| | e. Click the **Use the following IP address** option button. In the IP address text box, type **172.16.1.5**. In the Subnet mask text box, type **255.255.255.0**. |
| | f. Click **OK** twice, and then close any open dialog boxes or windows. |

13

*(Continued)*

**Table 13-2** **Possible actions to be performed by an instructor or classmate (*Continued*)**

| Action | Instruction |
|---|---|
| Change the DNS server on *WORKSTATION1*. | a. On *WORKSTATION1*, click the **Start** button, click **Control Panel**, click **Network and Internet**, click **Network and Sharing Center**, and then click **Change adapter settings**. (In Windows XP, click the **Start** button, point to **All Programs**, point to **Accessories**, point to **Communications**, and then click **Network**.) The Network Connections dialog box opens. |
| | b. Right-click **Local Area Connection**, and click **Properties**. The Local Area Connection Properties window opens. |
| | c. Double-click **Internet Protocol Version 4 (TCP/IPv4)**. (In Windows XP, double-click **Internet Protocol (TCP/IP)**.) The Internet Protocol Version 4 (TCP/IPv4) Properties window opens. |
| | d. Click the **Use the following DNS server addresses** option button. In the Preferred DNS server text box, type **192.168.154.1**. |
| | e. Click **OK** twice, and then close all open dialog boxes. |
| Change the DNS entry for *www.netpluslab.net*. | a. Log on to *SERVER1* as the administrator. The Windows Server 2008 desktop appears. |
| | b. Click the **Start** button, point to **Administrative Tools**, and then click **DNS**. The DNS Manager window opens. |
| | c. In the tree in the left pane of the window, click the **plus sign (+)** next to *SERVER1* to expand the tree underneath it. |
| | d. Click **Forward Lookup Zones** in the tree in the left pane. Icons for the forward lookup zones appear in the right pane. |
| | e. In the right pane, double-click **netpluslab.net**. More icons appear, including an icon for www. |
| | f. Right-click the **www** icon, and then click **Properties**. The www Properties window opens. |
| | g. Type **172.16.1.200** in the IP address text box, and then click **OK**. |
| | h. Close the DNS window. |

© Cengage Learning 2013

12. If there is no network connectivity, at the command prompt on *WORKSTATION1*, type `ipconfig` and then press **Enter**. IP addressing information is displayed. Verify that the IP address is correct.

13. If you cannot find a problem with the IP addressing information on *WORKSTATION1*, repeat the previous step on *SERVER1* and *SERVER2*.

14. If you have verified network connectivity between *WORKSTATION1* and the Web server, on *WORKSTATION1* type **http://172.16.1.2** in the Address bar in Internet Explorer, and then press **Enter**. If you can open the Web page, this indicates a problem with DNS.

15. At the command prompt on *WORKSTATION1*, type `ipconfig /all` and then press **Enter**. Look through the IP addressing information to verify that *WORKSTATION1* is configured to use *SERVER1* (at 192.168.54.1) as its DNS server.

16. If *WORKSTATION1* is using the correct DNS server, type `nslookup www.netpluslab` `.net` and then press **Enter**. The IP address for www.netpluslab.net is displayed. Check to see if this matches the IP address of the Web server (172.16.1.2).

17. By this time, you should have been able to identify the problem. Fix it and repeat Steps 5 through 16, asking your instructor or classmate to perform a different action listed in Table 13-2.

## Certification Objectives

Objectives for the Network+ Exam:

- 1.8 Given a scenario, implement the following network troubleshooting methodology: Identify the problem, establish a theory of probable cause, test the theory to determine cause, establish a plan of action to resolve the problem and identify potential effects, implement the solution or escalate as necessary, verify full system functionality, and, if applicable, implement preventive measures, and document findings, actions, and outcomes.
- 2.5 Given a scenario, troubleshoot common router and switch problems.

## Review Questions

1. What does the `nslookup` command reveal?

   a. A client's current connections

   b. A client's routing table entries

   c. The IP address of a given host name or vice versa

   d. The NetBIOS name based on a computer's IP address

2. If the link light on a switch port is not lit, what can you assume about the client connected to that switch's port?

   a. There are no connectivity problems with the client.

   b. The client cannot exchange data with the network.

   c. The client can exchange data only with other nodes on its segment.

   d. The client can exchange Network layer data, but not Transport layer data.

13

3. If a client does not have the correct DNS server address specified in its TCP/IP properties, which of the following will occur?

   a. The client cannot log on to or exchange data with the network.

   b. The client can exchange data with nodes on its local network, but not with nodes on other networks.

   c. The client can exchange data with nodes on local and external networks, but not by name.

   d. The client can exchange data with most, but not all, nodes on both its local and external networks by name.

4. What would happen if you assigned your Web server a new IP address that didn't match its DNS entry?

   a. It would be unavailable to clients.

   b. It would be available only to local clients but not to clients accessing it over the Internet.

   c. It would be available to clients accessing it over the Internet but not to local clients.

   d. It would still be available to all clients.

5. Which of the following tools issue a simple pass/fail indication for a Cat 5 UTP cable?

   a. Cable checker

   b. Time domain reflectometer

   c. Multimeter

   d. Tone generator

6. Suppose you ping the IP address of a known Web server, and the response to your command indicates that the Web server is responding. It then follows that the Web server would successfully respond to HTTP requests from clients. True or False?

# ENSURING INTEGRITY AND AVAILABILITY

## Labs included in this chapter

- Lab 14.1 Understanding Malware
- Lab 14.2 Using Uninterruptible Power Supplies (UPSs)
- Lab 14.3 Configuring RAID
- Lab 14.4 Backing Up a Windows Server 2008 Computer
- Lab 14.5 Backing Up a Linux Computer

## Network+ Exam Objectives

| Objective | Lab |
| --- | --- |
| 4.6 Explain different methods and rationales for network performance optimization. | 14.2, 14.3 |
| 5.4 Explain common threats, vulnerabilities, and mitigation techniques. | 14.1, 14.4, 14.5 |

# Lab 14.1 Understanding Malware

## Objectives

Malware can infect computers in a variety of ways. For instance, a malicious program can infect a client (or a server) by running an infected executable file, by reading e-mail with an e-mail client that has not been upgraded with the latest patches, by browsing the Web with a Web browser that has not been upgraded with the latest patches, or even by running certain services on the Internet. Keeping a file server free of viruses can be even more challenging because your users might try to store infected files on its shared drives. Sometimes users save infected files to a shared drive, have their computers cleared of viruses, and then reinfect their computers from the files on the shared drive.

To complicate matters, virus scanners can't do their work if you fail to keep them up to date. Many virus scanners require that you periodically update the virus definition files they use to search for viruses. If you do not, the virus scanner cannot find newer viruses.

After completing this lab, you will be able to:

- Describe different types of malware
- Use malware-scanning software

## Materials Required

This lab requires the following:

- A computer running Windows 7 or XP Professional named *WORKSTATION1* with an Internet connection
- AVG Free Edition 2012 Anti-Virus (available from *http://free.avg.com),* or the current version, installed on the computer

Estimated completion time: **30 minutes or more depending on the size of the hard drives**

## Activity

1. Log on to *WORKSTATION1* as an administrator. The Windows desktop appears. Connect to the Internet, if necessary.

2. Click the **Start** button, point to **All Programs**, click **AVG**, and then click **AVG 2012**.

3. Click **Update now**, as shown in Figure 14-1.

4. If new updates are found, click **Update**.

5. After AVG downloads and installs the updates, click **Close**.

6. Click **Scan for Threats** in the right pane to open the Scan for threats section.

7. Click the **Whole computer scan** tab that appears under the Scan options tab. The scan begins showing the progress of the virus scan. Do not click any buttons or press any keys until the scan is finished; this might take several minutes. The amount of time required for the scan depends on the power of the computer's CPU and the number of files on the computer. After the scan is finished, the computer shows a summary of the scan, including the number of files scanned, the number of viruses found, and the number of files repaired, quarantined, deleted, or excluded.

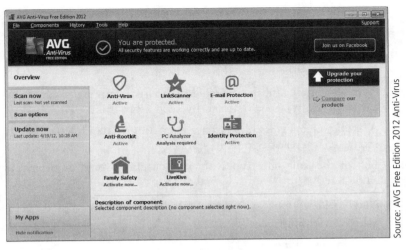

Source: AVG Free Edition 2012 Anti-Virus

**Figure 14-1**    AVG Anti-Virus Free update manager

8. Click **Close results** to return to the AVG Anti-Virus Free Edition 2012 main window.

9. Close AVG Anti-Virus Free Edition 2012.

10. To gain an understanding of virus-related terms, you access the Webopedia Web site. Start Internet Explorer. In the Address bar, type **www.webopedia.com** and press **Enter**. The Webopedia home page opens.

11. Type **macro virus** in the search box, and then click **Search**. Scroll down and click the **What is macro virus?** link. Record the definition in your own words.

_____

_____

_____

12. Repeat Step 11 for the term **worm**.

13. Repeat Step 11 for the term **Trojan horse**.

14. Log off.

## Certification Objective

Objective for the Network+ Exam:

- 5.4 Explain common threats, vulnerabilities, and mitigation techniques.

## Review Questions

1. If you receive an infected file as an executable program attached to an e-mail message, which of the following is this program likely to be?

    a. A macro virus

    b. A Trojan

    c. A worm

    d. A boot sector virus

2. What is the difference between a Trojan and a true virus?

   a. A Trojan does not automatically replicate itself, whereas a true virus does.

   b. A Trojan causes harm by simply being on the computer's hard disk, whereas a true virus file must be executed by the user.

   c. A Trojan often can't be detected by a virus-scanning program, whereas a true virus can almost always be detected by such a program.

   d. A Trojan changes its binary characteristics to avoid detection, whereas a true virus's binary characteristics remain static.

3. Which of the following types of virus checking requires frequent database updates to remain effective?

   a. Signature scanning

   b. Heuristic scanning

   c. Rotation checking

   d. Integrity checking

4. If a virus is polymorphic, what is it able to do?

   a. Replicate itself over a network connection

   b. Change its binary characteristics each time it's transferred to a new system

   c. Modify the network properties of a client or server

   d. Remain inactive until a particular date

5. What is unique about a time-dependent virus?

   a. It changes its binary characteristics at regularly scheduled intervals.

   b. It can be eradicated only by applying a virus fix at certain times of the day.

   c. It is alternately detectable, and then undetectable, by virus-scanning software, depending on the date.

   d. It remains dormant until a particular date or time.

6. A macro virus is most apt to affect which of the following programs?

   a. Microsoft Client for Networks

   b. Microsoft Outlook

   c. Microsoft Excel

   d. Microsoft SQL Server

# Lab 14.2 Using Uninterruptible Power Supplies (UPSs)

## Objectives

A sudden power failure or outage can cause numerous computer problems. If power were interrupted while a computer's files were open, for instance, those files might be corrupted. An uninterruptible power supply (UPS) is a power supply that uses a battery to ensure that any device attached to it can function for some length of time despite a power failure. If the power outage lasts only a few seconds, the UPS prevents the attached devices from losing power. If the power outage lasts more than a few seconds, the UPS affords you (or a software program) the opportunity to shut down the attached devices gracefully. Alternately, use of a UPS might allow a backup generator time to get up to full operating power.

Depending on the power requirements of your network devices and servers and the amount of power produced by a UPS, you might be able to use one UPS with multiple devices. However, you should check the power requirements of each device against the specifications of the UPS before attempting to do this. You should usually overestimate the power consumption to provide a healthy margin of error. A device's power consumption is commonly measured by its Volt-Amp (VA) rating. It can also be measured in amps. The VA rating can be found by multiplying the current consumed by the device (measured in amps) by the incoming voltage. For devices in the United States, this is 120 volts, but for international devices, this is usually 220 volts. In general, estimating the actual power consumption of a network device is difficult because an individual device might use more or less power than its manufacturer indicates that it should.

Some servers come with multiple power supplies. If one power supply fails, the other power supply continues to power the computer. For truly critical servers or network devices, you might find that attaching multiple power supplies to a single UPS is insufficient. If the UPS fails, the device would also fail during a power outage. However, if you plugged each power supply into a separate UPS, the failure of a single UPS would not cause the computer to lose power in the event of an overall power failure. Some data centers might also plug each UPS into a different circuit and each circuit into a different generator. However, these fault-tolerance measures increase costs considerably.

In addition to the smaller UPSs you investigate in this lab, you can also purchase large models designed to support many devices in large data centers.

After completing this lab, you will be able to:

- Perform a cost comparison of UPSs
- Discuss the characteristics of UPSs

## Materials Required

This lab requires the following:

- A pencil or pen
- A computer with access to the Internet and online retailers who sell UPSs, such as *www.apcc.com, www.tripplite.com,* or *www.emersonnetworkpower.com*

Estimated completion time: **60–90 minutes**

## Activity

1. You are the network administrator for Hollisville Manufacturing. Table 14-1 shows the types of devices in your data center, the number of each device, and the VA rating per each device. Calculate and record the total VA rating of the devices in the data center.

2. Using the Internet to perform research, choose a model of UPS that exceeds the total power rating for all of the devices in the data center. Record the vendor name.

**Table 14-1 Power consumption of network devices in the Hollisville Manufacturing data center**

| Device | Number of devices | Volt-Amp (VA) rating per device |
|---|---|---|
| Router | 2 | 120 |
| Server | 8 | 285 |
| Workstation | 20 | 250 |
| Switch | 5 | 90 |

© Cengage Learning 2013

3. Record the model number.

4. Record the price.

5. Record the amount of time that the UPS keeps a device running after a power failure.

6. Record whether the UPS comes with software that automatically shuts down a computer after a power failure.

7. Repeat Steps 2 through 6 with two other models of UPSs.

## Certification Objective

Objective for the Network+ Exam:

- 4.6 Explain different methods and rationales for network performance optimization.

## Review Questions

1. What is line conditioning?

   a. The regular testing of the integrity of electrical systems

   b. The periodic application of a large amount of voltage to electrical systems to clean the lines

   c. The continuous filtering of an electrical circuit to protect against noise

   d. The intermittent fluctuation of voltage on a circuit, which over time causes power flaws for connected devices

2. Which of the following devices, when used in conjunction with one or more UPSs, allows other devices to continue running indefinitely after a power outage?

   a. Surge protector

   b. Circuit breaker

   c. Generator

   d. Circuit mirror

3. Which of the following power conditions equates to a power failure?

   a. Sag

   b. Line noise

   c. Surge

   d. Blackout

4. Which of the following power conditions would not necessarily cause a power failure but might adversely affect computer equipment? (Choose all that apply.)

   a. Sag

   b. Line noise

   c. Brownout

   d. Blackout

5. What specification is necessary for you to determine the amount of electrical power that your computer devices require?

   a. Capacitance

   b. Impedance

   c. Resistance

   d. Wattage

6. What is the difference between a standby UPS and an online UPS?

   a. A standby UPS engages when it detects a power failure, whereas an online UPS continuously provides power to its connected devices.

   b. A standby UPS requires that the network administrator connect it to key devices when a power failure is detected, whereas an online UPS can remain connected to devices indefinitely, even when not in use.

   c. A standby UPS continuously provides power to its connected devices, whereas an online UPS engages when it detects a power failure.

   d. A standby UPS can remain connected to devices indefinitely, even when not in use, whereas an online UPS requires that the network administrator connect it to the devices when a power failure is detected.

7. Suppose you are working on several documents in Microsoft Word when your Windows XP Professional workstation loses power. Suppose also that you are not relying on a UPS or other alternate power source. Which of the following is a significant risk?

   a. The installation of the Word program on your hard disk might become corrupt and require replacement.

   b. Your computer's operating system might fail to recognize the Word program in the future.

   c. The Word documents you were working on when the power failed might become corrupt.

   d. Your computer's power source might become damaged.

# Lab 14.3 Configuring RAID

## Objectives

If a hard drive on a computer fails, either the computer itself will fail or the computer will lose data. RAID (redundant array of independent disks) allows you to improve disk reliability by combining multiple disks. Depending on how RAID is configured, it can also help improve disk performance. In this lab, you configure RAID in software. Keep in mind, however, that RAID is also commonly available in hardware. Hardware RAID has several advantages over software RAID, including greater reliability, better performance, and often the ability to swap out hard drives while the computer is still running. Most modern network operating systems (NOSs), including Windows, Linux, and UNIX, support software RAID. Windows server operating systems such as Windows Server 2008 support all forms of software RAID, but workstation operating systems such as Windows 7 or Windows XP Professional support only some forms.

Each possible RAID configuration involves a different arrangement of disks and is called a level. RAID level 0 is called disk striping and requires at least two physical disks (almost always of the same size). Because the computer writes parts of each file to both physical disks at the same time, RAID level 0 results in higher performance. As in all levels of RAID, the disadvantage is that less disk space is available to the computer because it sees only one logical disk that is the size of just one of the physical disks. RAID level 0 does not provide any fault tolerance, and data on both disks will be lost if either of the physical disks fails.

RAID level 1, which you configure in this lab, is known as disk mirroring. It requires at least two physical disks and provides 100% redundancy. Each time the computer writes data to its hard disks, the same data is written to each disk at the same time. If one disk fails, the computer can continue running normally because the other disk has precisely the same data. As in RAID level 0, the computer sees only one logical disk that is the size of one of the physical disks. In a variation of disk mirroring known as disk duplexing, the disks also have redundant disk controllers so that the failure of a single controller does not result in the loss of data.

RAID level 5 (commonly known as RAID 5) writes data to three or more physical disks. It also writes parity data to each disk. If one of the physical disks fails, the data and parity data written to the other disks can be used to recover any lost data. In RAID level 5, an amount of disk space equal to the space on one physical disk is unavailable. Although disks in a RAID level-5 configuration take longer to recover from the failure of a disk than disks in a RAID level-1 configuration, RAID level 5 allows the computer to have more disk space than RAID level 1.

To configure a RAID array in software in Windows Server 2008, you must use two or more dynamic disks. The exact number of disks required depends on the level of RAID you want to use. A dynamic disk can be used in volumes that can be resized as needed without rebooting the server, or they can be included in RAID arrays. The disadvantage of using dynamic disks is that other operating systems, including versions of Windows prior to Windows 2000, cannot locally read these disks (although they can read data stored on them if it is shared over a network). In contrast, a basic disk can have primary and extended partitions and logical volumes, which can be read by other operating systems.

After completing this lab, you will be able to:

- Configure RAID level 1 on a Windows Server 2008 computer

## Materials Required

This lab requires the following:

- A computer running Windows Server 2008 named *SERVER1* with two hard disks of equal size installed; one of the hard disks should contain the Windows Server 2008 installation
- The second hard disk should have no partitions or logical volumes configured
- Access as the administrator to the computer

Estimated completion time: **45 minutes**

## Activity

1. Log on to *SERVER1* as the administrator. The Windows Server 2008 desktop appears.

2. Click the **Start** button, point to **Administrative Tools,** and then click **Computer Management.** The Computer Management console appears.

3. In the left pane, click **Disk Management.** Information about the disks installed in the computer appears in the right pane, as shown in Figure 14-2. If the Initialize Disk Wizard opens, ensure that the **Disk 1** check box is checked. Click **OK.**

4. In the middle pane, you see a list of the physical disks on the system. Right-click an area in the gray box around Disk 0, and then click **Convert to Dynamic Disk.** The Convert to Dynamic Disk dialog box opens.

5. Click the **Disk 1** check box so that both the Disk 0 and Disk 1 check boxes are checked. Click **OK.** The Disks to Convert dialog box opens, listing the disks to be converted to dynamic disks.

6. Click **Convert.** The Disk Management dialog box opens, indicating that after conversion you will be unable to start other operating systems installed on those disks. Click **Yes.**

7. If the Convert Disk to Dynamic dialog box opens, indicating that any file systems on these disks need to be unmounted, complete the following steps. Otherwise, skip ahead to Step 13.

8. Click **Yes.** The Confirm dialog box opens, indicating that the computer will be rebooted to finish the conversion process.

9. Click **OK.** The computer reboots.

**Figure 14-2** Computer Management console

Source: Microsoft Windows Server 2008

10. After the computer has rebooted, press **Ctrl+Alt+Del** to display the Log On to Windows dialog box. Log on as the administrator. The Windows Server 2008 desktop appears. The System Settings Change dialog box opens, indicating that you must restart the computer before the changes you made can take effect.

11. Click **Yes**. The computer reboots again.

12. After the computer has rebooted for a second time, repeat Steps 1 through 3. Both Disk 0 and Disk 1 now appear as dynamic disks.

13. Right-click the rectangle with the green bar at the top next to Disk 0, and click **Add Mirror** on the shortcut menu. The Add Mirror dialog box opens.

14. Click **Disk 1** to select it. Click **Add Mirror**. The bar at the top of the rectangles next to both Disk 0 and Disk 1 turns red, and text in each rectangle indicates that each disk is resyncing. After a few minutes, each disk is marked C: with a status of healthy. You have successfully created a RAID level-1 set of disk mirrors.

15. Close the Computer Management dialog box and log off *SERVER1*.

## Certification Objective

Objective for the Network+ Exam:

- 4.6 Explain different methods and rationales for network performance optimization.

## Review Questions

1. Which of the following levels of RAID offers disk mirroring?

    a. 0

    b. 1

    c. 3

    d. 5

2. Why is RAID level 0 not considered fully fault tolerant?

    a. If a hard disk fails, its data will be inaccessible.

    b. It cannot stripe files whose size exceeds 64 MB.

    c. It is incompatible with modern NOSs.

    d. It cannot verify whether its fault-tolerance activities are successful.

3. RAID level 0 achieves performance benefits by simultaneously writing to multiple _____.

    a. NICs

    b. Hard disks

    c. Processors

    d. Instances of RAID software

4. Which of the following RAID levels provides fault tolerance while also making a large amount of disk space available?

    a. 0

    b. 1

    c. 3

    d. 5

5. What is the minimum number of physical hard disks required for disk mirroring?

   a. 1

   b. 2

   c. 4

   d. 5

6. What is one disadvantage of using RAID level 1 compared with using RAID level 5?

   a. RAID level 1 is not fault tolerant, whereas RAID level 5 offers at least some fault tolerance.

   b. RAID level 5 requires a third-party software program, whereas RAID level 1 is provided with every NOS.

   c. RAID level 1 requires more physical hard disks than RAID level 5.

   d. RAID level 1 makes a higher percentage of disk space unavailable when compared with RAID level 5.

# Lab 14.4 Backing Up a Windows Server 2008 Computer

## Objectives

In this lab, you use the Backup utility on a Windows Server 2008 computer to back up files to a shared network folder or a second hard drive. Then you restore the files from the backup media. Many companies supply software for backing up data. Examples include Symantec Backup Exec and Tivoli Storage Manager. The capabilities (and the cost) of these programs vary widely. Some software allows you to back up a single machine, while other software allows you to back up an entire data center. Almost all backup software allows you to schedule a backup for a time when activity on the machine is low.

The usefulness of backups is limited if they are not performed regularly. If you need to restore a user's file and you have not backed that file up in six months, the file will not contain any changes the user has made in the last six months. This might be as unhelpful to the user as no backup at all.

Backups should be stored in a safe, offsite location because they are useless if the backup media have been destroyed. For instance, if backup media are kept near the servers that store the original data, a fire in the data center could destroy both the server and the backup tapes. For this reason, many organizations regularly rotate copies of their backups to offsite locations or back up to remote drives over the Internet so that at least one good copy is available even after a disaster. Your backup location should also be secure because your backup tapes will contain any sensitive information on your servers.

After completing this lab, you will be able to:

- Back up data
- Restore data

## Materials Required

This lab requires the following:

- A computer running Windows Server 2008 named *SERVER1* with Windows Server Backup installed
- Access as the administrator to the computer
- Access to a remote shared folder or a second local drive large enough to back up the local volume

Estimated completion time: **30 minutes**

## Activity

1. Log on to *SERVER1* as the administrator. The Windows Server 2008 desktop appears.

2. Click the **Start** button, point to **Administrative Tools,** and then click **Windows Server Backup.** The Windows Server Backup window opens, as shown in Figure 14-3.

3. Click **Backup Once** in the Actions pane. The Backup Once Wizard opens.

4. Make sure that the **Different options** button is selected, and click **Next.** The wizard asks what you want to back up.

5. Click the **Custom** option button, and then click **Next.** The wizard asks you what volumes you want to back up. Select only your system volume, and click **Next.**

6. The wizard asks you to specify the destination media. Choose the backup media appropriate to your system, and click **Next.**

7. Choose the destination volume. Click **Next.**

8. If a message appears noting that the selected volume is also included in the list of items to back up, click **Yes** to exclude the volume.

9. Click **Next** to accept the default VSS copy backup option.

10. Click **Backup.** The Backup progress window opens and the status box indicates the various backup states being completed.

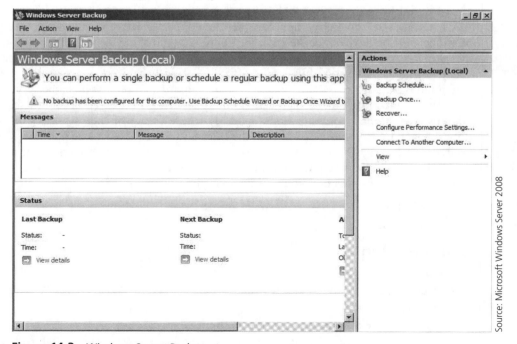

**Figure 14-3** Windows Server Backup

11. After a few minutes, the Backup progress window indicates that the backup is complete. Click **Close**. The Backup progress dialog box closes.

12. Now you test the backup by restoring some of the files you have just backed up. Click **Recover** in the Actions pane. The Recovery Wizard opens.

13. Choose the server you are on, and click **Next**.

14. Select the date and time that the backup was made, and click **Next**.

15. Click the **Files and folders** option, and click **Next**. In the Select items to recover window, expand the **SERVER1** node, click the **Local disk** node, select **autoexec.bat**, and then click **Next**.

16. Click **Next** again to accept the recovery options, and click **Recover**.

17. When the recovery has completed, click **Close**.

18. Log off *SERVER1*.


## Certification Objective

Objective for the Network+ Exam:

- 5.4 Explain common threats, vulnerabilities, and mitigation techniques.


## Review Questions

1. Assume that a company has 50 users (at a single location), a limited budget, and significant security concerns. What method would it most likely use to back up its server data?

   a. Online backup

   b. DASD

   c. RAID level 5

   d. DVD

2. Which of the following types of backup requires the most attention to the security of data while the backup is taking place?

   a. Online backup

   b. DASD

   c. RAID level 5

   d. DVD

3. Why do network administrators prefer not to back up every file on their servers every day? (Choose all that apply.)

   a. It would take too much time.

   b. It would be less accurate than periodic backups.

   c. It would be more costly.

   d. It's hard to configure backup software to perform daily backups.

4. Which of the following methods will back up only data that has been changed since the last backup?

   a. Full

   b. Incremental

   c. Differential

   d. Interval

5. Which backup method backs up data regardless of whether the data has been changed?

   a. Full

   b. Incremental

   c. Differential

   d. Interval

# Lab 14.5 Backing Up a Linux Computer

## Objectives

As with Windows, you can back up a Linux server with either commercial software or built-in commands. The `tar` command, short for "tape archiver," is one of the most common methods for making a backup. In addition to making backups of files on tape, the `tar` command (like the zip program) is also commonly used to package software for distribution. A file created with the tar program is often called a tar file. A tar file can be updated incrementally with any files that have changed since the tar file was created.

The `tar` command is commonly used with one of two compression programs, gzip and bzip2. Each program uses a different algorithm to compress files. The bzip2 program creates smaller compressed files, but the gzip program is faster. A compressed tar file made with the gzip program usually ends with the suffix .tar.gz or .tgz, whereas a compressed tar file made with the bzip2 program usually ends with the suffix .bz2.

Another useful command for backing up files on a Linux server is the `rsync` command. The name `rsync` is short for "remote synchronization." This command can be used to copy files from one machine to another and to copy files incrementally. An incremental backup copies only the files that have changed since the last backup. To copy files remotely, the `rsync` command typically uses the capabilities of another command. In this lab, the `rsync` command uses the `ssh` command to copy files to the remote server.

After completing this lab, you will be able to:

- Back up files on a Linux server with the `tar` command
- Back up files on a Linux server with the `rsync` command
- Compress files on a Linux server with the `gzip` and `bzip2` commands

## Materials Required

This lab requires the following:

- A computer running a current version of Fedora Linux named *LINUX1. NETPLUSLAB.NET,* configured with no firewall, and the GNOME Desktop Environment

- *LINUX1.NETPLUSLAB.NET* configured with an IP address of 192.168.54.5 and a subnet mask of 255.255.255.0
- A computer running a current version of Fedora Linux named *LINUX2. NETPLUSLAB.NET*, configured with no firewall, and the GNOME Desktop Environment
- *LINUX2.NETPLUSLAB.NET* configured with an IP address of 192.168.54.6 and a subnet mask of 255.255.255.0
- Access as the netplus user and as root to both *LINUX1.NETPLUSLAB.NET* and *LINUX2.NETPLUSLAB.NET*
- Both computers connected to a switch or hub with straight-through Cat 5 (or better) UTP cables
- No firewall software enabled on either computer

Estimated completion time: **35 minutes**

## Activity

1. Log on to *LINUX1.NETPLUSLAB.NET* as the netplus user.

2. Open a terminal window, type **su -** and press **Enter**. The password prompt appears.

3. Enter the password for the root account, and press **Enter**. The prompt now ends in a pound sign (#), indicating that you are logged on as the root user.

4. Type **echo "*Your name*" >/usr/local/netplus.txt**, replacing *"Your name"* with your name, and press **Enter**. The computer creates a text file named netplus.txt containing your name.

5. Type **ls /usr/local** and press **Enter**. The computer displays a list of the files in the /usr/local directory, including the file netplus.txt.

6. In the terminal window, type **tar -zcvf backup.tar.gz /usr/local** and press **Enter**. As shown in Figure 14-4, the computer creates a tar file named backup.tar.gz, backs up all the files in the /usr/local directory, and compresses the files with the gzip program. It displays a list of files as it backs them up. Note that all the files and directories located within the /usr/local directory are included in the archive.

7. Type **mv backup.tar.gz /tmp** and press **Enter**. The computer moves the file backup. tar.gz to the /tmp directory.

8. Type **cd /tmp** and press **Enter**. The computer changes your directory to /tmp.

9. Type **tar -zxvf backup.tar.gz** and press **Enter**. The computer unarchives and uncompresses all the files contained in backup.tar.gz.

10. Type **ls /tmp/usr/local** and press **Enter**. The computer displays a list of the files that you have just extracted from the tar archive. Note that the tar command has preserved the directory structure of all the files it has archived.

11. Type **cd usr** and press **Enter**. The computer changes your current directory to the /tmp/usr directory.

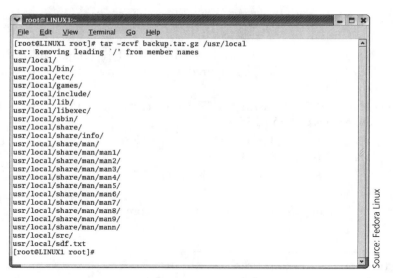

**Figure 14-4** Creation of a tar file

12. Type **cd local** and press **Enter**. The computer changes your current directory to the /tmp/usr/local directory that was created when backup.tar.gz was untarred. (Do not type cd /local because that will change your current directory to the /local directory instead.)

13. Type **cat netplus.txt** and press **Enter**. The computer displays the contents of the netplus.txt file.

14. Type **tar -jcvf backup.tar.bz2 /usr/local** and press **Enter**. The computer creates an archive as it did in Step 6, with a name of backup.tar.bz2 and using the bzip2 program.

15. Now you back up files to a remote machine. Type **rsync -zav -e ssh /usr / local 192.168.54.6:/tmp** and press **Enter**. The -z option tells the rsync command to compress the files like the gzip command, the -a option tells the rsync command to archive all the files, and the -v option tells it to be verbose, or display detailed messages explaining what the command is doing. The -e option tells the rsync command to use the ssh command. The last two options tell it to copy the /usr/local directory to the /tmp directory on 192.168.54.6. If the "Are you sure you want to continue connecting (yes/no):" prompt appears, type **yes** and press **Enter**. The password prompt appears.

16. Enter the password for the root account, and press **Enter**. The rsync command indicates that it is building a list of files to transfer to the remote computer, lists the files it transfers, and then summarizes the size and speed of the transfer.

17. Type **echo "New file" >/usr/local/newfile.txt** and press **Enter**. The computer creates a text file containing the text "New file."

18. Repeat Steps 15 and 16. The rsync command indicates that it is building a list of files to be copied and displays the names of the files and directories that have changed. (A directory in Linux changes when files are added to or removed from it.)

19. Log on to *LINUX2.NETPLUSLAB.NET* as the netplus user. Open a terminal window, type **su** - and press **Enter**. Enter the password for the root account, and press **Enter**.

20. In the terminal window on *LINUX2.NETPLUSLAB.NET*, type **cd  /tmp** and press **Enter**. This is the directory to which the rsync command copied files from *LINUX1.NETPLUSLAB.NET*.

21. Type **cd local** and press **Enter**. The computer changes the current directory to /tmp/local.

22. Type **ls** and press **Enter**. The computer displays a list of all the files and directories copied from *LINUX1.NETPLUSLAB.NET*.

23. Type **cat netplus.txt** and press **Enter**. The computer displays the contents of the netplus.txt file.

24. Type **cat newfile.txt** and press **Enter**. The computer displays the contents of the newfile.txt file.

25. Log off both computers.

## Certification Objective

Objective for the Network+ Exam:

- 5.4 Explain common threats, vulnerabilities, and mitigation techniques.

## Review Questions

1. Which of the following commands could *not* be used in the process of creating backups on a Linux computer?

   a. tar

   b. rsync

   c. bzip2

   d. cat

2. Which of the following commands would create an archive file named march13.tar.gz containing the directory /usr and all of the files and directories within it and compressed by the gzip command?

   a. tar -jzvf march13.tar.gz /usr

   b. tar -zxvf march13.tar.gz /usr

   c. tar -jcvf march13.tar.gz /usr

   d. tar -zcf march13.tar.gz /usr

3. Which programs are likely to have made a file named foo.tar.bz2?

   a. Rsync and bz2

   b. Ssh and bz2

   c. Tar and gzip

   d. Tar and bzip2

4. Which of the following programs would be used to back up data to a tape drive on a Linux computer?

a. Tar

b. Gzip

c. Rsync

d. Cat

5. You are a network administrator working for Red Rectangle Manufacturing. Red Rectangle has 12 servers, which it would like to back up to a single server attached to a tape library capable of backing up many computers. How would you use the tools in this lab to accomplish this task?

a. Use the `tar` command every night to back up each server individually, and then transfer the tar files to the backup server with floppies.

b. Use the `tar` command every night to back up each server individually, and then transfer the files using the `ssh` command.

c. Use the `rsync` command each night to back up each server to the backup server, and then use the `tar` command to create an archive file for each server.

d. Use the `rsync` command each night to back up each server to the backup server, and then use the `tar` command to write each backup to a separate tape.

# IMPLEMENTING AND MANAGING NETWORKS

## Labs included in this chapter

- Lab 15.1 Creating a Project Plan
- Lab 15.2 Planning an Upgrade
- Lab 15.3 Observing a Network Upgrade
- Lab 15.4 Installing and Removing Updates on Windows Server 2008
- Lab 15.5 Researching Network Solutions

## Network+ Exam Objectives

| Objective | Lab |
|---|---|
| 1.8 Given a scenario, implement the following network troubleshooting methodology. | 15.2, 15.3, 15.5 |
| 4.5 Describe the purpose of configuration management documentation. | 15.1, 15.2 |
| 5.4 Explain common threats, vulnerabilities, and mitigation techniques. | 15.4 |

# Lab 15.1 Creating a Project Plan

## Objectives

When planning a project—particularly a large, technical project—you must keep track of details pertaining not only to the hardware and software involved but also to the people responsible for tasks, the time each task might take, and which tasks rely on other tasks. To track all these details, it's helpful to use project-planning software.

Microsoft Project Professional 2010 is one of several project-planning software packages available. An advantage of using such software is that it allows you to create charts and timelines easily. For example, you could create a Gantt chart that displays the timelines of all project tasks and their relationships.

After completing this lab, you will be able to:

- Create a project plan using Microsoft Project Professional 2010

## Materials Required

This lab requires the following:

- A Windows 7 or Windows XP Professional computer with Microsoft Project Professional 2010 installed
- Access to the Windows computer as an ordinary user

Estimated completion time: **20 minutes**

## Activity

1. In this lab, you use Microsoft Project Professional 2010 to create a Gantt chart, which provides a graphical diagram of a project. Review the task list in Table 15-1.

2. Log on to the Windows 7 or XP computer. The Windows desktop appears.

3. To open Microsoft Project, click the **Start** button, click **All Programs**, click **Microsoft Office**, and then click **Microsoft Project 2010**. (In Windows XP, click the **Start** button, point to **All Programs**, point to **Microsoft Office**, and then click **Microsoft Project 2010**.) You might find Microsoft Project located elsewhere on your Start menu.

4. If a new project does not open, click the **File** tab, and then click **New**. The New tab opens in Backstage view. Click **Blank project**, and then click the **Create** button. A new project opens. Close the task pane, if necessary.

5. On the left side of the window, look for the Task Name column. You can enter task information in this column. On the right side of the window, a chart appears after tasks have been entered, marking the tasks on the calendar with boxes and showing precedence information. Figure 15-1 shows the window after task information has already been entered. You enter the same information in the following steps.

**Table 15-1 Project task list**

| Number | Task description | Predecessors | Duration |
|--------|------------------|--------------|----------|
| 1 | Order and ship server hardware | None | 7 days |
| 2 | Order and ship server software | None | 7 days |
| 3 | Install server hardware | 1 | 1 day |
| 4 | Install server software | 2, 3 | 1 day |
| 5 | Add server to LAN | 4 | 1 day |

© Cengage Learning 2013

**Figure 15-1**   Microsoft Project Professional 2010

Source: Microsoft Project Professional 2010

6. In the Task Name column, enter the first task description given in Table 15-1, and press **Tab**. Microsoft Project automatically updates the chart as you enter this information.

7. If necessary, click the cell in the Duration column next to the first entry you've made. Up and down arrows appear in the cell. Click the up arrow until the duration matches the number of days given for that task in Table 15-1.

8. In the Predecessors column, enter the appropriate number(s) from the Predecessors column in Table 15-1. (Leave the column blank if Table 15-1 indicates that the task has no predecessors.)

9. Right-click the first task, and click **Information** on the shortcut menu. The Task Information dialog box opens.

10. Click the **Resources** tab. In the top line of the Resources text box, enter your name or the name of your lab partner, and then click the **green checkmark**.

11. Click **OK**. The name you entered in Step 10 appears in the chart in the right pane of the Microsoft Project window.

12. Repeat Steps 6 through 11 with the remaining tasks. When repeating Step 8, be sure to enter the appropriate information in the Predecessors column.

13. On the Ribbon, click the **File** tab, and then click **Save As**. The Save As dialog box opens.

15

14. Enter a unique filename in the File name text box. Click **Save**. The computer saves your project.

15. Close Microsoft Project and log off the computer.

## Certification Objective

Objective for the Network+ Exam:

- 4.5 Describe the purpose of configuration management documentation.

## Review Questions

1. What is the name of the task that must be completed before another task is begun?

    a. Successor

    b. Predecessor

    c. Antecedent

    d. Dependent

2. In a significant network upgrade project, which of the following tasks takes place first?

    a. Identify which tasks are dependent on other tasks.

    b. Complete a needs assessment survey.

    c. Test the proposed solution on a pilot network.

    d. Assign tasks to the most qualified or appropriate people on the project team.

3. Which of the following best describes contingency planning?

    a. Obtain support from high-level project sponsors before committing resources to the project.

    b. On a smaller scale, install software and hardware identical to that required by the project's proposed solution to test the feasibility of the solution.

    c. Identify a team and assign roles to that team in case of disaster.

    d. Identify steps that will minimize the impact of unforeseen obstacles.

4. You are a network administrator managing a network backbone upgrade. Your supervisor has scheduled a meeting to discuss the project's status with you. What is the advantage of taking a Gantt chart to the meeting?

    a. A Gantt chart helps the supervisor better understand the project's costs.

    b. A Gantt chart determines the maximum possible amount of time each employee can spend on each task.

    c. A Gantt chart allows the supervisor to see timelines of each task in addition to the project as a whole.

    d. A Gantt chart demonstrates why some tasks have taken longer to complete than first anticipated.

5. One way of predicting how long a task might take is by examining the time taken to complete previous similar tasks. True or False?

# Lab 15.2 Planning an Upgrade

## Objectives

Even when you make relatively minor changes, a project plan can be helpful. The potential benefits include minimizing downtime, creating an efficient implementation, and planning for when something goes wrong. For instance, a project plan for changing the NIC on a server might include contingency plans in case the new NIC is defective, the NIC is accidentally damaged during installation, or the server does not boot after installation. Alternately, a configuration change made on a remote router might cut you off from the router. Including contingency plans in your project plan ensures that you are better prepared to solve problems quickly and efficiently.

In environments in which downtime must be minimized at all costs, contingency planning is even more important. Although the odds of a problem occurring might be low, you must be prepared just in case. During a server upgrade, for example, you could have a spare server ready in case the server fails. (Note that you can also use network design to minimize potential downtime. For instance, you could use redundant servers.)

In this lab, you create a project plan for replacing the NIC in a Windows Server 2008 computer. Your project plan should include a task breakdown, which divides the project into smaller parts, and a list of dependencies—that is, a list of tasks that depend on the completion of previous tasks. Your contingency planning should cover situations such as a defective NIC, drivers that are not available for the NIC, a NIC or server that is damaged during installation, and a server that cannot boot after installation of the NIC. Also include a testing plan in which you outline your plans for determining whether the project or change was successful and whether the results of the project include any unforeseen side effects. Finally, your plan should contain a timeline, the resources required, and the project milestones.

After completing this lab, you will be able to:

- Make a project plan for a network upgrade
- Perform a network upgrade

## Materials Required

This lab requires the following:

- Pencil and paper or planning software such as Microsoft Project Professional 2010
- A computer running Windows Server 2008, Standard Edition named *SERVER1*, configured as a domain controller for the netpluslab.net domain with an IP address of 192.168.54.1 and a subnet mask of 255.255.255.0
- A shared folder on *SERVER1* named NETPLUS
- Access as the administrator to *SERVER1*
- An extra NIC (with a driver disk, if necessary)
- A computer running Windows 7 or Windows XP Professional named *WORKSTATION1*, configured as a member of the netpluslab.net domain, with an IP address of 192.168.54.3 and a subnet mask of 255.255.255.0
- An ordinary user account in the Domain Users group in the netpluslab.net domain

- Both computers connected to a hub with straight-through Cat 5 (or better) UTP cables
- Both computers should have Network Discovery enabled
- A toolkit with a Phillips screwdriver, a ground mat, and a ground strap

Estimated completion time: **60 minutes**

## Activity

1. First, you verify that the network works properly. Log on to *WORKSTATION1* with an ordinary user account. The Windows desktop appears.

2. Click the **Start** button, and then click **Computer**. (Click **My Computer** in Windows XP.) The Computer (or My Computer) window opens.

3. Click **Map network drive** on the toolbar. (In Windows XP, click **Tools** on the menu bar, and then click **Map Network Drive**.) The Map Network Drive dialog box opens.

4. If necessary, select **Z:** (or the first available drive letter) from the Drive drop-down menu. In the Folder text box, type **\\192.168.54.1\netplus** and click **Finish**. The computer maps the NETPLUS shared folder.

5. If necessary, return to Computer (or My Computer). The netplus (\\192.168.54.1) (Z:) now appears under Network Location (In Windows XP, the netplus on (\\192.168.54.1) (Z:) now appears under Network Drives.

6. Right-click the **netplus on '192.168.54.1' (Z:)** icon or the **netplus on (\\192.168.54.1) (Z:)** icon, and then click **Disconnect** on the shortcut menu. The drive mapping disappears as the computer disconnects the network drive.

7. On a separate piece of paper, or in project-planning software such as Microsoft Project Professional 2010, write the project plan that will cover the activities in Steps 8 through 17. Use Steps 2 through 5 as your testing plan.

8. Power down *SERVER1*, and remove the power cable. Place the computer on the ground mat.

9. Place the ground strap on your wrist, and attach the strap to the ground mat underneath the computer.

10. Remove any screws, as necessary, to open the cover of the computer case.

11. Remove the computer case cover.

12. Unscrew the NIC from its slot in the computer, and carefully remove it.

13. Place the new NIC in the slot.

14. Attach the NIC to the system unit with the Phillips screwdriver to secure the NIC in place.

15. Replace the computer case, and reinsert any screws you removed in Step 10. Remove the ground strap and the ground mat.

16. Plug in the computer and turn it on.

17. To verify that the network is working properly, perform the steps in your testing plan.

18. Review your project plan, and note anything that did not work according to the plan.

## Certification Objectives

Objectives for the Network+ Exam:

- 1.8 Given a scenario, implement the following network troubleshooting methodology: identify the problem; establish a theory of probable cause; test the theory to determine cause; establish a plan of action to resolve the problem and identify potential effects; implement the solution or escalate as necessary; verify full system functionality and, if applicable, implement preventative measures; and document findings, actions and outcomes.

- 4.5 Describe the purpose of configuration management documentation.

## Review Questions

1. What is the purpose of identifying milestones in a project plan?

   a. They indicate when project staff changes must occur.

   b. They mark significant events of the project's progress.

   c. They offer a quick assessment of how successfully the project is staying within budget.

   d. They help predict the result of a project.

2. Which of the following are examples of resources related to a project plan that proposes to upgrade the network cards inside each workstation on a network from 100 Mbps to 1000 Mbps? (Choose all that apply.)

   a. NIC device drivers

   b. A team member's time

   c. IP addresses

   d. NICs

   e. Switches

3. Which of the following are examples of project stakeholders whose purpose is to upgrade an entire network from 100 Mbps to 1000 Mbps? (Choose all that apply.)

   a. Network users

   b. Software vendors of applications running on the client machines

   c. High-level managers who approved the project

   d. IT staff who helped implement the change

   e. Network cabling vendors

4. Which of the following tools might you use to assess the success of a project whose purpose is to upgrade an entire network from 100 Mbps to 1000 Mbps?

   a. Network Monitor

   b. Sniffer or packet analyzer

   c. Microsoft SQL Server

   d. System Monitor

15

5. Which of the following obstacles could halt or seriously impair your progress in upgrading the NICs in all workstations on a network from 100 Mbps to 1000 Mbps?

   a. The use of two different NIC models

   b. The use of different installation personnel on different shifts

   c. Management's requirement that the cost of each NIC remain under $75

   d. A large group of defective NICs

# Lab 15.3 Observing a Network Upgrade

## Objectives

Observing a network upgrade can help you appreciate the complexities that can arise in a real-world situation. Depending on the project, you might be able to observe only a small part of an upgrade at any one time. For larger projects, the networking professional is more likely to have a formal project plan; for smaller projects, the plan might be very informal.

After completing this lab, you will be able to:

- Explain how a network upgrade is performed

## Materials Required

This lab requires the following:

- Pencil and paper
- A person (such as a network professional) willing to allow you to observe a network upgrade
- Alternatively, an instructor can play the role of a network administrator and demonstrate a network upgrade in the classroom environment

Estimated completion time: **2 hours**

## Activity

1. Visit the site where the network upgrade will be performed.

2. Ask the network engineer who is allowing you to observe the upgrade to discuss any project plans that might be used during the upgrade.

3. Ask the network engineer to discuss any contingency planning that might have been done as part of the upgrade.

4. Record any changes occurring at the site. For example, the upgrade might involve replacing Cat 5 cable with Cat 6 cable. Another change might involve altering the IP addressing scheme.

5. Record the time required for the network upgrade.

6. Thank the network engineer who allowed you to observe the upgrade. Follow up with a thank-you note or e-mail.

## Certification Objective

Objective for the Network+ Exam:

- 1.8 Given a scenario, implement the following network troubleshooting methodology: identify the problem; establish a theory of probable cause; test the theory to determine cause; establish a plan of action to resolve the problem and identify potential effects; implement the solution or escalate as necessary; verify full system functionality and, if applicable, implement preventative measures; and document findings, actions and outcomes.

## Review Questions

1. Which of the following best describes project management?

    a. Recording and analyzing the time and resources required for each task in a project

    b. Assessing network statistics before and after a project is completed

    c. Monitoring the needs of users prior to the beginning of a project, and then later assessing how the project's completion met those needs

    d. Planning for and handling the steps required to accomplish a goal in a systematic way

2. Which of the following projects is most likely to be driven by a company's security needs?

    a. Doubling the RAM in a key file server

    b. Installing a firewall on a connection to the Internet

    c. Upgrading the version of client software on each workstation

    d. Changing from the use of static IP addressing to DHCP on an entire network

3. What is one good technique for assessing the feasibility of a suggested project deadline before the project begins?

    a. Begin calculating task timelines from the deadline, working back to the start of a project.

    b. Issue a survey to key staff asking their opinion of the suggested deadline.

    c. Use the Web to research similar projects completed by other companies.

    d. Calculate the ratio of the number of project milestones to the proposed project duration, in months, to check that it does not exceed 2:1.

4. In a very large company (for example, one with over 10,000 employees), which of the following staff is most likely to decide whether a project such as an entire network upgrade will be funded?

    a. Network administrator

    b. Personnel director

    c. Chief information officer

    d. Accountant

15

5. Which of the following situations might necessitate changing all the IP addresses on a company's networked workstations?

a. The company has divided its network into several smaller subnets.

b. The company has hired 50 new employees.

c. The company has decided to use Network Address Translation (NAT) for all connections to public networks.

d. The company has decided to establish a Web server with e-commerce capability.

# Lab 15.4 Installing and Removing Updates on Windows Server 2008

## Objectives

Keeping software up to date both on servers and network devices is an important part of maintaining and upgrading a network. Usually, software updates consist of patches or other fixes to problems that users and administrators have encountered when using the software. In other cases, a software update might solve a potential security problem, or it might even add a new feature.

Microsoft typically releases its software updates in one of two forms. The first form is a hot fix, which is an update to a specific piece of software that is often used to correct a specific problem. For instance, a hot fix might solve a problem with Internet Information Services (IIS), which is the Web server sold by Microsoft. The second form is a service pack, which is a group of numerous software updates. You might install a service pack as part of a server's regular maintenance.

Both forms of updates are accessible through Microsoft Windows Update service. In addition, you can automate the installation of hot fixes so that no user intervention is required. Automatic updates can often prevent security problems from occurring because they can fix a security vulnerability as soon as it is discovered. However, a software update might also cause problems. For instance, you might run a certain application on your Windows Server 2008 computers. If this application relies on a piece of software that has been changed in a service pack or hot fix, the application might no longer work after the update has been applied. As a result, you might have to back level, or revert to the previous version of the software, after the upgrade. Thus, if at all possible, you should verify that a software upgrade works in a test environment prior to applying it to production machines. In addition, you should carefully consider the implications before scheduling automatic updates on important servers. Automatic updates are more safely scheduled for workstations, but it is also possible that an update installed automatically could cause problems on all workstations in your organization. You should carefully weigh the benefits of scheduling automatic updates before you implement them.

After completing this lab, you will be able to:

• Install updates to a computer running Windows Server 2008

• Remove updates from a computer running Windows Server 2008

## Materials Required

This lab requires the following:

- A computer running Windows Server 2008, Standard Edition with access to the Internet
- At least one update or hot fix that needs to be installed on the computer
- Administrator access to the computer
- Internet Explorer security set to High (the default)

Estimated completion time: **30 minutes**

## Activity

1. Log on to the server as the administrator. The Windows Server 2008 desktop appears.
2. Click the **Start** button, click **Control Panel,** and then double-click **Windows Update** to open the Windows Update window shown in Figure 15-2.
3. Click **Check for updates.** The Windows Update dialog box indicates that it is checking for updates.

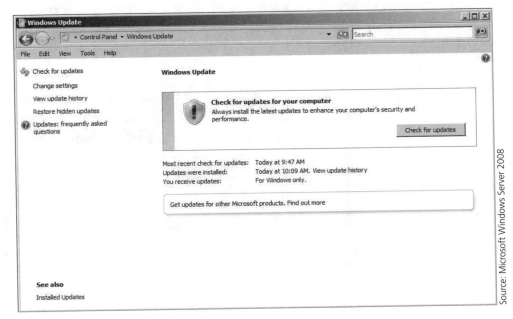

**Figure 15-2**   Microsoft Windows Update

4. When Windows has finished checking for updates, click **Install updates**.

5. Select **I accept the license terms**, and click **Finish**.

6. Depending on the updates required, the installation process might vary somewhat from this step. Often, not all of the required updates can be installed at the same time. Some of the updates might require other updates to be installed first and the computer rebooted before they can be installed. As a result, you might have to update your computer in stages.

7. If Windows indicates that you need to restart the computer to finish installing the updates, click **OK**. After the computer reboots, press **Ctrl+Alt+Del** to display the Log On to Windows dialog box. Log on as the administrator. The Windows Server 2008 desktop appears.

8. Now you remove an update added earlier. Click the **Start** button, click **Control Panel**, and then double-click **Programs and Features**.

9. Click **View installed updates**. A list of installed updates appears, as shown in Figure 15-3.

10. A number of hot fixes are listed, followed by the number of a Microsoft Knowledge Base article describing the problem solved by the hot fix. Click a hot fix chosen by your instructor.

11. Click **Uninstall** for the selected hot fix, and then click **Yes**. Windows begins to remove the hot fix. Depending on the hot fix to be removed, additional steps might be required.

12. If a dialog box opens, indicating that some programs might not function properly after the removal of the hot fix, click **Yes**. The wizard finishes.

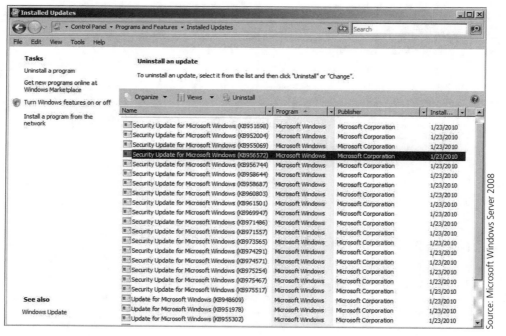

**Figure 15-3** Installed Updates window

13. Click **Finish**. The wizard closes.

14. Repeat Steps 2 through 7 to reapply any necessary hot fixes.

## Certification Objective

Objective for the Network+ Exam:

- 5.4 Explain common threats, vulnerabilities, and mitigation techniques.

## Review Questions

1. In which of the following situations would it be wise to back level?

    a. You have just performed a complete backup of your server's data directories, and you cannot confirm that the backup was successful.

    b. You have just applied a fix to your network operating system (NOS) and have discovered that the fix resulted in a lack of network access for half of your users.

    c. You have just installed a database program on one of your servers and have discovered that you neglected to install an optional component that your users need.

    d. You have just installed Windows Server 2008 on a new computer, and you cannot get the operating system to recognize the NIC.

2. Which two of the following can typically be accomplished by applying a patch to an NOS?

    a. Replace all the NOS's program files.

    b. Modify an existing feature.

    c. Remove an old feature.

    d. Fix a known bug.

3. What should you do before installing a major NOS patch?

    a. Remove all protocols installed on the server.

    b. Prevent users from logging on.

    c. Disable Internet services.

    d. Disable network connectivity.

4. In Microsoft terminology, what is a hot fix?

    a. A patch that replaces all or a portion of the NOS

    b. A patch that requires that the server be connected to the Microsoft Web site as it is installed

    c. A patch that updates a specific type of software, often the operating system

    d. A patch that can be installed while users are logged on without causing adverse effects

15

5. What is the primary difference between a software upgrade and a patch?

a. The software manufacturer issues a patch, whereas an upgrade may be issued by any organization that has the software's source code.

b. A patch fixes a specific part of a software program, whereas an upgrade typically replaces much or all of a software program.

c. A patch typically does not require that the network administrator test its changes before applying it to a server; an upgrade does.

d. A patch typically is not supported by the software manufacturer; an upgrade is.

# Lab 15.5 Researching Network Solutions

## Objectives

In this lab, you research network solutions by examining business case studies on vendor Web sites. By examining these case studies, you can get an idea of how each vendor uses its product line to help customers solve problems or fulfill business needs. It is important to keep in mind, however, that few vendors are objective about their products. When considering a solution, you should look for information from multiple sources. In addition, you might find it helpful to talk to someone who has attempted to implement a solution like the one you are considering.

When looking at case studies, you will often find it helpful to look for organizations that are similar to your own. For instance, a large bank with thousands of employees and a high-security network environment is likely to have different needs than a small, nonprofit organization. Seeing how an organization similar to your own has solved certain problems might help you solve similar problems in your organization.

It is also important to try to anticipate future network trends when researching network solutions. A solution that might help you solve future problems tends to be more cost effective in the long run than a solution that addresses only an immediate problem. For instance, suppose you are researching software packages that diagnose potential problems in business productivity software on user workstations. If you have noticed a trend toward greater user support of personal digital assistant (PDA) applications, then software packages that also diagnose potential problems in PDA software might prove more useful than ones that do not.

After completing this lab, you will be able to:

- Review case studies of networking companies
- Identify the needs of the customer in a case study
- Identify the solutions provided by the networking companies

## Materials Required

This lab requires the following:

- Pencil and paper
- A computer running Windows 7 or Windows XP Professional with Internet access
- An ordinary user account on the computer

Estimated completion time:  **20 minutes**

## Activity

1. Log on to Windows as an ordinary user. The Windows desktop appears.

2. Perform whatever steps are necessary for the computer to access the Internet.

3. Start Internet Explorer.

4. Go to **www.microsoft.com**.

5. In the Search text box, type **case study** and then press **Enter**. A list of links for this search term is displayed.

6. Select a case study from the search results by clicking the case study's title. The case study's page appears. Scroll through the page, and read the details of the study. Record the name of the customer and the type of business you reviewed.

7. Record background information on the company in the case study. This information might include the type of business, its size, and the networking hardware or software used.

8. Record the business need or challenge for the company that was the customer in the case study.

9. Record the Microsoft solution. Be sure to identify the software or hardware solution used.

10. Record the results of the solution.

11. Close your Web browser.

## Certification Objective

Objective for the Network+ Exam:

- 1.8 Given a scenario, implement the following network troubleshooting methodology: identify the problem; establish a theory of probable cause; test the theory to determine cause; establish a plan of action to resolve the problem and identify potential effects; implement the solution or escalate as necessary; verify full system functionality and, if applicable, implement preventative measures; and document findings, actions and outcomes.

## Review Questions

1. You are trying to decide whether to purchase a software package from a vendor. Who among the following is most likely to provide objective information about the software package?

   a. The vendor's sales staff

   b. A business partner of the vendor

   c. A current customer of the vendor

   d. A vendor who makes a competing product

2. You are researching a new Internet access router for your company's network. You have also noticed a trend toward greater use of your company's network resources from home. Given this, which of the following features would you expect to be most valuable in a new Internet access router?

   a. Support for additional routing protocols

   b. Support for virtual private networks

   c. Support for additional security features

   d. Support for multiple protocols

3. When implementing a network solution, why is it important to anticipate future trends as much as possible?

   a. So that the solutions you implement meet the future needs of your users

   b. So that the solutions you implement meet the current needs of your users

   c. So that the solutions you implement are more scalable

   d. So that you can justify the purchase of the solution to management

4. You work for the Best Roast Coffee Company, which has one hundred employees in nine retail stores. You are looking at case studies for a product you are researching. Which of the following case studies is most likely to be helpful?

   a. An automobile manufacturer with hundreds of thousands of employees

   b. A candymaker with 200 employees that sells candy in 13 malls across the country

   c. An insurance company with thousands of employees in three locations, plus hundreds of agents all over the country

   d. A small school district with 300 employees and 10,000 students

5. When investigating a network solution, which two of the following should you do?

   a. Get information about possible solutions from only one source.

   b. Get information about possible solutions from multiple sources.

   c. Look at the product lines from only one vendor.

   d. Talk to someone who has implemented a similar solution.

# INDEX